MICHAEL OWEN

MICHAEL OWEN

OFF THE RECORD • MY AUTOBIOGRAPHY

with PAUL HAYWARD

HarperSport
An Imprint of HarperCollins*Publishers*

First published in hardback in 2004 by
HarperSport
an imprint of HarperCollins*Publishers*
London

First published in paperback in 2006
and fully revised and updated

1

The Author asserts the moral right to be
identified as the author of this work

A CIP catalogue record for this book is
available from the British Library

ISBN 0 00 218940 2

Set in Linotype Sabon by
Rowland Phototypesetting Ltd,
Bury St Edmunds, Suffolk

Printed and bound in Great Britain by
Clays Ltd, St Ives plc

The HarperCollins website address is
www.harpercollins.co.uk

*To my mum and dad, Janette and Terry.
My inspiration through childhood,
and the reason for where I am today.*

Contents

Acknowledgements ix

Introduction 1

1 The Goalscorers – Dad and Me 7

2 Little Big Man 24

3 Lilleshall and Louise 35

4 Liverpool: Sugar and Spice 55

5 France 98 76

6 Wonder Goal 90

7 Proving a Point: 1998/99 105

8 Hamstrings: Fact and Fiction 121

9 All the Pretty Horses 128

10 Dark Clouds: 1999/2000 144

11 Euro 2000 – the Low Countries 152

12 The Treble: 2000/01 166

13 My Greatest Day 180

14 Hat-trick! 190

15 Houllier's Heart 203

16 Big in Japan   217
17 Back to Hell   231
18 Gambling – the Truth   244
19 New Life: 2002/03   253
20 Gemma   268
21 Life and Death   274
22 Farewell to Houllier   291
23 Euro 2004   310
24 Magic of Madrid   332
25 Black and White   352
    Career Record   370
    Index   389

Acknowledgements

One good reason for my decision to write an autobiography at such a relatively young age was as a way of saying thank you to the people who have helped me achieve my dream.

I know exactly where to start: with my mum and dad, Janette and Terry, my fiancée, Louise, and our daughter Gemma and our son James, who I miss like hell when I'm away. Louise and I are reflections of one another; my mum and dad gave me the grounding that I'm taking into the future as a father and a husband.

I also need to find room on the same high platform of affection for my brothers and sisters, Terry, Andrew, Karen and Lesley, who helped me understand the benefits of growing up in a large family, and who are always there to keep my boots on the ground.

In my development as a footballer and a person, a number of important people intervened at the stage where my life could have taken any number of directions.

At the Football Association's Lilleshall academy, Keith Blunt helped turn me from a schoolboy goal-machine, fresh off the parks of North Wales, into a Premiership footballer, comfortable with the tactical and technical demands of the game at the highest level. In the dormitories at Lilleshall,

Gilly and Tony Pickering stood in for my mum and dad and made sure I was cared for as I learnt the rules of life's game.

At Liverpool, Steve Heighway oversaw my journey from youth team player to the first XI, and remains a trusted friend. I'll always keep a place in my heart for Roy Evans, my first Liverpool manager, who, when I was still 17, gave me a chance in that famous red shirt. Later, Gérard Houllier made sure that I continued to mature as a player.

Around the time that Roy ushered me into the Liverpool first XI, I joined forces with Tony Stephens, my agent, who has guided me round the rocks of a life in sport, and who arranged with publishers HarperSport for this book to be written. My thanks to Tony, and to all those at SFX who have assisted me along the way.

Anyone who has ever played football will understand the importance of team-mates, of dressing room friends. At Anfield I've had many good pals, but four deserve special mention: Jamie Carragher, Didi Hamann, Steven Gerrard and Danny Murphy. Together, we've ridden the waves.

Introduction

On Friday 13 August, a private plane touched down at the small airport of Hawarden, a ten-minute drive from my home in North Wales. From there I was flown into a military airport in Spain where a car was waiting to take me to a new life – a new world – as a player with Real Madrid. At 24, I waved goodbye to the area I had grown up in, and to the only football club I had known.

We set off towards Madrid in convoy, pursued by radio and television camera crews, and made our way towards the hospital where I underwent, with some trepidation, a four-hour medical examination. It turned out to be a formality, though a long one. That night we retired to our hotel with some of the club's directors, members of my family and my agent, Tony Stephens, to enjoy my first meal as an Englishman abroad.

The following day, my fiancée Louise and my mum and dad joined me in a chauffeur-driven Audi for the short drive to the Bernabeu, where I walked through Gate 54 of the stadium in which so many legends of the game have performed, to formally sign for Real Madrid. I suppose it was a scary moment, but the real significance of that day was that I was stepping out of the comfort zone: challenging myself and moving onto the next phase of my life. And it felt good. It was up to me to show that I belonged.

On that first visit I didn't stay long. I hadn't been there twenty-four hours before I returned home for England's friendly against Ukraine, in which I scored my twenty-seventh international goal. After twenty-four years of living in the same area of North Wales – and thirteen with Liverpool Football Club, where I had grown from a child into a man – I had the overwhelming sense of moving into another stage of my footballing career as well as my life with Louise and our daughter Gemma. The truth is that I felt proud of myself for taking that step.

There were people who were saying, 'Yeah, but will Michael Owen get in the team?' I regarded that as a direct challenge to me as a professional and as a man. I was heading off to play with many of the world's best players, disappointed, I have to say, by some of the negative things that were said about me leaving Liverpool. I had given many years of loyal service at Anfield, and told the Spanish media at my unveiling that Liverpool 'would always be in my heart.'

I was trying to better myself. In our game, too many people stay in their own little cocoon and don't want to mix with other players or in new environments. I had broken out of that – and I was going to have to push myself to learn a new language, understand a different culture, make new friends, and adapt to a new style of football. I was ready for all of that.

But first came the introductions. In front of more than fifty journalists, I said I was relishing the thought of joining Ronaldo, Morientes and Raul – the club's other main strikers – and announced: 'My dad has been telling me about the great Real Madrid players of the 1950s and 1960s: Di

Stefano and Puskas, two strikers who were just unbelievable, and Gento, who was the quickest No 11 he had ever seen. Today I am so proud to be wearing his No 11 shirt.' That fine white jersey was handed to me by Alfredo Di Stefano himself, which was such a thrill.

The intention was to find a house as soon as possible. As a family we had no wish to live in hotels – even luxury ones – any longer than we had to. That wouldn't be fair on Gemma, our one-year-old daughter. My sister Karen had recently given birth to her second child, so my mum felt a responsibility to stay at home and help her with the demands of motherhood. But I knew both our families would be coming over to see us regularly. I knew I would have plenty of support.

So how did I go from being a Liverpool player of thirteen years' standing to a team-mate of David Beckham and Jonathan Woodgate in a foreign city in such a short and dramatic period? Until a few days before I left Liverpool, I had every reason to think I'd extend my contract with the club beyond May of 2005. Talks were going well, and a new Premiership season was approaching fast. I'd heard previously, through the grapevine, that I was on a list of five strikers Real Madrid were interested in but always assumed they would go for either Thierry Henry or Ruud Van Nistelrooy ahead of me. So I didn't take too much notice of those rumours.

Fast forward to Liverpool's pre-season tour of America, where we were due to have another round of discussions with my existing employers. The key stage came in New York, where we played AS Roma on 3 August. It was then that Tony Stephens told me he believed there was firm interest from Real. He said there was a genuine possibility that an offer could be forthcoming, but added, 'We can't find out more without getting permission from Liverpool.' I was still under contract – it had ten months left to run – and we wanted to follow the rules.

Tony met Rick Parry, the Liverpool chief executive, and things moved quickly from there. We had been close to agreeing a deal with Rick, but this really set the cat among the pigeons. It certainly turned my head. *This is Real Madrid!* I was thinking. After Tony and Rick talked, we were given permission to talk to the appropriate people in Spain to find out how serious they really were. From that point on it took about ten days for the move to be signed and sealed.

Obviously it wasn't a foregone conclusion. I met with the new Liverpool manager, Rafael Benitez, plenty of times. I talked to Rick, too. Mr Benitez was tremendous with me. All the while he was saying: 'I'd like to keep you, but I do understand what Real Madrid means to a player. We need to do what's best for all parties.' He never stood in my way. It was all very amicable.

I told him: 'A large percentage of me wants to stay, and if I want to be in the comfort zone it would be easy for me to put pen to paper and remain here for another few years.'

The problem is, I've never been in the business of picking up money for nothing. I've always wanted to test myself at the highest level, and in club football there is no higher level than Real Madrid. I told Mr Benitez that this was a once-in-a-lifetime opportunity, and that I couldn't afford to turn it down.

Rick understood my position, but was anxious that Liverpool should receive a fee to compensate them in the event of me leaving Merseyside to go abroad. The last thing the club wanted was for me to leave on a 'Bosman' free transfer. I'd always assured Liverpool that I wouldn't go that way, and I did so again.

When Rick gave us permission to talk to Real, we also knew of interest from other big Italian clubs, who were hoping to sign me on a Bosman, without a fee. But I was always adamant that I didn't want to leave Liverpool with nothing from my move – even though I hadn't actually cost them anything in the transfer market. I was a home-grown lad; Liverpool had always been really good to me, and we'd enjoyed a strong relationship.

When I look at it now, if I'd had two or three years left on my contract, I don't suppose Real Madrid would have come in for me with £25 million to put on the table. The benefit, for them, of me having only a year left on my contract, was that my price was bound to be reduced and would therefore be more appealing.

The fact that Liverpool had a Champions League qualifier against AK Graz while the drama unfolded did complicate things. That game on 10 August came at an awkward time. It may have left a sour taste with some Liverpool fans to see me sitting on the bench for such an important match – yet the reality is that we had come to an amicable arrangement, which protected all sides.

Had I stepped foot on the field that night in Austria, I would have been ineligible to play for Real Madrid in Europe. Obviously, they wouldn't have wanted a striker who was cup-tied, so the deal might have fallen apart. Equally, Liverpool needed to protect the transfer fee of 12 million euros (£8 million). So there was no choice but to watch my team-mates from the bench. I really didn't enjoy not being able to help my mates.

Strange though it sounds, I didn't talk to my family much when the initial interest became apparent. I kept them informed as best I could, but they didn't know the full extent of it until the deal was quite close to being sealed. I think it hit my mum and dad quite hard. Louise was less affected. She's more easy-going. My parents, though, were a bit anxious, to say the least. I think my dad wanted me to stay at Liverpool for at least another couple of years.

Maybe that would have been a good solution. But if I'd signed an extension for, say, two seasons there might have been a chance that Real would not be interested in me in 2006. Life moves on so quickly. There was one opportunity staring me in the face, and it was the right time and the right place. It took my mum and dad a good couple of weeks to get their heads round it. It was an adventure for us all. A new beginning.

1

The Goalscorers – Dad and Me

All through my childhood I was certain I was heading for a career in football. My father Terry, an ex-professional himself, was with me every step of the way; we worked as a two-man team to turn promise into reality. As a boy, I always felt I was playing for my dad more than anyone else, to make him proud.

I've lived in North Wales all my life, but I'm English by birth and by blood, though there is a Scottish branch to my dad's family tree. There was never a possibility that I would end up playing for the country I'm happy to call home. I love the area around Hawarden where I grew up – it's near Mold in Flintshire, only a few miles from the border with England – but it's a fact that my birth took place in England, in the Countess of Chester Hospital.

I entered the world at 10.20 p.m. on the night of 14 December 1979 weighing 7lb 15½oz. My mum Janette worked in the family clothes shop until 7 p.m. on the night of my birth and didn't arrive at the hospital until 8 p.m. It was all over 140 minutes later. For three of her five pregnancies the two options for maternity hospitals were Chester and Wrexham, each of which was about 10 minutes away from the family home. But Chester was more convenient, and it had the added advantage of being in the country where both my parents were born. My other two siblings were born in Liverpool and Bradford, so all the Owen children are English, though our roots have been put down outside the land I represent on the football pitch.

My addiction to football developed in this large, happy and hard-working family environment I shared with my brothers Terry and Andrew and sisters Karen and Lesley. When people learn that my dad played professional football for 14 years, from 1966 to 1980, with Everton, Bradford City, Chester, Cambridge United, Rochdale and Port Vale, they tend to assume I took over the family business after watching endless tapes of his career, or listening to his stories about football in the old days. Not so. My dad never made a point of telling us that he was a former professional. I can tell you what teams he played for, but I can't tell you in what order, or how many goals he scored for each club. He's not one to bombard anyone with the minute details of his career. Nor would he insist on telling us in great detail how to play the game. There were a few old photos lying around the house, but you had to dig deep to find them. There was nothing on the walls or on prominent display elsewhere. I know what sort of person he is – quiet and quite shy – but I don't really know what kind of footballer he was. If I hadn't found out from my older brothers, I might never have discovered at all that he had played the game for a living. It's possible that he wouldn't even have mentioned it. He never felt the need.

I always wanted to be a footballer so I always had an appetite for knowledge, but I never pressed Dad with technical questions. He was always on hand to guide me with subtle advice, but playing football came naturally to me. In recent years, however, I've pressed him a bit harder on the details of his life on the circuit. I know, for instance, that he scored for Chester against Aston Villa in the first leg of a League Cup semi-final. He calls it a 'scrappy goal'. I've also discovered that he had his happiest times at Chester, which is why he settled a few miles from the club when his playing days were over.

I think a lot about what it must have been like for him playing in such a different era. He'll admit that he was something of a journeyman pro, touring the old Third and Fourth Divisions, and I can certainly imagine how hard that must have been. When he stopped playing he was forced to go straight out to work to support the five young children in our family. I have all my dad's traits, so during my school years I was no more inclined than he was to discuss foot-balling careers in front of my friends. If they found out about my family's footballing history, it was through the local newspapers, which commonly referred to me as 'Michael Owen, son of former Chester striker, Terry'.

Beyond Dad, there's no history of playing football in the family. His father, Les Owen, who was in the navy, died in 1983 when I was three. I have only one memory of him, standing by the back door of the utility room in our family home smoking his cigar. I gather that Les loved his boxing. Later, when I had two fights in the ring, my dad told me that Granddad would have been so proud to see me box. That brought a tear to my eye, because I've never really had a granddad around. My mum's father, Roland Atkins, though he was always known as Tommy, died when she was 12. He was a sergeant in the army during the Second World War and fought in Germany; during peacetime he ran the clothes business my mum eventually took on.

Tommy's wife, my mum's mum and my nan, Isabel Atkins, came to live with us in an extension to the family home when she was 68. She was an avid fan of mine. Like my dad, she had this urge to be at all my games. She would give me a bar of Dairy Milk before the match to provide me with energy. You wouldn't do that now of course, but it seemed a great idea at the time. Also, if I scored she would give me 10p a goal. She would stand there on freezing cold days, even when she was getting too old to do things like that. She died in 1994, just before I started playing for England U-15s, so my dad's mum, Rose Owen, is my only living grandparent. She was the one who sent over a pile of sweets every Friday when Dad came home from work in Liverpool. Pocket money from her was a pound a week. She's gone downhill in recent years and is now suffering from Alzheimer's disease.

I have two uncles and an aunt, too: Dad had two brothers, John and Tommy, and a sister, Margaret; Mum was an only child. Margaret married José, who is Spanish, and they had three girls who are my only cousins. José and Margaret run a restaurant called Antonelli's near Crosby, where they all live. My connections with the city where I play are stronger than some might realize. People are constantly coming up to me saying, 'I know this or that member of your family in Liverpool.' By an amazing coincidence, Jamie Carragher, my friend and colleague at Anfield, was a big fan of José and Margaret's restaurant. When I told him about my family connection, he said, 'That's where I eat virtually every day after training!'

My mum's side of the family owned a clothes shop in Liverpool, and Mum and Dad took over the business until it ran into financial difficulties. They sold clothes on credit, and were undone by imports that were cheap enough to be bought without a loan. Mum then moved on to Iceland frozen foods, where she worked in the head office on Deeside, and Dad sold policies for Co-op insurance. He's quite reserved, so he hated knocking on doors and trying to sell people things. But we weren't the wealthiest of families, and as the business had gone belly up he had to do something to earn a living. There was no nest egg from his time in the game. We lived in a nice house in Hawarden, but with a mortgage and all the usual financial obligations. It was only when I made money out of football that I paid that mortgage off to enable them to live without debt. From what I can gather my parents had a lot of financial pressures, and had I not made it as a footballer it's possible we would have had to sell up and move somewhere more modest.

From my point of view, Dad didn't make any mistakes in my upbringing. I think of him as the perfect father. He encouraged me, above all, simply to enjoy playing football, and now I'm a professional, and I'm happy with the way I am as a person and with how I play. I sometimes look at other players and wonder how they could have made it to such a high level without the kind of parental support I received.

There is no one like my dad. He would go to absolutely every game I played. Mum attended almost all of my matches as well, and my younger sister Lesley was equally loyal. She would sit there in a snowsuit, trying to keep warm. At the Ian Rush tournaments for school-aged club teams that I played in, she became Liverpool's mascot. We didn't have a pot to pee in, yet Dad would stump up money to travel as far as Jersey for a single match. He couldn't bear to miss a game, not even friendlies for the local club. And this fatherly encouragement wasn't available just to me. If my sisters were playing hockey or netball in the most far-flung location, Dad would be there. Karen was a good runner and played hockey for the county; Lesley's game was netball.

Dad's intention was simply to provide encouragement and

support. I went through a patch as a kid when I just couldn't play if he wasn't there. If he was late, I would virtually stand still looking for his car, waiting for it to pull up. He soon learned to be on time. Even when I was 14 or 15 playing at Lilleshall, the national academy at that time – I was an England schoolboy competing at quite a high level by that age – my dad had to be in his usual position behind the goal. If he was on the sidelines or not present at all, I couldn't perform. Other young pros might not want their dads to be at games. I can understand that point of view, if the parent puts pressure on the boy. Ninety-nine per cent of dads want their lads to be footballers. It's the dream. But I think my dad just knew I was going to make the grade.

I found out later that he'd told close friends I was definitely going to end up playing for England. Armed with that inside information, a few of them clubbed together and had a bet with the bookmakers on me wearing an England shirt. He was absolutely sure I would make it. But though he shared that confidence with his mates, he didn't have to say anything to me. I just knew he thought I was a special player. He wasn't the kind of father who would constantly tell me how proud he was. Words don't speak as loudly as actions with my dad. I had years and years of him expressing his feelings just through his presence. There was a special bond between us.

It sounds funny now, but every Thursday he'd give me a massive steak to build me up. Just to be strong. Just to be a footballer. He used to joke about me paying him back one day. While he was serving the steak, I'd join in the banter by saying, 'Dad, for everything you do for me I'm going to get you a Mercedes one day.' (I got him a Jaguar instead.) He did everything in his power to put me on the right track to become a footballer without actually saying that that was what he was doing. It was all about actions. My parents' work schedules were built around my games.

I never worried about getting special treatment because, as I said, Dad was consistent in his support for my siblings: no matter how important the match, he'd be there. When it became clear that my older brothers weren't going to be footballers, he didn't regard that as the death of a dream; he just wanted us all to do well at whatever we were doing. First and foremost, he wanted us all to be decent people. If you're good at engineering, as my brothers are, then good luck to you – well done, son. The same applies to my sisters. His main message was: just be a decent human being.

In some families there can be problems when one of the children is especially successful at something and becomes famous. That's not an issue with us, because I have very sensible brothers. I've looked after them as much as I can, and because they love the game they can appreciate what I do on the football field. And that's a good thing, because the phrase 'the love of money is the root of all evil' is the most true of all. If the family can't handle it, wealth can be horribly destructive. I hear stories in dressing rooms about money and fame driving people apart. That's where I'm so lucky. My family is so normal and sensible. There's no jealousy with us. In fact, I find it hard to believe that the word 'envy' can appear in the same sentence as 'brother' or 'sister'. It's alien to us in the Owen family. But it's out there. I see it in football all the time.

As brothers and sisters, the five of us weren't competitive with one another. Terry and Andy work at British Aerospace in Broughton, making wings for airbuses and assorted planes. Terry is nearly 10 years older than me and Andy nearly nine, so I was out of my depth when it came to child-hood activities. Every Sunday, though, we'd go to the park together to play football, and I suppose I did try to close the age gap so I could be as good as them. My dad was obviously head and shoulders above the three of us, my brothers came next, and I was plainly the worst of the four players. The two decent ones would line up against the very good and the rubbish (that was me). So maybe I was always stretching myself to the limit to reach their level. Around the house Terry and Andy stuck together, and it would never have crossed my mind to take them on. Certainly I never started any fights with them because they seemed immense. My sister Karen was born between Andy and me; there are three and a half years between us. Karen was studying to be a solicitor, then had a baby, and now works part-time. Then there was my kid sister Lesley, who is three and a half years younger than me. I looked after her a lot, and played games with her, sometimes football. If I was in an aggressive mood, Lesley would probably take the brunt of it, and vice versa. She's training to be an interior designer now.

Many of my strengths were honed in the park with my dad and brothers, or with my mates after school. At the time, though, I didn't think of it as an academic process; I just saw it as fun. I didn't think, 'Oh, I'm not so good with my left foot so I'd better practise,' or anything like that. I was so much quicker than everyone else as a small boy that I could run on to a through-ball and have endless time to set up the shot. I could put it where I liked. My right foot was the strongest, so I barely kicked a ball with my left foot until I was 16. The only technical area my dad worked on was my heading. On Sundays in the park he'd send in a few crosses for me to nod in. All kids hate heading the ball, and I was no different. But Dad used to love it when I scored a diving header, because he had scored a few himself in his own career. So I used to do it just to please him.

As a finisher, it was all about smelling blood, seeing the chance and seizing it. Verbally, I was a bit of a rebel. I was always answering back to referees. I had a temper on me. I was a tough tackler. I had a few good battles with centre-halves on the North Wales schoolboy circuit. My first real tussle, though, was with Richard Dunne, who was at Everton schoolboys when I was in my early teens and playing for the equivalent age group at Liverpool. Richard is a fairly stocky figure, and he wasn't much different back then. He was the first opponent who really made me think the day before about what I was facing the following afternoon. He was the one I had my first real ding-dongs with. Around 14 is when things start to get serious physically. By that age you know what's going to hurt someone. You wise up and start to understand what the game is all about. You're no longer an innocent kid chasing the ball around. If someone kicks you, you know where it hurts and how it hurts, and consequently you learn how to hurt them back.

Not that Mum and Dad encouraged that side of things to blossom. Still, they weren't rigid about family discipline. To be a 'cheeky little bugger' was fine up to a point, but if we were in the company of adults we would be expected to say please and thank you and to show respect. They wanted me to be my own person while also teaching me good manners and making sure I knew how to conduct myself. In fact, they wanted us all to have a personality, and they knew how to provide fun for us as we grew up. If my dad had a spare fiver, he would want to take us on a day out.

Mum was in charge of the day-to-day parenting and instruction. She knitted the whole family together, and she still rules the roost. To get into the Owen family you've got to get past my mum. She had five children and worked as well, so she was always a grafter – still is. Even though she worked eight till five, she always seemed to be there, every minute of the day. She, more than my dad, shaped my everyday behaviour.

If we got a rocket from Dad, it was once in a blue moon, which made you want to avoid it even more. He was never a shouter, though. With me, he would prefer to go quiet. He just wouldn't speak to me. And that's the worst thing in the world. There is no one you want to impress more than your dad. If he's not talking to you, life's not worth living.

I wasn't a naughty kid, but if it was Halloween, say, I might be tempted to throw an egg at a window like any other mischievous young boy. I got up to my own tricks. If there was a weaker boy I might take away his ball. It's embarrassing to remember that now. Of course I stepped out of line many times as a child. If I smashed a window with a football I might run off without owning up to it, and the owner would come knocking on the door. In the neighbour-hood I was known as 'the footballer', so unfortunately it was always obvious that I was the culprit. But it would take a lot to push my dad so far that he would stop talking to me altogether.

After games, he had his own way of conveying his feelings about my performances. If I played badly, he might not talk to me about it until my next game. Now that I'm an adult I can see that had a very positive effect, but it didn't half hurt at the time. It wasn't deliberate on his part. Even now, if I play badly the level of conversation drops. He'll try, but it's in his nature not to speak quite so freely. I've talked to him about it and he's assured me he doesn't mean to go quiet. We have a laugh about what his silences were like when I was a kid, and he insists, 'I genuinely didn't do it on purpose.' He just wanted so much for me to do well. If I played badly he was disappointed for me rather than in me. He knew I wanted to please, and I never experienced his occasional silences as pressure to succeed. It was just ingrained in me to try to please my dad.

I wouldn't be allowed to touch my football boots. That was Dad's job. He took great pride on a Saturday in me having the shiniest boots. If you're proud of the way you look and feel, I suppose you've got more chance of doing something well; if you're always scruffy you might play that way. Plainly, I didn't think about life like that when I was a child, but now I can see the point in investing time and care in your appearance. As soon as I got home I'd take my boots out on to the patio and he'd get to work with the brushes. Right from the start that job wasn't mine. For some reason Dad seemed to enjoy it.

These days he reads papers and listens to phone-ins to monitor what kind of coverage I'm getting. He feels proud when someone says something good about me and fiercely angry if anyone says anything bad. He knows me back to front and he sees me as a decent lad, so when people accuse me of being a cheat or dishonest in any way he must see it as a slight against himself. A few years ago people were calling me a diver and he just couldn't accept people questioning my honesty. You could say that if we expect praise we should be able to take the reverse as well, but quite frankly he's not asking for praise, and nor am I, so I'm not sure that principle stands up. I get paid so well I can't ever complain about my job. Ninety-nine per cent of people will assume it's great to be famous. I'm not so sure. I never ask for plaudits, and likewise I don't welcome people having a go at me.

It wasn't all football. Dad was an avid golfer. As a kid, if I didn't have a football match I wanted to do what my dad was doing. On Sundays he would go off to play with a few mates and I would be his caddy. Sometimes he probably wanted to be away from the family, just with his friends, but more often than not he would take me along. Afterwards I would sit in the corner with a glass of Coke and a packet of crisps while he played snooker.

I used to love looking for lost golf balls. Sometimes I would be 50 yards down the fairway rummaging through the bushes while he was taking his shot. We had a ritual: late on a Sunday afternoon, after the football, we would go up to the course and head straight for the rough; we would spend two or three hours looking for golf balls and would be disappointed if we didn't find 20 or 30. He used to play games with me, saying, 'Oh, I'm sure I can feel something under my foot. Oh, maybe not.' On the way home we'd stop for a can of Lilt at the local garage. Later I became quite competitive about it. Whoever found the most balls would get first pick after we'd scrubbed them clean with Fairy liquid. When they were bright white we would lay them out on the patio and take turns to choose. I couldn't imagine a better way to spend a Sunday evening than doing all that with my dad. With my own son I will do those sorts of activities. I didn't want to be taken to Spain to lie on a sun-lounger. Hunting for golf balls, or feeding horses, are the priceless things you remember from childhood.

Through those early experiences on the course I learned a few lessons about the etiquette of golf – where to walk, where to put your bag and so on. It was a good grounding, because golf is a gentleman's sport with lots of etiquette. I soon progressed to wanting to hit balls myself. 'Go on, Dad,' I would say, 'just give me one go.' Eventually, on warm Sunday evenings, he would let me play a few holes, all the while still looking for lost balls. Dad then got me a membership at Hawarden Golf Club, the local course, and my friends began to join too.

There were so many new juniors that the club began to send us away on courses. During the school holidays we were there morning, noon and night, playing 36, sometimes 54 holes. It's an incredible thought. These days, I can't walk 18 holes without feeling knackered. By the age of 13 my handicap was down to nine, and I began taking lessons from David Vaughan, a professional based at Llangollen. At one stage Dad became a bit concerned about the number of hours I was spending with a club in my hand. He was worried that I was starting to prefer golf to football. In the summer it was golf, golf, golf. He didn't stop me playing, but he did remind me a couple of times, 'Football's your game, don't get too distracted.'

The snooker club was another of our regular haunts. We'd pay £2 for an hour of light above the table. We would always have black-ball games because Dad would let me get close to winning so there would be a decent climax. Every game was tense. The people who owned the hall must have been sick of us because every time I would run down the stairs with 50p to ask for 15 more minutes' worth of light just so we could squeeze in the end of the frame. I'm sure Dad paid for an hour just to add to the drama; he knew how excited I'd be getting when the sixtieth minute was approaching. When the lights went out, you were in pitch darkness, so I was constantly badgering him for that extra 50p.

I'm not sure whether he went through these routines to encourage me to be competitive or whether it simply amused him to see me getting so worked up. But certainly, if I didn't find as many golf balls as my dad I would be fuming. I'd still remember it as a great day, but there would be something missing. To get first pick of the washed balls was, to me, a major prize. I'd like to think he shaped me as a man, but not by waking up in the morning and thinking, 'Right, how can I form Michael's character today?' It was much more natural than that. All the activities he wanted to do I fell in love with too. And every time I played I wanted to win. It's the fierce nature I've always had.

I'll give any game a go. I played for Hawarden Cricket Club and made it into the senior side at 13. I love darts and bowls, too. Once a month we'd go to the tenpin bowling alley in Chester. Boy, was that competitive. My dad used to be brilliant, with a smooth action that helped him hit the middle pin every time. Now his action has gone, and we always take the mickey out of him for it.

I'm proud to be able to summarize my childhood as fun and character building, with family life to the fore. My parents gave us everything they could. I can recall plenty of examples. In my early teens, Dad wanted to take me to visit a few clubs to open my eyes to how football worked. One day we were invited to Sheffield Wednesday to have a look round, and as we were about to leave the youth-team manager stopped us and said, 'Right, here's your expenses.' Twenty quid, I think it was. So off we raced, straight past home and on to Rhyl pleasure beach to spend the money on rides before returning to the house. I'll never forget that day.

When I look back on my childhood, that incident sums up my parents. Any spare penny they had was spent on the kids to make them as happy as could be. They never spent a thing on themselves. Sometimes I wonder whether Mum wore the same clothes for 20 years.

Whatever your mum and dad say or do, for most people that's the gospel. I would never want to spoil my kids because giving in to every wish or demand was something my parents never did. But any time I get a spare minute

I want to spend it with my children, to make them as happy as we were. Now, of course, I'm scoring goals for England and having a great life, yet being a kid is really hard to beat, if you're lucky enough to have grown up in the kind of parental environment I experienced. It's wonderful to have such a comfortable existence now, and to live in such a nice house, but if somebody said to me 'You've got to give it all back and live the life you had as a child', I could think of worse things. I would have no problem with my daughter Gemma or son James growing up that way. If money is tight in a family things are given to kids only for the right reasons; no child is going to get anything just because they cry for it. It's easy to brush problems off with money ('here's a couple of quid, go and buy some sweets'), but the best things in life are free, as everyone knows. For my dad to take me, on the back of his bike, to feed some horses in a field for half an hour was my idea of a treat; Dad spending £40 on one activity, or paying for an expensive holiday, just didn't have the same appeal. Give me a simple train ride any day.

I won't deny that my wealth from football has enabled me to help the whole family financially. When I was 18 and building a house a mile from the family home, a new estate with some really nice houses was being constructed nearby. It was always my intention to buy homes for members of my family, and it was just coincidental that a chance to do so arose so close to where I was building on the plot of land I had found. Mum and Dad liked the show house we went to inspect. Initially I bought two show homes because my brother Andy has always liked his own space; the idea was that the family would live in one while Andy took the house next door. At first I didn't think any further ahead than that, but soon I started to feel it was unfair on my other brothers and sisters. So I bought the next two houses along, for my older sister Karen and my brother Terry. Lesley was very young, so I didn't need to buy one for her, but subsequently the next one in the close became available and I acquired that one as well. The next house along also came on the market, but we didn't have enough family members to fill it. So there is one non-Owen in the street. He's a very nice fella and doesn't seem to mind sharing the close with my whole family. The arrangement probably won't last for ever. If Lesley's boyfriend or Karen's boyfriend moves away through work it's possible that one or both of them will move on. But at least it has given them a start on the property ladder. If they wanted to move, obviously I wouldn't take offence.

I've always liked investing in property. In 2003 I bought a couple of plots of land in the Algarve, near where Paul Ince has a place. Having poured all my energy into my new home in North Wales, initially I didn't make much headway in terms of building on the land in Portugal, but it's an exciting project for the future. The house will be open to all the family, and I like the idea of us going there in the summer with all the kids for a major holiday. I'm also buying a place on The Palm in Dubai. When we visited the city before the 2002 World Cup, members of the England team were offered the chance to buy in the resort. Half a dozen of us said yes.

But I don't see myself as special in any way. One of my brothers drilling the wrong hole on an aeroplane wing is a much more serious issue than me having a bad time in a football match. When I pick up an injury I don't expect a stream of sympathy from them. Missing a goal is part of the job; being a hero or a villain is part of the job. We're all good at something. It just happens that I'm good at football and that has a high public profile, so everyone notices what I do. I'm skilled at football, my brothers are skilled at engineering. Neither talent is more valuable or important than the other. In the Owen family we just get on with life and look out for one another.

2
Little Big Man

From my earliest days as a footballer I was up there with the big boys – we're talking size and age here, not fame. Almost from my first serious kick I left my own generation behind to take on older lads – perhaps starting a trend that ended with my World Cup goal against Argentina when I was only 18.

My first memories of my life in football date from when I was seven. I started properly with Mold Alexander, five miles from the family home, though people often trace my beginnings to Hawarden Pathfinders, who were my local cub side. They played every few months, so fixture congestion was hardly a problem. When Dad took me to Mold he was told that the youngest age group was Under-10s, which didn't look too promising given that I was still only seven. But after a couple of training sessions I managed to force my way on to the substitutes bench, from where I would often come on and score.

Things started to get serious when I was chosen, at the age of eight, to represent Deeside Schools under the management of Bryn Jones and his assistant Dave Nicholas. Their motto was 'first to the ball', which they stuck to the dressing-room door. Though playing for Deeside seemed a huge promotion at the time, I realize now that you don't really leave an imprint in football until you become a professional. How many people, for instance, could name the record goalscorer for England Under-15s? (It's me, by the way.) Still, for me to be the youngest boy to be picked for Deeside Schools felt like an immense achievement at the time, even if it doesn't now. I beat Gary Speed's age record and then, in my third year, Ian Rush's highest total for the number of goals in a season. To be in the local papers at 10 or 11 in the same sentence as Ian Rush was about as good as it could get.

For a while, then, I was an eight-year-old playing in an Under-11 county side. I could score goals at that age and at that level, but I think Bryn Jones and other administrators of Deeside Schools felt they needed to be fair to the older boys in that age group and not allow them to be ousted by an eight-year-old kid. For my second season, however, I was made captain and I played every game. I scored 50-odd goals in 30 or so games, and then in my final year I hit 92. The papers were full of it. I actually broke Ian's record at a tournament in Jersey, and my dad and younger sister were there to witness the event. In an equivalent number of games I beat Rushie by two, but we played a lot more matches than he did in his record-setting year so I ended up pulling 20 clear.

I can still remember the decisive strike that day, though all my goals at that age were virtually identical: a ball over the top, followed by a sprint and a finish. I was quicker than everyone else at that time so it was always a one-on-one, with a finish to the side. You don't get many crosses or diving headers in Under-11 football; you're always running on to through-balls, with the full-backs mysteriously playing everyone on side. When I scored against Argentina at France 98, and in the 2001 FA Cup final against Arsenal, I can recall jogging to the touchline trying to assess the meaning of what I'd just done. The first time I went through that mental process, I suppose, was when I scored in Jersey to surpass Ian Rush in Deeside's record books.

I hadn't yet met Rushie when I improved on his earliest achievement in football, and I didn't cross his path for a long time after I arrived at Liverpool. By then he had left Anfield, though I did see him occasionally in the players' lounge, or doing a stint on local radio. I didn't get to talk to him properly until January 2003, when he rejoined the club as the strikers' coach. I've had a couple of rounds of golf with him since and he's a mate now. When he was first unveiled as Liverpool's striking coach we both did interviews about each other, and the Deeside scoring record was usually the first question to be asked.

There's a funny story attached to my second proper association with a local club side. After Mold Alexander, I moved on to Hawarden Rangers and scored about 116 goals in 40 games in their colours. We won everything. When the club's annual awards came round, I was desperate to be Player of the Year, as all young boys are. I just knew I was head and shoulders above the other lads in the team. But the winner was . . . our goalkeeper. We were winning 10–0 virtually every week, and our keeper, who was two years younger than everyone else, had barely made a save all season. It wouldn't bother me now if someone got Player of the Year ahead of me, but when you're 12 it really hurts. It's life and death. You wait all week for Saturday to come.

Dad was livid. 'You're not playing for them again,' he told me. The following season I was going to confine myself to the county team (though I was also by that time play-ing Liverpool youth games at the weekend). However, the manager of St David's Park, another local side, was especially persistent and promised Dad that if I joined them I wouldn't be asked to play too many times.

'Just let him play in four or five,' he pleaded.

'Oh, go on, then,' Dad replied.

St David's were about to play Hawarden Rangers, and the manager came on to ask me to play against my old club – the one that had deprived me of the Player of the Year award. I wanted to spite them so much that I agreed to make myself available. We beat them 4–3 and I scored all four of our goals. There were rumours that the Hawarden manager was going to report the St David's manager for tapping me up, though it never came to much. You can imagine the feeling of smugness as Dad and I walked back to the car.

When you're the top man at football in primary school, you attract a certain amount of respect from your peers; once you get into secondary school, however, not everyone's quite so fascinated. At Hawarden High, many of my contemporaries developed an interest in fighting and smoking, but I had to stay off that path. If you're a prospect, it's then that you have to retain your focus on the game. It was around that time that I started to become aware of jealousy in other children. I was well liked at school, but when it was announced that I was leaving to go to Lilleshall, in my third year at senior school, a couple of the tougher lads would occasionally snarl at me. I assumed it was envy because I was doing so well and moving on. It didn't turn physical and I didn't tell my parents, though my dad seemed to be aware that I had stirred up some animosity in one or two kids. Anyway, schools are full of cliques and hierarchies. I had my own. I certainly never went home crying, saying people were picking on me.

My best friend from my school days is Michael Jones,

who I met at infant school. He lived about three miles away from us, so until I was allowed to ride off on my bike I had to rely on Mum to drive me to his house. Later we played golf every other day. Whenever I'm not working we go out for a meal with our partners, or he comes round to watch a match. We always look out for each other. Didi Hamann, at Liverpool, has become good friends with Mike, and he often joins us on the golf course. Mike turned pro in 2003 and has been to South Africa to play in the Sunshine Tour. His plan is to join the Pro Tour, which is two levels below the European Tour. He's got a bit of climbing to do, but at least he has a sponsor to see him through his first year.

I didn't really enjoy the academic side of school, though I quite enjoyed maths. I also liked geography. General knowledge interested me too. At home on winter nights Mum and Dad would set quizzes. It was the formal aspect of being taught through lessons that turned me off. In those environments I would find myself looking at my watch, gazing through the windows and waiting for PE – anything, really, except classroom teaching.

It was at the age of 10 that boxing was added to my list of sporting activities. A little known story about me is that I boxed in two proper club fights, one in front of the dickie-bow brigade. It was Dad's intention to make me stronger physically and toughen me up mentally, so he took me to the local boxing gym – the Deeside Boxing Club, above a pub in Shotton – where I watched a training session one afternoon and joined the following day. Organized fighting tends to be a fad for a lot of boys. They come in for a session or two and then disappear, often when the going gets really tough. But I stayed with it for three years because I enjoyed it so much.

The first of my serious bouts came after I'd played for Deeside Primary Schools that same day. The fight was in the evening, and I found myself opening a 10-fight bill in Anglesey in front of an audience wearing dinner jackets and bow ties. Never mind taking a penalty in the World Cup, nothing compares to being in a boxing match. My first opponent had already had a couple of fights, and I was much lighter than him, so I made sure I protected myself down below by inserting the proper guard. I wore all the body armour I could to make the weight. I just about managed to get close enough to him on the scales for the bout to go ahead, and the next thing I knew I was climbing through the ropes for the opening contest in the short but eventful boxing career of Michael Owen.

I won on a split decision. It should have been unanimous, or so I believed. My corner and my family thought so too. A couple of experts came up to me that night and said, 'Fantastic performance. That should get you the boxer of the night award.' But a heavyweight who won the final bout of the night just beat me to it. By then I was becoming passionate about the sport.

My victim wanted a rematch. This time we met on my home ground, at Connah's Quay Civic Centre, in front of a thousand spectators. I didn't box quite as well but won on a split decision again. Home advantage probably helped. And this time I was named boxer of the night. I still have the programme, which cost 20p, for this, my second and final bout. The date on it is 14 March 1990, it was billed as 'An Evening of Boxing on behalf of Guide Dogs for the Blind', and it was organized by the R & B Golf Society. There, among the 'senior' bouts consisting of three two-minute rounds, is S. Kavanach of Anglesey v. M. Owen of Deeside. I wonder what happened to my great rival, S. Kavanach?

With two wins under my belt, my next fight was scheduled for Wrexham, but my opponent failed to show. By this time, however, football was beginning to take over and I was moving up through the ranks. A place at Lilleshall, the Football Association's national academy, was on the horizon, so my life as a boxer was brought to a premature end.

I'm certain that putting myself through the trial of a proper boxing match had a beneficial effect. I didn't know at the time that it was Dad's intention to toughen me up. He now admits that the idea was to give me an extra layer of protection against the jealousy I aroused at school. I wouldn't say boxing increased my muscle bulk or changed me physically, but it helped me learn how to look after myself. It was certainly more mentally challenging than rugby, cricket or athletics, which I also took part in (when it came to school sports I grabbed whatever was going). If I got kicked and stayed down when I wasn't properly hurt I got a rollicking from Dad. In fact, I only needed to do it once to learn not to do it again. Apparently he was a fearless player who wouldn't be afraid to put his head where it hurt. He came from a tough part of Liverpool, and his mentality was that you don't go down unless you're in real pain.

I suppose I'm quite old-fashioned when it comes to playing the game. Umbro, one of my major sponsors, are always trying to twist my arm to get more colour into the boots they make for me, and as I've grown older I've let them inject a little more white. Football is full of passing fashions, such as coloured boots, or pulling your socks up above the knees, but I'm not the sort of player who would shave one eyebrow for effect. I'm not into trends. I'm not saying that makes me better than anyone else, but my attitude is similar to my father's: just play the game like a normal man.

One of the worst things to have crept into football in recent years is the crowding of referees. If you do that, and push and shove one another, you make the incident look more serious than it is. When I first came into the Premier League players had plenty of respect for one another; it would have been unthinkable to try to get an opponent sent off. Nowadays if you even touch a goalkeeper the whole defence comes over and pushes you around. The crowd starts shouting, the ref feels an exaggerated sense of urgency, and red and yellow cards start flying. There just isn't as much mutual respect among players as there used to be.

But back to my childhood. A major feature of my footballing repertoire is explosive speed over short distances. Third in a county race at the age of 12 was the full extent of my honours as a young sprinter, though I did once cover the 100 metres in 11.4 seconds. My size helped. In my early teens I was half the height of most of my contemporaries, which helped me achieve that extra pace. But it wasn't until I was about 18 that I started to become not just fast but powerfully quick. By then I was growing into my frame. Dad tells the story of how he took me to the local leisure centre for an indoor match when I was five. He sat up on the balcony watching, and remembers noticing that I side-footed the ball into the goal rather than blasting it. Later he told Mum, 'If Michael's got pace as well, he's going to be some player.' Soon it became apparent that I could burst away over 40 or 50 yards.

My two brothers were also good footballers. They had a lot in the locker. As he would tell you himself with a smile, my eldest brother, Terry, did what many keen footballers do and became a bit too fond of smoking and drinking. Andy had attributes that would be highly valued today. He was blisteringly fast. These days, if you're quick and you can kick a ball in the right direction you can make a decent living in the lower leagues. I wouldn't say Andy went off the rails, but he got himself a girlfriend he was passionate about and didn't want to put in the time on the training ground. He was at Chester (Third Division) for a while, and he played for Holywell Town (Welsh Premier League). You're not a mug if you're competing at that level. Both Andy and Terry got paid for playing.

When the family get together, we fall about laughing when the talk gets round to 'what might have been' for my brothers. When Andy has had a couple of drinks he starts saying, 'I could have been as good as Michael if I hadn't found a girlfriend or hit the ale.' It's hilarious, and he knows it too. There's nothing funnier in the world than Andy telling us how fast he was and how many goals he scored. He will turn to Dad and say, 'Come on, Dad, tell 'em how fast I was!' And Dad will back him up, playing him on a string. Terry doesn't make the same claims; he's happy to have chosen the easier life, without football as an obsession. Even at 32, though, Andy insists he could still make the grade for a couple of years. Usually when he's had a couple of drinks.

Speed is the key to my battles with the game's best defenders. The tough ones are the quick ones. Size doesn't bother me, because my main weapon is pace; it's the fast ones who negate some of my natural swiftness. Marcel Desailly springs to mind in that respect. In his prime, he was a beast to play against. Martin Keown was also quick on his feet. At his peak, you wouldn't find yourself sprinting past Martin. Of the current generation, John Terry is not as quick as some, but he gets very tight to you and it's difficult to turn against him. Rio Ferdinand is fast, but he also likes to give you a chance. He likes to play a bit. He wouldn't mind you thinking you were on to a good thing and then reaching the ball first to do a Cruyff turn. You think you're going to get round him but then he sticks out one of those long legs and steals

the ball. Jaap Stam was also a really world-class defender, on account of his speed, size and aggression. That's the real modern defender. Football's moved on from the age of the big stopper always heading the ball. Walter Samuel, of Roma and Argentina, is another to have given me trouble. We've had a few good tussles.

Anyone who lets me get a run on them, lets me turn and face them one on one, is playing to my strengths. But a defender who glues himself to me and doesn't let me turn is starting to make it difficult to make those runs. When they do that, I love a ball to be plonked in behind the defender because I will always fancy my chances of beating him in a sprint. In those instances it's all about the midfielder picking the right pass to play to the striker – the killer pass.

Gary Lineker was my favourite player when I was a kid, and Everton were my team, though for my card collection I'd go after any big name from any club. However, if I compare my allegiance to Everton to, say, that of my Liverpool friend and colleague Jamie Carragher, I didn't come close to being a real diehard fan. He tells me about the lengths he used to go to in order to follow the Blues. When Jamie was five his dad was already carting him off to away games, even in Europe. When he tells me that, I think, *Oh, OK, I wasn't really a fan after all*. Between the ages of five and 15 he'd be physically sick if Liverpool beat Everton. For the first 20 minutes he could hardly watch. He would hide in the toilets. I supported Everton, but if they lost it wouldn't devastate me. I would look forward to my own game more than the Everton result.

The stars at Goodison Park when I was a kid were Trevor Steven, Kevin Sheedy, Kevin Ratcliffe, Neville Southall and, above all, Lineker, mainly because he scored goals. I didn't know much about him though. I'd have been buzzing to meet him and get his autograph, but I didn't really idolize anyone when I was young. I didn't study any individual with a view to learning his secrets and the details of his life, I just loved football. I didn't look at the players of that time and think, *I'm desperate to be like you.*

At that time, Lineker was the England striker, followed, of course, by Alan Shearer. I'd like to think I'm the main England striker now. People always assume you're best pals with players who were prominent in previous England set-ups, which isn't always the case, though I do speak to Gary and Alan on the phone from time to time. Not for advice, though Gary has certainly called me a few times just to chat. When I put the phone down I sometimes think he was passing on wisdom without ramming it down my throat. But I would never ask anyone for guidance. If that's a fault, so be it. It's not that I think I can do everything perfectly, it's more that I regard advice as a favour given, and I don't like asking for favours. I can never phone anyone and, say, ask for match tickets. My dad is the same. He would never have called Everton, as an ex-player, to ask for tickets, or put in a call to Liverpool to say, 'My son's on your books, can you get us in to the game?' We would stand in line like everyone else. If I'm struggling for form or fitness, I batter my way through it. If someone wants to give me advice I'm a happy listener, but I just can't ask for it. That's just the way I am.

3

Lilleshall and Louise

Lilleshall has disappeared off the list of big breeding grounds for talent, but it was the academy where I changed from a boy to a man. It was the Football Association's university for England's most promising youngsters. For me, it was the bridge between my exploits with Deeside Schools and the start of my professional career with Liverpool. And I loved every moment of it.

The two years I spent under the direction of Keith Blunt and his staff were, for me, an enormous transitional stage. I learned a vast amount about life, football, everything. Keith was the head coach, and he taught me about the discipline of football as well as how to be as a person on the pitch. My graduation was notable for one other life-changing event: when I returned to Hawarden, my relationship with Louise Bonsall, who was around throughout my formative schoolboy years, found shape, and it put us on the path to parenthood in our early twenties. Today, we have our daughter Gemma and son James to show for all the happy years we have spent together.

In large measure, Lilleshall made me the player I am today. By the age of 14, at the FA's hothouse in the Midlands, I was playing football full-time – training every single day and playing matches at weekends. Up to the ages of about 12 or 13, you play football purely for the enjoyment; around 14, you start thinking about it more seriously. It becomes more of an academic process. So in my first year at Lilleshall I felt myself passing through that door into professionalism. It was during these years that I made my debuts for England U-15s and U-16s, and I managed to score on both occasions.

Keith Blunt taught me a tremendous amount about being a striker. He stressed the importance of keeping possession of the ball and highlighted all the technical areas where I needed to improve. He was a coach who wouldn't complicate things but insisted on the basics being done properly. He wanted the defenders and midfielders to move the ball quickly to the strikers' feet. That totally transformed my game. Up to the age of 14, I was running on to balls chipped over the top; now I was learning the serious stuff. I was finding out how to take a ball into feet, how to turn, how to keep it away from a defender, side-on, and how to use my strength and link the play. Lilleshall was where my game really took off.

It may seem unlikely, given that effectively I had to leave home at 14, but I have immensely happy memories of being a student there, and I was heartbroken when I heard it was to close as a national centre of excellence. Just look at the players who have emerged from its halls. It was a place of phenomenal achievement. I remember watching an international five or six years ago and counting half a dozen players who had been through Lilleshall; Ian Walker, Sol Campbell, Andy Cole and Nick Barmby were among them. From my generation there was me, Wes Brown (Manchester United), Michael Ball (Everton), Kenny Lunt (Crewe) and Jon Harley (Chelsea). Every year they were churning out good players, so I was dumbfounded when they closed their doors and the Premiership clubs assumed responsibility for guiding the country's best young players. At Lilleshall we developed both as footballers and as young men. We lived and breathed the game.

I say all this with a large measure of hindsight, because the first couple of months living away from friends and families was hell. An absolute killer. In the first two or three weeks I often cried. Everyone in our group fantasized about going home. But soon enough I found those feelings reversed: when I was at home, I couldn't wait to get back to Lilleshall. I just loved that place. Some of my fondest memories are of the lads with whom I shared those years. We were like 15 brothers. When I left, at 16, again I couldn't stop crying. The wrench was leaving people with whom I'd shared so much.

Those two years between 14 and 16 are serious ones in any teenager's life. Whatever you want to do, that 24-month period will probably tell you whether or not it's going to work out. The coaches at Lilleshall were quite clear with the parents. They were told that if we were lucky one of us might turn out to be a top-flight pro. One in 16 was, they said, the average. So the parents were under no illusions. But these warnings were delivered with a certain kindness in the voice. The care we received was just excellent. They sent us to a very good local school, Idsall High, and made sure we didn't neglect our education. I managed to pass all 10 of my GCSEs, with C and D grades. Had football not dominated my thoughts, I'm sure those grades would have been higher.

The days were highly structured. In our dormitories we would be woken up at 6.45 a.m. and have to be down for breakfast by 7.30 to give us time to board the bus to school. Often, on Saturdays, we would head off to watch a Premiership game – usually Aston Villa or Coventry, because they were the nearest grounds. Our own matches would be on the

Sunday, then it was back into training on the Monday. On the third Saturday and Sunday in every month we came home. There were three main influences on us, none of whom we will ever forget: Craig Simmons, the physiotherapist; Keith Blunt, the head of football; and Tony Pickering, the housemaster on the two upstairs floors of bedrooms and bathrooms. Tony and his wife Gilly looked after us as if we were their kids. They were lovely.

One day at Lilleshall I became extremely poorly, and Gilly called my parents to ask them to drive down. Mum and Dad said they would be there in 40 minutes. When they arrived, Gilly told them, 'I've never known a kid have so much faith that his parents were coming.' She thought that was very special.

In the dorms we had some great parties – and usually got caught by Mr and Mrs Pickering just as we were getting into full flow. The friendships with the other lads remain, but we haven't always kept in close contact. You always think you are going to maintain that close connection, but life moves on. It's sad, because I'd love to speak to a few of them now. I see Wes, obviously, with England and we chat about Lilleshall occasionally, though not often enough. I'd love to get everyone back together. Maybe we'll have a big reunion when we're all finished.

Everyone looked out for one another. We had to, because we encroached on a normal local school where there was a great deal of jealousy. In addition, we naturally took all the prettiest girls because we were young footballers playing for England schoolboys. We had one or two serious problems with the local kids, and some fights. I didn't get involved in any punch-ups, but there was a lot of general animosity – threats, say, from the older brothers of boys at the school we'd fallen out with. I remember a big group coming down

with baseball bats one day, and us having to run off. There were even attempts to confront us up at Lilleshall. But maybe the threats weren't as serious as they seemed at the time. After all, we were extremely fit athletes, so I can't imagine the locals wanting to take us on. My only previous experience of that kind of jealousy was during my last few weeks at school in North Wales when, knowing I was about to leave, some of the older boys made things uncomfortable for me. This is where my boxing experience came in useful – not that I had to make physical use of it, though.

That aside, Lilleshall was a time of opportunity and growth. I even managed to pick up an FA Youth Cup winner's medal with Liverpool while I was there. I was on Centre of Excellence forms at Liverpool, and had been attending informal training sessions at the club since the age of 11; it was like a mini-club, always with the same lads. I wasn't on schoolboy forms with Liverpool at the time, though, because the authorities at Deeside had a rule against boys having formal associations with clubs. Still, Liverpool had a right to request my services from time to time, and on this occasion Keith Blunt took a call from Anfield asking the FA to release me for a game against Sheffield United in the fourth round of the FA Youth Cup. The Liverpool strikers at that time were a few years older than me, and the team had just scored four against Bradford City and five without reply against Luton, so I was especially honoured to be summoned so young. The Liverpool youth side of the time had some very decent players too, particularly David Thompson and Jamie Carragher. John Curtis, who was also at Lilleshall, made the same jump from Lilleshall to FA Youth Cup games, but it was still unusual for someone as young as me, just 16, to be playing in U-18 football. For that reason I was pretty shocked by the club's request. One of the youth coaches came to pick me up, and that night I slept in digs before playing against Sheffield United in a match we won 3–2. I scored two goals. Then it was back to Lilleshall and full-time training.

The fifth round came, and the phone rang again. This time we played Manchester United at Anfield and I scored a hat-trick in a 3-2 win. That is one of my special memories. Then we beat Crystal Palace in the semis, with me scoring three goals over the two legs. For the first leg of the final against West Ham I was away with England U-16s, but in my absence Liverpool won 2–0 in front of more than 15,000 spectators. I was back for the second leg of the final at Anfield to face Rio Ferdinand and co. in the West Ham defence. Now there were 20,600 in the stands. Within two minutes of the whistle going, Frank Lampard scored and narrowed our lead to 2-1 on aggregate. Then I managed to force in a header, and we scored again through Stuart Quinn. So we were crowned 1996 FA Youth Cup champions in front of a huge Anfield crowd.

If anyone asks me, I still regard that trophy as one of my major honours, up there with the FA Cup. The Youth Cup is the whole focus of junior and academy football, and to be exposed to that experience so young left a considerable mark on my development. Jamie Carragher and I still talk about it to this day.

My main friends from my Liverpool days are Carra, Danny Murphy, Didi Hamann and Steven Gerrard. I think of the other players as mates, but the four I've just named are my closest friends. But when I first joined the club everyone seemed to be everyone else's close pal. In those days I would have struggled to pick out four names for fear of offending the rest. There were fewer foreign players back then, and the squad changed less frequently. Carra, as we all call him, has been my mate all the way through. We started to become close when I was at Lilleshall and coming back to Liverpool for those FA Youth Cup games. He made his debut in the first team a while before me, but then dropped away a bit before returning permanently around the time I joined the first eleven. We've been room-mates ever since, and have become closer and closer. I regard him as my best mate at Liverpool.

He's an amazing character. He's the resident joker and the social secretary, and makes the club tick behind the scenes. If we have a night out, Carra's the one to organize it. He's invaluable for team spirit. He's very knowledgeable about football, and quite opinionated, too. He eats, sleeps and drinks the game. My relief, when I go in to training, is talking to Didi about horse racing, but if you talk about anything other than football to Carra he's not interested. He won't even pretend to be interested. He'll tell you to shut up. But if you ask him to tell you the starting line-ups for the 1965 FA Cup final he would reel them off. He gets every football magazine and every book. If Sky showed a documentary about, say, the FA Cup glory years, Carra would be glued to it.

I could never be like that. I would burst. When Carra's injured or suspended, he nearly explodes. Without his football he's like a time-bomb waiting to go off. When we talk about what he's going to do when he finishes playing, he's deadly serious about being one of the supporters, travelling to every away game. He's a fan through and through who is just living the dream. On a couple of occasions my parents have spotted him in the crowd, at Middlesbrough and Chelsea. If he's suspended, he'll go to the game with his friends and sit among the supporters. He keeps it quiet because the manager worries he might have a drink on the way to the match. Carra's just a diamond like that. Deep down, he might still have a feeling for Everton, who he supported as a boy, but he loves Liverpool Football Club. Above all, he's a fan of football. He loves the lads and he loves the craic of getting on the team bus to head off for a game.

He works incredibly hard, too. He's a solid, reliable full-back. We all take the mickey out of him, calling him the stereotypical club pro, Mr Dependable. He believes he's got more in his locker than that. He gets irate if someone who isn't playing as well as him gets heaps of praise. Carra's an unsung hero, there's no question about that. He's always the last Liverpool player to be sung to by the crowd, yet he has given as much to the team and the club as anyone currently at Anfield. It gets him down, because he feels like one of them. He sees himself as one of the supporters and asks himself why they don't love him as much as they should.

But all this, of course, was still to come back in the mid-1990s. When Carra and I met I was still a young dreamer working my way towards a career in the Premiership.

I honestly think I did as much as I possibly could as a schoolboy and youth footballer. I don't see how I could have added much more to my CV. I think I'm right in saying that only Terry Venables and I have represented England at every age level. I played only one Under-21 game for England, and then went straight into the senior squad. Similarly, I played only 10 reserve games at Liverpool before being promoted to the first eleven. As soon as I left Lilleshall it was bang-bang-bang: A-team, reserves and first team within minutes of one another, or so it seemed.

The issue of my nationality was a theme of my early days in the game. Given my goalscoring record for Deeside Schools – an average of three per game – it was inevitable that the Welsh schoolboy selectors would take an interest and try to persuade me to pledge my allegiance to them. I always knew when a scout was present: I had only to look over to Dad's usual vantage point to see whether he had company. Nobody would talk to my father during a game because he would make it clear that he wanted to concentrate on the match and on how I was doing. Mum would make all the conversation with the other parents, who wouldn't intrude on Dad's privacy in his spot behind the goal. So I had an early warning system: if anyone stood next to my dad, it had to be a scout. To anyone else he would have said, 'I don't mean to be rude, I'd just like to watch the game.' I glanced up often, for reassurance, so no scout could have slid up to my dad without me knowing.

When I was first approached by Wales I was playing for Flintshire schoolboys. I ended up at the national trials, two years younger than I should have been. I didn't enjoy trials; I never have. You would end up staying in a college for two days, not knowing anyone, very much on your own. But you have to put yourself about if you're going to get anywhere in football. So I went to a training session, then the first trial, then the final one, not thinking much of it. For the equivalent trial with England a couple of years later it felt like life or death, but with Wales, at the age of 13, I think I regarded it as an elaborate football course rather than as an audition for international representation. I didn't feel a weight of expectation, which probably helped.

During the final session my dad approached the organizer and said, 'If you're thinking of picking him, you should know that Michael's not going to be available to play for Wales.' Dad had spoken to Steve Heighway at the Centre of Excellence, as well as to a representative from Lilleshall. The advice was that if I got tied into the Welsh schoolboy system it would prevent me from playing for England at the same junior levels.

In that final trial, I knew it wasn't going to lead to a place in the Wales team. And the following year, of course, I was selected for Lilleshall after a windswept trial at Chester's Deva Stadium, which meant that I was away for two years and studying at an English school. Besides, the only option I ever had was to play for Wales schoolboys; it was never going to be possible for me to go on and represent Wales at senior level because there's no trace of Welsh blood in me, though my surname has Welsh overtones. I'm English, with Scottish ancestry on my dad's side. I always try to make that clear to people who may wonder whether I turned my back on Wales.

So, in international terms it was England or no one, and I had a really successful youth career. I broke the Under-15 scoring record that had been shared by Nick Barmby and Kevin Gallen, and at Under-16 and Under-17 I also scored plenty of goals. You hear so many rave reviews about young players who are going to make it, but experience teaches us that a lot of them disappear. I'm so pleased that I managed to escape that fate, not to mention proud that I lived up to the promise I showed as a kid.

That aspect of football has changed dramatically even from when I was a teenager. Then, if you got offered a two-year deal and £500 a week you were ecstatic. And you had to be some player to be offered a formal deal at 15 years old. Nowadays, it's so important not to let a Michael Owen or Steven Gerrard slip through the net that clubs employ a scattergun approach, offering lucrative contracts to just about anyone. In one sense it devalues what it meant when I was a teenager. The grapevine is alive with stories about how much teenagers are being offered these days, and I'm not sure every young player who gets that kind of deal necessarily deserves it. People are getting paid left, right and centre on the basis of promise rather than achievement. In the past, you got the money when you made it to the top; now, there are people getting paid well for being good one year and ordinary two seasons on.

But there will never be any lack of gratitude on my part at how football has changed the lives of the Owen family. And it's my mum and dad who deserve the credit. Throughout those early years, my parents were a constant presence. Interestingly, the highlight for them, of my whole career so far, remains an Under-15 England v Scotland game in Newcastle on 28 April 1995 in which I scored in a 2–1 win. Right from the restart after Scotland had equalized the ball came to me and I ran all the way through their team to score. What made it so special for them was that all the Owens and the Donnellys had gathered to watch the game. The Donnellys were my dad's Scottish relatives, and many of them came south to watch the match. He got dozens of tickets and was as proud as punch just to see me in an England shirt in that setting. When the final whistle went I ran up to the crowd, found Dad and hugged him. He was crying; in fact, the whole family was sobbing. It just meant so much to us. It was only Under-15s, so nobody outside the family will remember it, but the Owens will never forget that day. (I should add that Mum has her own private highlight: the day I won the 1998 BBC Sports Personality of the Year award.)

The most meaningful international goal I've scored was either the one against Brazil in the quarter-finals of the 2002 World Cup or the one I struck against Argentina four years earlier, but that goal against Scotland in Newcastle was certainly the finest. I may never score one of higher quality. I ran through the entire Scotland team and smacked it into the top corner. I'm not sure the Donnellys appreciated how good it was, but the Owens certainly did.

Long before I signed professional forms for Liverpool, which I did on my seventeenth birthday in December 1996, I did the rounds, checking out some of the clubs who had expressed an interest in me while I was at Lilleshall. I didn't particularly enjoy that process because I've never relished the experience of turning up at a place where I don't know people. But I always felt comfortable at Liverpool. I'd been there in my school holidays and, of course, had signed Centre of Excellence forms. This was a fairly loose arrangement and didn't commit us to each other, but already a bond was being formed. I was becoming reassuringly familiar with the players, the coaches and the other staff at the academy. As I said, one of my dreads in football has always been walking into a dressing room where I don't know anyone. The thought kills me. But, quite rightly, Dad wanted me to accept a few invitations to visit other clubs and extend my education.

I went to Manchester United and spent a week or two there undergoing trials. I always had the impression that United wanted to bring me into their successful youth system. It was when I went to watch a game at Old Trafford that I first came face to face with the man who had shaped the careers of David Beckham, Ryan Giggs, Paul Scholes and the Neville brothers, Gary and Phil. Plainly I was in an environment where homegrown talent was valued very highly.

It's here that I have to make a confession that many readers will find odd. I had no raging desire to play for Manchester United ahead of all other clubs, and even in Sir Alex's formidable presence I couldn't pretend that I did. Before the match we had the traditional meal in the stand, and then we went to Ferguson's office. I will always remember him looking me straight in the eye and asking, 'So, do you want to play for Manchester United?' The question was so big and so simple that it threw me off balance. I was sitting opposite one of the world's leading managers, and I wanted so much to become a professional footballer. But I was a kid, and I didn't want to lie, so something stopped me from giving him the straightforward answer he was seeking. The truth was that I didn't want to play for Manchester United more than any club in the world. I had no special feeling for them. There was no basic allegiance of the sort a local lad might have felt. So my answer was 'sort of', followed by a meandering 'yes'. I just couldn't have stood in front of him and said, 'Oh, yes, Mr Ferguson, I've always been dying to play for Manchester United.'

As much as I respected him, I was extremely nervous in his company. It wasn't a fear of being bullied; more a case of finding the whole routine uncomfortable. It required me to hold conversations I wasn't ready to have. So, generally, I found myself agreeing with a lot of what managers said – being diplomatic, I suppose.

'Do you want to be a professional footballer, son?'

'Yeah, I do.'

That's pretty much the way it would go. You only really give one-word answers when you're a kid, don't you?

I don't know what Alex Ferguson made of it, but I do know that Brian Kidd, his assistant, had been to watch me lots of times and had got to know my dad quite well. For a while, if United didn't have a game on the Saturday Brian Kidd would often be on the touchline to see me play. The United scouts stayed in touch and asked Dad to let them know when it was decision time on which club I was going to choose. If I'd been older, I might not have been quite so naive in front of Sir Alex, but at that tender age I was listening to my heart more than my head. I wasn't old enough to make calculations about who was the biggest club or who might have the brightest future.

I also went for a week's trial at Arsenal, and then, later, to Highbury to watch a match against Coventry, who won the game with the help of a hat-trick by Mickey Quinn. We watched from one of the new executive boxes at the Clock End, with smoked salmon and other delicacies to tempt us. I'd never seen smoked salmon before, and I'm not sure my parents had either. We were all pretty nervous in that environment. An hour before kick-off Arsenal's chief scout took me out of the box and down to the dressing room. The Arsenal players were getting ready for the match, and I especially remember Ian Wright making a big fuss of me. As he bounded over, there was a cry of, 'Hey, how are you, mate?' Being naturally shy, my response probably didn't quite match Wrighty's enthusiasm.

From the changing rooms I was taken to meet George Graham, still the Arsenal manager at that time, who shook my hand and said, 'I hear you're a good player, we'd love to sign you.' But he was speaking, of course, to a child, and I just about managed to mumble, 'Oh, great, thanks.' I never went to these clubs to give them a tick or a cross on my list of possible destinations. It wasn't about finding the right team; it was more a case of my dad wanting me to see these great clubs and meet the people who had made them what they were. It was an educational process, and I didn't experience it as pressure. I just assumed that the big clubs provided that kind of welcome for every promising young player. Only now do I realize that no manager would waste his time with a kid unless he was really keen to have him on the books. It's only now that I understand how privileged I was to be given time by some of the most prominent people in the English game.

At Arsenal I didn't have to prove what I could do. I think I scored four in a game my team won 5–4, but they were already making a huge fuss of me before I actually pulled on one of their shirts. They had a scout in North Wales who must have been sending down glowing reports, because the Arsenal staff couldn't do enough for me. At some clubs you have to prove your worth in a formal trial. They don't automatically take the scout's word, but Arsenal clearly did. So my time there was more about the club showing how much I would be valued and what a terrific youth system they had.

Chelsea was another stop on the tour. I went there for a game against Sheffield United, and this involved another dressing-room visit. I couldn't believe how small their players were. In those days they had John Spencer, Gavin Peacock and Dennis Wise, who all seemed about the same size as me. Glenn Hoddle was the manager. It would have been stretching even a child's imagination to believe that this was the start of an association that would take us both to the 1998 World Cup as England striker and manager. When I walked into his office, Hoddle had written my name on a board. He studied me for a while, then said, 'Look, there are a lot of youngsters we're after, but as you can see, you're top of our list.' Later I did ask myself whether he'd written the list a few moments before I entered his room, or whether I really was Chelsea's number-one target.

I also went training with Everton. I didn't get to meet the manager, though Joe Royle, who was in charge at Goodison Park, did phone my dad to express his admiration. (As an ex-Everton player, Dad takes plenty of good-natured stick for allowing me to sign for their arch-rivals. I think he's got used to being teased as a 'turncoat' when he goes back to his old club.) I called in on Oldham and Norwich too, and I trained with Wrexham and Chester because they were local. I did quite well at Manchester City, whose youth development officer had seen me at the early England get-togethers. I went away with City for a week for a tournament in France, which we won. Again, I can't remember ever meeting the manager, though their representative was the most persistent: he called Dad often to invite us to City games.

So why did Liverpool stand out from this crowd? Three names: Steve Heighway, Hughie McCauley and Dave Shannon. They were the three youth coaches. I'd worked with them on and off for several years before decision day and I liked them all. Steve Heighway had a huge influence on me and is still at the end of the line for a chat. We have a special bond. My parents think the world of him, too. He's dead straight with the mums and dads of boys at the Liverpool academy. He would never make any false promises. My parents liked that. My academy experience also meant that I was never nervous when I walked into a Liverpool dressing room. I knew all the lads. I like routine and I hate being knocked out of my stride, so I just thought, 'Why change?' Another factor was that I'd been away at Lilleshall for two years, and I faced the prospect of having to stay away from home again if I joined a club other than Liverpool. As much as they wanted me to live in club accommodation, they were willing to sign me on the basis that I could commute from home.

I suppose I was fortunate to escape the cycle of grotty pocket-money jobs that go with being a teenager. I was away from home from the age of 14, and when I returned I went straight into being a full-time YTS trainee on £42.50 a week. In that sense I was a full-time footballer from a very early age, and £42.50 would just about see me through so I didn't go out hunting for spending money. Thanks to Mum and Dad, I was used to not spending my cash on frivolous things.

When it was time to leave Lilleshall, I received my international cap from Jimmy Armfield, one of the elder statesmen of English football, at a graduation ceremony which dispersed our band of brothers across the professional game. I was now ready for life at Liverpool. But another big change was on the way: the full blossoming of my relationship with Louise Bonsall.

We lived about 15 doors away from each other on our estate in Hawarden, which was brand new but not at the mega-expensive end of the market. All the children of the same age from those houses became good friends, and Louise is just two months younger than me. We went to the same infant, junior and then secondary schools. Louise's dad, John, thought of me as the cheeky kid who was always wandering round the estate with a ball under his arm.

People always try to put a date on when Louise and I started going out together, but this begs the question: when you're a kid, what does 'going out' really mean? When you're eight, if you kiss someone on the cheek you're supposedly going out with them. When I was a child, my whole focus was football, so I didn't have an eye for a girl until I was 13 or 14. Then, of course, your interest in the opposite sex starts to get a bit more serious, and it was then that Louise, through a friend, asked me to 'go out' with her. I really don't know why I said this, but I told her mate, 'I'll think about it.' Maybe I wanted to be chased even more. I had every intention of saying yes because I fancied her right the way through. I'm not sure exactly what her friend relayed to Louise, but, as I discovered later, it was positive.

I heard nothing from her for a week, but during that time Louise must have assumed we were an item. I was playing football in the playground one day and can only have been entranced by the game because all I heard of Louise shouting my name was a faint 'Michael'. I turned round immediately to see her walking away in a huff, so she must have called my name a few times. I was a bit too embarrassed to chase her, so I carried on with my game. Later, I spoke to her friend and said, 'Sorry, I didn't even know we were meant to be going out with each other.' She replied, 'Don't worry. Forget about it.' And that was that. Things didn't progress any further before I went off to Lilleshall. If it had, maybe it would have been difficult for me to be away from home for two years.

When I came back permanently I spotted Louise in the local pub when I was there with my brothers. This time I asked a friend of mine to find out whether she was still interested in me. When the answer came back as yes, I went over and asked for her number. But within a couple of days I had to go to Ireland on a pre-season tour with Liverpool. I called her from there, and was very nervous; I just about managed to arrange a date for when I got home. By the time I returned it was quite late, so I had to drop the idea of taking her to a bar in Chester – which I'd come up with in an attempt to seem cool. We went to the local instead and had a nerve-racking chat for an hour before I drove her home and went into the house to carry on the conversation. That's when we relaxed and began to speak more freely.

Louise was in college at that time, and then she went to work for MBNA bank whose headquarters are in Chester. She stopped working a couple of months before Gemma was born. On 14 February 2004 we became engaged, on Valentine's Day, which also happens to be Louise's birthday.

We had no fixed date or venue in mind because my football commitments make things complicated. A brief window in the summer is the only clear time for us to get married – preferably in a non-championship year.

Our relationship has been a stable element throughout my adult life. If you start to become a man at 17, then I've been with Louise ever since I began that process. She was with me when I had nothing, so I've never had the problem that some prominent people have of wondering about my partner's motives for being with them. The question 'Is she here just because I'm famous?' has never arisen because we go back such a long way. We can look each other in the eye and know we're together for all the right reasons. It's sad even to have to mention that element, but I do so because it's one of the many advantages we have.

A lot of people treat me differently just because of who I am. Some of them fall over themselves to be friendly. That's the way society is. In football and life you encounter a certain amount of falseness. With your girlfriend, your family and your friends, that's never a problem. A lot of famous people marry other famous people because they understand the process of living in the public eye. Fortunately, Louise and I met before I achieved a high profile, and this was one of the foundations of our marriage in the summer of 2005.

One of the inconveniences we've had to put up with is reporters knocking on Louise's door asking if we are ever going to get married, or split up, and offering her enormous sums of money to spill the beans. I don't think my dislike of celebrity will ever change. I'd be happy if I could be left alone for the rest of my life. I'm content to get on with my job and my life with Louise, Gemma, my family and friends. I don't really like the flashing lights, the arm round the girl-friend for the cameras. It's not my scene.

Having a steady girlfriend has also helped me in my playing career. For a young footballer, the pitfalls start to open up at around 17 or 18. A lot of my time around those ages was spent with Louise. I'm not saying I would have been out drinking or doing things I shouldn't have been, I just know that I wouldn't have wanted it any other way. Stability has certainly helped me as player.

In my eyes, Louise is so down to earth. Like me, she has no desire to be in the limelight. We've moulded ourselves around each other. She's wonderful with Gemma and great to be around – really good company. She has no desire to compete with anyone in terms of fame or wealth and would never show off or boast about new clothes or possessions. I'd like to think that if she was in the players' lounge talking to the family of someone who had just joined Liverpool, they would come out saying, 'I've just met Michael Owen's girlfriend and she's so down to earth. She really made me feel welcome.' She would go out of her way to make anyone feel included. And she would speak to everyone on the same level. I'd like to think I'm like that as well. I'd like to think that I am everything Louise is.

4

Liverpool: Sugar and Spice

My Liverpool career started in earnest on my seventeenth birthday, when I went into chief executive Peter Robinson's office to sign my first professional contract. They gave me the classic red shirt with my name and number on, and that was the best part of the ceremony. Never mind the money.

I had always been a number 9, right the way through my FA Youth Cup years, but I was about to say goodbye to the centre-forward's traditional number. I was number 18 in the full Liverpool squad to begin with, but the following year, when John Barnes was retiring, Ronnie Moran, the assistant coach, approached me one day and asked, 'Do you want the number 10 shirt next year?' Robbie Fowler was number 9, and plainly he wasn't going to be giving up his jersey any time soon, so I moved up to 10. Funnily enough, I went through the same routine with England. Alan Shearer was the resident number 9 at international level and there was no chance of getting that one off him. So it was number 10 twice. And I've held it ever since.

Ten is, of course, a special number for a footballer, because everyone associates it with Pelé, Zico and Maradona. But in the English game the number 9 has a particular association. It's the old symbol of the strong and determined

55

centre-forward. Not that I get too fussed about these things. The number on your back provides no clue as to how many goals you're going to score. It's numbers on the board that count.

Peter Robinson had already been telling my dad for some months that I ought to appoint an agent, but at the time I was still only 16 and was initially reluctant to take one on. Still, Peter was adamant. 'Michael will need an agent,' he told Dad. Dad then spoke to Simon Marsh of Umbro, who had been supporting me since I was 15. Simon said he knew someone who might be ideal, and suggested both sides meet without knowing who the other one was. So, on my seventeenth birthday, with my new number 18 shirt with Owen on the back, the door opened and Simon and Tony Stephens walked in. My parents were there, too, and they sized up Tony to see whether he was the right man. They had a gut feeling that he was the one for me. Because Tony didn't know much about me he wanted to go away and do some research, but Mum and Dad stopped him and said, 'Well, we want you, so we want to know now whether you want us.' They didn't like the idea of him going off to think about. So he said yes there and then. Tony already had David Platt, Dwight Yorke, Alan Shearer and David Beckham on his books (this was before he merged himself into the big SFX organization).

Tony was impressive when we began talking to him more. I soon forgot that he had asked for more time to think about taking me on. I knew I could prove to him that he'd made a good decision. Ninety-nine per cent of the public don't know what Tony looks like. If his picture appears in the paper he kicks himself because he tries to avoid being photographed. He never gives interviews. Most agents can't wait to shout their mouths off to get business, but he does everything privately and low key. That's a plus point I really value. His experience at the negotiating table is invaluable too. He has arranged huge transfer deals for Shearer, Platt, Yorke and, of course, Beckham. But that's not the main reason I'm with him. If ever you have a problem, he seems to be the ultimate authority. It doesn't matter what the topic is, he's always knowledgeable. If you're ever in trouble he knows all the right people. Life's about contacts half the time, and Tony's are second to none. He's very rarely proved wrong. He'll select deals that fit with your image and he'll never send you down the wrong line. Shearer and Beckham, for example, were aimed in totally different directions. I couldn't see Alan doing a deal with Brylcreem or a sunglasses company. It's all very well saying, 'It's easy when you've got good clients,' but it's still possible to make big mistakes. Sure, Tony has all the right ammunition, but he knows how to use it.

The first contract I signed was with Malcolm Douglas from the watch company Tissot, who I'm still proud to be with. I was really pleased to attract their interest when I was on £500 a week, and I like the people associated with the company. Umbro's support enabled me to buy my first car. Simon Marsh and Martin Prothero were there from the very beginning and became really good friends and golf partners. Jaguar were another good contact of Tony's. Alan Shearer joined them first, and Beckham and I then signed similar deals. I've been driving a Jaguar since I was 18. I get two free ones every year. Walkers Crisps is another firm I linked up with – and they even named a flavour after me: Cheese and Owen. My first substantial soft-drinks contract was with Lucozade Sport. I've also written a column in the *News of the World* with Dave Harrison, a trusted friend, and had a link with Topps, who make sticker cards for kids. I was with

Yamaha for a while, too, and I now have an arrangement with a Japanese suit company, Aoyami, as well as Vivid Imaginations, who make children's football toys, and most recently Persil and Asda. My dad's personal favourite is my annual calendar deal with Danilo.

Four months after my visit to Peter Robinson's office, and with only a handful of reserve games behind me, I was summoned for a first-team trip to Sunderland. Initially I was under the care of Ronnie Moran, the head coach. Ronnie loved the kids. 'Don't worry, son, you're only young, it's just down to experience. Make sure you learn.' That's what he would say to us, and it was exactly what we needed to hear at that age. He treated us so well, and knew absolutely everything about the game. Sammy Lee, who played in some of the greatest Liverpool teams, was also around. Ronnie left the club when Roy Evans left, in November 1998, and after that the men in charge were Patrice Bergues, then Jacques Crevoissier, then Cristian Damiano, who was previously with Jean Tigana at Fulham. Since Ronnie, we've had two coaches on account of the increased numbers in the squad. When I first joined, Sammy was the reserve-team manager; then he became the main first-team coach before leaving Anfield in the summer of 2004 to take up a post at the FA.

'Bring your gear, just in case there are any injuries,' Ronnie added before that mid-April 1997 Sunderland game. A few hours later he told me I was in the first-team squad. I assumed, of course, that I'd been included for educational purposes. It was just to give me a look round, so I told Mum and Dad not to bother making the long journey north, and didn't ask for any tickets. Roy Evans, the manager, duly announced his team, and naturally I wasn't included, but when it came to calling out the substitutes I suddenly heard my name. In those days we were allowed to have a mobile phone with us until we entered the dressing room an hour before the game. I didn't own one, but I did manage to borrow one from a team-mate and called my parents from the centre of the pitch. Dad said, 'It's only an hour until kick-off – shall we try to get up there for the second half?' I told them not to bother, which turned out to be the right call. It wasn't the sort of game in which a reserve striker gets on.

Next time out for me was Wimbledon away on 6 May, and I was on the bench again. This time a fresh striker was needed in the later stages of the game. We were 1–0 down, and with about half an hour to go the manager said, 'Go and get warmed up.' I rose, shook myself down and took a couple of steps. I'd jogged about 10 yards when Wimbledon scored again. I didn't have time to reach the corner flag before I heard a shout of 'Michael!' As I turned they were gesturing at me to get ready to go on. So no warm-up; just straight into the thick of it for my League debut.

To run on to a football pitch in a Liverpool first-team shirt for the first time is a massive moment in anybody's life. It's one of those crests that is instantly recognizable across the world. But as a kid that day, I didn't think of Bob Paisley and Bill Shankly and all those European Cups; I was living for the moment. I looked around and saw Stan Collymore beside me and John Barnes just in behind. It was only after the game that I thought, 'I've actually played for Liverpool Football Club today.' Scored, as well, because I got off to the best possible start. It was the kind of goal I'd been scoring for 10 years. I was looking for gaps when Stig Inge Bjornebye played a perfectly weighted ball which I barely had to touch. I just ran round the outside of it and placed it in the corner. For the remainder of that game I felt just great – fresh and dangerous. The downside was that we couldn't set up an equalizer.

It was in the next game five days later, when I started against Sheffield Wednesday in a match we needed to win to reach the Champions League, that I started to feel vaguely important. I was 17, and they were showing how much they believed in me. I was so proud, running out at Hillsborough as one of the starting eleven. I can remember the whole day vividly. Sheffield Wednesday's pitch is massive and I was exceptionally tense. Twenty minutes into the match I was struck by horrendous cramp. I'd never had it before, and I'd always assumed it was something that tended to attack in the eightieth or ninetieth minute. It started in my calf, then spread to my hamstrings, my groin and my thighs. By half-time I felt as if I had cramp in every muscle. It must have been sheer nerves and tension. I was considering saying to the physios, 'Look, I can't carry on. Every time I break out of a walk my legs lock up.'

As we sat down, the manager announced he was going to make a change. I automatically thought, 'Well, I'm the kid, and I'm surrounded by big, established stars, so it's bound to be me.' Instead, Roy Evans looked at Stan Collymore and said, 'Stan, you're coming off.' I was in shock. It wasn't in my nature to analyse Stan's deteriorating relationship with the manager or the club; I just thought, 'I must be playing better than Stan Collymore!' which gave me a fresh injection of confidence.

I played the full 90 minutes, and won the free-kick from which we scored our equalizer. The 2–1 loss at Wimbledon had put us out of the championship race, and the draw with Sheffield Wednesday deprived us of a Champions League place, yet there I was coming off the pitch with a beaming smile.

Stan left Liverpool under something of a cloud, but to the best of my knowledge there was no tension between him and the rest of the players. As a kid looking in, my guess was that he found it hard to be close to people, though he was always friendly and shared our laughs and jokes. He was good pals with Jamie Redknapp and Phil Babb, among others, but it's fair to say he was a loner. I did admire him as a player, though. What he did at Nottingham Forest got him his move to Liverpool, and his whole career was built around that. He was by no means a failure at Anfield, where he made a cracking start. He was always fit and made and created plenty of goals. But Robbie Fowler was on fire at that time and was plainly the main man. It's possible that Stan found it hard to play the supporting role, and certainly there was friction between him and the manager; as a player, you can just sense it. There was no single falling-out between them; it was just a gradual icing over of the relationship. The manager starts bringing a player off early in a game, the player gets resentful; if he's two minutes late for training the next day, it seems a bigger issue than it really is. I should say that as far as I was concerned Stan was never a problem in terms of not turning up for training, or arguing with the staff. He was just one of those characters who live within themselves.

Although I'd trained a few times with the first team, because Liverpool had a system of plucking the odd player out from the reserves to practise with the seniors, I certainly hadn't been a regular companion for them on the training ground. I didn't really know the men I joined in the closing stages of the 1996/97 campaign, and the squad at that time was packed with big names and big personalities. With those first few kicks at the end of my debut season, I didn't have time to form firm opinions about the lively characters around me, but in retrospect I can appreciate that it was a great laugh coming into that dressing room. We had a terrific team spirit, which can count for a lot.

There was a negative aspect to the 'Spice Boys' image that some players acquired, but I honestly don't think anyone did anything to the detriment of the team. Yes, they came in and talked about girls, or said, 'Hey, come and have look at my new car.' If you look at the Melwood car park now and compare it to the one we had in my early days they are simply miles apart. It's true that before Gérard Houllier took over Liverpool players were less self-conscious about showing off their wealth. The culture was more laddish, closer to the stereotype of how young footballers behave. It wouldn't be unusual to see the odd girlie mag lying around the changing room. But it was harmless lads' behaviour. I know from talking to my brothers, who work in factories, that pranks and jokes are a feature of the workplace everywhere. I couldn't condemn it, not least because I was part of it. I enjoyed being one of the lads and going out for a drink from time to time. It was definitely a different atmosphere to the one we have now. Enjoyment was a large part of the training routine. If someone played badly in practice we'd make a joke of it to lift his spirits. These days, if a player is awful on the training ground it's no laughing matter. He'd probably be dropped.

David James, or Jame-o, our goalkeeper at the time, is a great lad and always one for the banter. When I first arrived in the Liverpool dressing room he wasn't the first to put his arm round me or go out of his way to make me feel comfortable. For that reason I often felt a bit nervous in his company. He was so lively, and he would take the mick out of anyone, no matter how important they were. If he had it in for you, you'd be on the wrong end of his chat for quite a while. When you develop, you can give it back, but at that stage he was a bit too big and clever for me to be taking on. I didn't have much to do with him in those days, but he lives quite near me now and we often speak on the phone. We're good friends. But I admit I was very wary of him at first. He wasn't nasty, but he could take the mick out of you in front of the other players. I tried to avoid him doing that to me.

The main difference between English and foreign players is the sense of humour. If you get up to a prank with someone's toothbrush in the team hotel, a lot of foreign players just won't find that funny. But I'm laughing even as I say this. In my early days Steve Harkness was the biggest prankster. Didi Hamann has an Englishman's sense of humour, but apart from him I've yet to meet one overseas player who laughs at the things we do. In training, if you make a silly mistake the English lads will laugh their heads off, whereas the foreign lads are much more serious in their approach. They are all good guys so I'm not trying to label them in any way. I'm just trying to highlight the difference between the two cultures. I can remember Robbie Fowler getting thrown into a puddle and covered in mud at countless training sessions. They were just harmless, laddish things. I'm not saying it was better or worse, just different. The trick, I think, is to strike a balance. It's scientifically proven that alcohol is not good for you too close to a game. But then, our occasional nights out helped us to develop such a strong team spirit. We would have died for one another.

According to Liverpool tradition, training wasn't practice for the game on Saturday. We had a different mindset. The warm-up would last five minutes; now it's half an hour. Five-a-side used to be the centrepiece. Only on Fridays did we prepare for corners and other set-pieces. Otherwise five-a-side was the religion.

I didn't know it then, but Liverpool were coming to the end of this boot-room era, in which the manager's job would be passed along the line by men who had been around the club for years and understood Liverpool's unique culture. If anyone was to point the finger and say, 'You partied too much, you did this or that wrong,' it was certainly outweighed by the team spirit we built up. From every negative you can draw a positive. If you do everything by the book – train every minute, eat only the healthiest food, sleep for 10 hours a night – it might be great for your physical preparation, but if your mind goes stale and you're not enjoying your life then it can become counter-productive. If a get-together on a Tuesday night before a Saturday game brings players closer together, you won't find me always condemning that as wrong.

I'm not a big drinker myself, and on a Thursday or a Friday alcohol ought to be out of bounds. But it's too simplistic to condemn all socializing as irresponsible or unprofessional. In part, I remember those early days for the amount of time I spent laughing and enjoying myself. We looked forward to training because the camaraderie was so good. Also, people forget how good some of the Liverpool performances were during those years. I can remember going to watch the first team between the ages of 14 and 17 and being entertained every week. We were winning games 4–3 and playing fantastic stuff.

Temptation is a fact of any young Premiership player's early career. Suddenly there is money and a thriving social life on offer. But I think of my elders during my first two seasons at Anfield as really good men. A myth has grown up that some of them were rebels who didn't care about the job. It really wasn't like that. I was 17 years and 144 days old when I made my first appearance – Liverpool's youngest debutant – and the senior players could see I was a decent player who needed looking after. If anything, they protected me. If we had a night out, there was no peer pressure to get drunk or behave stupidly. If you wanted to drink Coca-Cola all night then that was fine. They wanted me to do well and they looked out for me. They didn't try to lead me astray. Quite the opposite, in fact.

I did, however, have to grow up fast. I was mixing with 25- and 30-year-olds who were a lot more worldly than me. That forced me to be more mature than I otherwise might have been. I learned the rights from the wrongs very quickly.

Robbie Fowler was the top man. When I joined the club properly he was the one I looked up to. Even though Ian Rush was still a legend at Anfield, he wasn't around when I was breaking into the first team, whereas Robbie had always been present, and I had studied him closely when he was 15 and 16 and I was only 10 or 11. He was such a good player that he became the one whose standards I wanted to match. It wasn't a question of trying to take his place, more 'Robbie Fowler's the best, try to get alongside him'. Sadly his career has been blighted by injuries, but in his prime he was a wonderful finisher – really sharp. He was never one to take players on and beat them for pace, but then he didn't need to. He could finish with both feet from any range. Whether it was placement or power or chipping the keeper, he was awesome to watch.

Robbie and Steve McManaman were joined at the hip – off the pitch and often on it too. I didn't point it out to them at the time, but if Macca had the ball and Robbie and me were both making runs with a fifty-fifty chance of receiving the pass, it would rarely come to me. You could tell they were best mates because Macca was always looking to feed Robbie. It got a bit frustrating at the end. But Robbie was a great lad, and one of the chief jokers in the team.

His most infamous scrape was pretending to snort a line of cocaine off the pitch during a Merseyside derby. When he made the odd mistake, it was always through naivety. People forget that footballers are normal lads, and Robbie was from Toxteth, a particularly tough district of Liverpool. We forget how much stick he took from opposition supporters. Take it from me – and I don't even live there – Liverpool is rumour city. Everything is recorded, distorted and passed on. If you're seen going into a toilet, it must have been to take drugs; if you're seen outside a casino, you must have just lost two million quid. Bearing in mind that half the city is red, and half blue, it's an easy line of attack to spread some gossip about one of the enemy's players. Robbie took the full brunt. Every time we played Everton their fans sang songs about him being a 'smackhead'. You can see how frustrated someone would get if they hadn't been doing that kind of thing. The upside, I suppose, is that because Robbie grew up in the heart of Liverpool – unlike me – he became very streetwise. I think that helped make him such a success.

When Liverpool fans see one of their own performing well in the team, that player develops a special status. The supporters can relate to him as a man as well as a footballer. Maybe they saw themselves in Robbie – a working-class lad, raised in Liverpool, who had come up through the ranks in the traditional way. Coming from Chester, I was a comparative outsider, so there was never much chance that I would be given a nickname to compare with that of Robbie, who was known to the fans simply as 'God'. When I was growing up, I thought he was God too. I was never jealous of him, but I did take note of the fact that the fans were less inclined to sing songs about me than him, even when I was making a big impact in the team. At times I did wonder why I wasn't regarded as another of the club's 'local heroes'.

Now, I have a different perspective. Towards the end of his Liverpool career, when he was slipping, Robbie fell behind some of the club's other strikers on the supporters' song list. They would chant about Titi Camara, or one of the other forwards the club had bought from overseas. Some of them hadn't scored a hundredth of the goals Robbie registered for Liverpool, and these days I ask myself, 'Was Robbie enough of a god to Liverpool fans?' He returned from Manchester City a hero, of course, in the winter transfer window of 2006.

But it happens in football. When you hear Ryan Giggs being booed by United fans, as he was one season, you know for sure that nobody is immune. I don't understand how people can ignore a player's achievements just because he's going through a sticky patch. When Giggs was being jeered, he had won seven championship medals and a European Cup. How can that be forgotten? People will say, 'He earns £50,000 a week and he's a millionaire now,' but it doesn't half hurt to be booed by your own people – the fans who grew up in the same communities as you.

On the cast list of big Liverpool characters, Robbie's mate Steve McManaman was also near the top. Contrary to popular opinion, he was a quiet and sensible lad. If someone was getting out of hand, he would be the one to have a word and tell him to calm down, or apologize to the people the player had just upset. You never saw Macca drunk. On the pitch, when he was in his prime I've never seen anyone like him. When I was 15 or 16 years old, watching from the stands, he controlled games. We used to play 3–5–2 just so he could have the run of the pitch. He used to win matches on his own. He was the best player I've seen live.

Paul Ince joined us a little while later. That was a fantastic signing. The basis of it was that we had tremendous flair going forward but could be a bit open at the back when all the midfielders were on the attack. It's true that we did need a bit of steel to break up opposition moves, and even in his mid-thirties, in a one-off game Incey could mix it with the very best. He was definitely one of the jokers, with a huge lust for life. If he had you under his wing you'd certainly find him putting a glass of champagne in your hand and offering you a cigarette (not that I smoked). I say this affectionately, because it was always light-hearted with Incey. He had a sense of fun. He was made captain almost straight away. The peak of his career was spent with Manchester United and Inter Milan, but he still did an important job for us.

In August 1997, during the summer before my first full season, John Barnes moved on to Newcastle, which left a big hole on the training ground. In games, you could count on the fingers of one hand the number of times he gave the ball away. In training, he was just majestic, a joy to watch. You ask anyone who's played alongside him, 'Who's the most gifted player you've ever seen in training?' I'll bet they say John Barnes. His passing, his touch, his finishing – everything was beautiful to observe. I didn't play with him in his heyday, but I've watched videos of him and he was awesome. He has to be among the top three players Liverpool have ever had. He does get recognition for his enormous natural talent, but not quite on the level he deserves. It might be because he didn't perform as well for England as he did for Liverpool. But, boy, could he play.

That same summer, I went to Malaysia with England for the World Youth Under-20 Championship, which was of some concern to Liverpool, who knew I was going to be playing a prominent part in the following League season and were worried about me not having a break. It was obvious that I would be playing every game for England in Malaysia.

Amazingly, when I got to the Far East it felt as if everyone knew me. Not many of the Under-20s had played for their club side, but I'd played twice, which seemed to be enough to earn me all this recognition. We sailed through the group stage, winning all our games. I scored in a 2–1 win over Ivory Coast and a 5–0 thrashing of the UAE, and then got the only goal against Mexico – which meant that the first of my great confrontations with Argentina came before the 1998 World Cup, because it was them we had to face in the second round. We were 2–0 down by half-time. Though Jamie Carragher reduced that deficit just after the interval, we lost 2–1. I had to wait another 12 months for my first goal against one of England's biggest rivals.

Really, after that defeat, from the end of June onwards, my mind was focused on the coming season with Liverpool. I couldn't wait to get back on to the training ground. Up front for the 1997/98 campaign it was going to be me, Robbie and Karlheinz Riedle, who had signed that summer from Borussia Dortmund. Stan had moved on to Aston Villa, and it was reasonable to assume that Karlheinz wouldn't be playing every game on account of his age. My expectation was that he and Robbie would be the starting strikers, but that August Robbie was struggling with an ankle problem so I ended up starting in the first eight games. In that particular pre-season I had been flying, scoring plenty of goals and playing really well. My confidence was up and I probably got ideas above my station, thinking, 'I could be in from the start this year.' But it was Robbie's injury more than my own good form that opened the door. So there I was on 9 August, lining up for the first game of the new season – against Wimbledon again.

It was Incey's debut in a Liverpool shirt, and he was soon being brought down by Vinnie Jones in the penalty area. The manager had already told me I'd be taking the penalties – which was an incredible honour, given my age. So, again, there I was, in the midst of all these Liverpool legends, being asked by Roy Evans whether I would accept one of the biggest responsibilities a manager can hand to a player. In baking conditions, my penalty went in OK, but over the next 10 or so games I was about to learn the difference between reserve- and youth-team football and the first eleven.

Below the senior team, I had been accustomed to scoring every week – often two or three at a time. I always, always look at my match and goal stats, and I can remember looking at my first 10 games for Liverpool and being worried that I wasn't scoring an average of a goal every other game. I was playing well, but I wanted to score every week. I started to become disturbed. One advantage I had was that I'd been given a good grounding in the basic skills and duties of a striker. If you don't have those you can't progress to the higher levels. Take following in, for example. Ninety-nine times out of a hundred a good goalkeeper will gather an incoming ball and hold on, but if he spills it just once you're going to end up with an extra goal. It's all right knowing the theory, but you may have a hundredth of a second to react to an event and then turn it into an opportunity. It has to be second nature. Now, as soon as the leg goes back, before a team-mate has even thought about shooting, I'm already thinking about where I should be positioning myself. If it hits the post or the keeper, where will the ball go next? It's about being one step ahead. The opposite's true in front of our own goal. I just don't have the instincts of a natural defender. If there's a corner and I go back to mark an opponent, I might find their striker running straight past me on the way to goal. Logically, there is no reason why I shouldn't be able to reverse my own thinking to second-guess an opposing striker when we're defending our own line, but it's easier said than done. I've had to work hard to improve my defensive capabilities.

In those early years I wasn't always in full control of my aggressive streak. All top footballers have one, and as you mature you learn how to use it within the laws and to your own advantage. To begin with I was no angel on the pitch. I was no thug, either, but I understood the concept of self-defence. That September, playing for Howard Wilkinson's England Under-18s against Yugoslavia in Rotherham, I was sent off for butting an especially annoying defender. The in-thing in those days was the sweeper system, which meant that there were permanently two man-markers on the two strikers. I don't know why I reacted, because I was used to that system and all the extra difficulties that came with taking on defenders at international level; but I was just continually being booted and pulled back. Frankly, I don't mind being kicked, because it happens to me every week, but I hate the shirt-pulling and the 'girlie' fouls. I prefer honest physical contact. If you're going to foul me, boot me in the air. It's equally irritating when you retaliate with a foul of your own and the defender rolls around on the floor. My head was exploding all the way through the game. Finally, my patience ran out, and after being fouled for the umpteenth time I rose to my feet close to the defender and pushed my head into his. Down he went, rolling around, and out came the red card.

I was so nervous about what my dad was going to say, because I had my whole family there that day to see me captain England. When I got sent off after 20 minutes half of them went home, though Dad stayed on to give me a lift. Not much was said in the car. I think he knew I would learn from it; he didn't need to ram home a lesson I had already learned for myself. In life, I suppose, you have to do stupid things to know what stupid things are. And it's better to learn at youth level than in the senior game.

But it wasn't a one-off. Seven months later I was sent off at Old Trafford for a two-footed lunge at Manchester United's Ronny Johnsen. I was going through a mad period. At Lilleshall, I had a six-month spell where I fell in love with the tackling aspect of football. I loved getting stuck in. I'd had enough of getting pushed around by defenders and decided to give some back, so I developed this passion for going in hard – sometimes unfairly. In December 1995, Keith Blunt had written a report that highlighted the need for me to control my aggression on the pitch. It read: 'Michael has shown outstanding qualities as a front player both at school level and as an international player. He is a very good finisher and a highly competitive boy who only needs to control the occasional outbreak of temper to become an outstanding player.' I still consider myself a tough player, but I no longer give back what I get. The Ronny Johnsen incident was a turning point for me. That was a head-down, lost-the-plot kind of day. Even an hour before the game I was sharpening my studs for battle. It was total red mist.

Ironically, at the time of the incident I had scored, we were 1–0 up and I was full of the right kind of adrenalin. Before the Johnsen tackle, I had jumped in on Peter Schmeichel and ended up hurting myself. I'd already been warned for a previous challenge on the United goalkeeper, but for some reason I remained determined to give him a dig. He reached the ball way before me, but I kept going and brought him down on top of me, which left six stud marks on my belly. That should have been my warning. Again, the ball had gone when I reached Johnsen, but I carried on with my challenge and the ref, Graham Poll, was totally right to show me the red card. Poll had warned me moments earlier: 'Calm down or I'm going to have to send you off.'

I can remember feeling devastated as I took a shower, but still bubbling, still fierce. After about half an hour I felt my shoulders suddenly drop and all the air leave my body, as if I was coming down off an aggressive high. And then it hit me. I understood what I had done. I felt the tension drain. As I walked back down the tunnel to watch the second half, I saw Ronny Johnsen being taken off to an ambulance and felt truly awful. I was too embarrassed even to say sorry. It's not an episode of which I'm proud.

A week after that England–Yugoslavia match in September I had a much happier experience: a goal on my debut in European cup competition, against Celtic in a 2–1 win in the UEFA Cup. Again, that was a special day for the Owen family and its Scottish branch. My dad was especially busy that week sorting out tickets for the Donnellys. My late uncle Terry was a mad Celtic fan and one of my biggest supporters. I didn't comprehend what a big game it was until the warm-up. I've played around the world since, but the atmosphere at Celtic Park was up there with the best. The noise during the warm-up was the loudest I've known. When they played 'You'll Never Walk Alone', both sets of supporters sang. It was ear-splitting, and my blood ran cold.

A month later I found myself training with the England senior squad for the first time – with no intimation, of course, that I was on a path to the 1998 World Cup. Although I seemed to be advancing in leaps, my first full season in that famous Liverpool shirt was all about consolidating a place in the team.

It was February 1998 before events developed a fierce momentum. I raced through seven days that shook my world. On 7 February I scored twice against Southampton, then made my England debut against Chile in midweek before hitting my first Premiership hat-trick, against Sheffield Wednesday. That was special to me, because having made my debut for England at such a tender age I couldn't bear the idea of not playing well for my club the following Saturday. I had a morbid fear of people saying, 'Oh, this international business has gone to his head.' I just had to do well.

Ten days later, Robbie Fowler was ruled out for the rest of the season with knee ligament trouble following an innocuous challenge on the Everton goalkeeper. Losing your main goalscorer always knocks the stuffing out of a team, especially in the last two months of the season. The consequence was that I was given more opportunities to play first-team football, which improved my chances of being picked in Glenn Hoddle's World Cup squad.

Liverpool eventually finished third in the Premiership, behind Arsenal and Manchester United. I would characterize it as an OK season. The year before we had finished fourth, so it seemed we were creeping back up with a good young team, terrific camaraderie and a fine manager in Roy Evans.

In those days it was easier to win Premiership games than it is now, when the standard is infinitely higher. Perhaps it's down to diet awareness, better equipment, improved tactical organization; whatever the reason, it's so much harder to win games nowadays. The Premiership isn't hugely better in a technical sense; the improvement has been physical, in fitness, stamina and strength. The only break you get nowadays is when top clubs rest their best players in the cup competitions. Everyone these days has got someone who can change a game, whereas when I started out it wasn't unusual to come up against a team who had two workhorses up front. Then, 18 League goals could win you the Golden Boot. Some of the leading strikers in those days wouldn't

be able to compete with a Ruud Van Nistelrooy or a Thierry Henry. I can compete with these guys, but I need a season without injuries to be fighting it out with them at the very top of the list.

I was joint-top scorer in the League in my pre-World Cup season with 18 goals, level with Dion Dublin and Chris Sutton and ahead of Dennis Bergkamp, Jimmy Floyd Hasselbaink and Andy Cole. I got 23 in all and shared the Golden Boot, as I did the following season. It's only now that I understand the scale of that achievement.

As a striker, you look at the scoring charts and have a mini-competition inside your own head. It's largely irrelevant what the others are doing, but still you don't want your rivals to be out-performing you. Until the day I retire I'll be looking at that chart, wanting to overtake anyone who sneaks in front. I'll cherish those two Golden Boots, together with the PFA Young Player of the Year Award, which I won in the spring of 1998.

Even better, of course, I was off to the World Cup.

5

France 98

Somehow, between February 1998 and June 2003 I managed
to cram in 50 England caps and score 20 times for my country. When I captained the team against Slovakia in Middlesbrough in the summer of 2003, the Football Association's
website reviewed that first half-century of appearances as if I
was a veteran. But I don't have to stretch my memory much
to recall an icy night at Wembley and the thrill of my senior
debut against Chile.

In the late winter of 1998, my career was on fast-forward.
I've had a few of those phases, but this was the one that
launched me towards my first World Cup and a life-changing
goal. Looking back at those weeks, it would be easy to
assume I made an effortless transition from England youth
football to the senior squad, to take my place alongside
Teddy Sheringham and Alan Shearer. But when I broke
into the senior group I was still young enough to feel a sense
of wonder, even though my earlier experiences at junior
international level had provided me with a grounding in what
life would be like in the first eleven.

I'd mixed with the senior squad on a couple of occasions
before. Under Glenn Hoddle's management, there was a
policy of bringing in one or two promising youngsters to

familiarize them with life at the very top. We don't extend that privilege any more, perhaps because Sven-Goran Eriksson has supported young players by selecting them as soon as they're considered to be good enough. I was already playing in Liverpool's first team when I was first invited to join the elite in training; it's not as if I was a kid from a school of excellence, meeting those famous names for the first time. I was already playing against them at Premiership grounds.

I was on a golf course at Curzon Park, Chester, with my dad when the good news filtered through. Doug Livermore, who was then one of the Liverpool coaches, called me and said, 'Michael, you've been picked for the England squad.' That was the end of my golf for the day. My performance was wrecked. I was on the fourth of the nine holes we had chosen to play and my game went to pot. I couldn't stop ringing people to share the news. With nine goals for Liverpool so far that season I was establishing myself as a Premiership striker. I knew I had been creeping closer to the full squad, but I hadn't expected the breakthrough to come so soon.

In my earliest days with the squad, Alan Shearer and Tony Adams were the two main leaders of the pack. When I went down for England get-togethers I tended to stick with Paul Ince, Robbie Fowler and Steve McManaman from our Liverpool squad, so I felt protected, though the sense I had was of going to a new school for the first time. It's worse than that, in fact, because at school everyone's equal and everyone's new. In an England squad you're surrounded by people you admire. For the first few visits, the one negative question in my mind was: *Do I deserve to be here?*

Glenn Hoddle told me early in the week that I was going to play against Chile – on the Monday night, before he announced the team to the rest of the players. He asked me, 'Do you feel ready, because I want you to start.' Again, I was straight on the phone to Dad, saying, 'Don't tell anyone, but I'm in the starting line-up on Wednesday night.' Hoddle instilled a great deal of confidence in me by telling me at such an early stage in the build-up. No messing – bang, you're in. That gave me the self-assurance I needed to feel I belonged.

A lot of Hoddle's practice sessions concentrated on technique. In contrast, Kevin Keegan tried to coach or shape you as a player. Hoddle focused more on the team and tactics and tended to work with individuals on technical aspects of their game. For one session he brought in half a dozen size-three balls. For the first half hour we would just keep the size three up in the air to improve our skills. He wasn't one of those managers who would come and wrap an arm round you. I'm not saying I needed that, but it was noticeable that Hoddle left the more human side of man management to John Gorman, his number two. Wherever Hoddle has been in management, Gorman has often followed him, and I think that might be because Glenn realizes he's not one to develop close personal relationships with his players. Gorman would come and tell the players things, and we knew a large proportion of it was coming directly from the manager. Gorman was the messenger, so often we were communicating with Hoddle second hand.

My inclusion for the game against Chile at Wembley on 11 February was, I suppose, at the expense of Robbie Fowler, my Liverpool mate, who sustained a serious knee injury later that month in a League game against Everton. My record-breaking age at kick-off was 18 years and 59 days – an achievement that has since been beaten by Wayne Rooney. It helped that I had a lot of history to back me up. I had scored on my debut at every other international age –

Under-15s, -16s, -18s, -20s and -21s. This time, though, the sequence was broken. I played in a three-man attack together with Dion Dublin and Sheringham. I had one decent chance, but my shot was saved. Marcelo Salas, who was about to join Lazio for £13 million, scored twice in a 2–0 win for Chile, but my reviews were good. I was on my way.

With my debut behind me, in March I appeared in a friendly against Switzerland in Berne, this time playing alongside Shearer for the first time, and then in another non-competitive match, against Portugal, at Wembley in April, though I only played for 13 minutes after Sheringham had been taken off. Our World Cup build-up intensified with the King Hassan Cup in Morocco in May, which turned out to be more memorable than the name of the tournament might imply.

Rooney has since deprived me of another place in history (not that I'm resentful, of course). My first senior goal for England came when I was 18 years and 164 days old, in the game against Morocco, our hosts. In between my debut and the trip to North Africa I had been sent off against Manchester United but had finished joint-top scorer in the Premiership with 18 goals. Given that this was my first full season, I could press for a place in Hoddle's World Cup squad knowing that I'd already made a good impact with my club. You can imagine the effect those 18 goals had on my confidence.

The goal in Casablanca was perfectly timed to remove any anxiety I might have had about going to France 98 without an international goal to my name. For a striker, a goal always brings an immediate flood of relief. From the moment the ball goes in, you're not asking questions of yourself. The pressure is off. I wasn't in the starting line-up that day but came on when Ian Wright was injured

25 minutes into the game. I've watched the goal since on tape, and Dion Dublin is standing right opposite me in a better position when Steve McManaman supplies me with the pass. Really, I should have passed it, but I swear I didn't notice Dion.

Fate, as well as the blinkers, played a role that day. I might have been taken off in that match before the goal-scoring chance came my way because I'd taken an almighty boot to the head in an earlier passage of play. There are various types of concussion, and this was nowhere near as bad as the aftermath of a blow I once took in a Premiership match at Derby County. After that incident I swore I would never use the word 'concussion' unless I was clinically unconscious. I had whiplash for a week. In Morocco I was more dazed and confused than concussed, though the photographs made it seem worse than it was because my head is down by my neck. People tell me I was groaning, 'I don't want to come off. I won't come off.'

By the time Hoddle began deliberating over who to take to France and who to leave behind, I was confident I would be in the 22. As soon as I took part in the Morocco tournament I knew I was part of the manager's plans. Someone asked him after my goal in Casablanca, 'Has he made your mind up now?' Hoddle's reply, as I recall, was, 'My mind was already made up.' When I heard him say that on television, it really put the issue to bed. If the manager doesn't fancy you, it doesn't matter how well you're playing, it's just hard coco. But I always had a sneaking sense that he wanted me in, and when we got to France I was sure I would see action.

Before the tournament itself, which began on 10 June, we made the infamous visit to the La Manga resort in Spain, where Paul Gascoigne fell off the edge of the squad and into one of the most troubled phases of his life. On decision day we all had individual slots to see the manager. Mine was middle to late, and they were all five minutes each. I didn't hear about the confrontation between Hoddle and Gazza until later, when it was the talk of the town. Hoddle's room certainly hadn't been trashed when I went in – or, if it had, it had been put back together and tidied up with great care. David Seaman was the one trying to bring Gazza down from the ceiling, and by the time we got to dinner it was the only topic of conversation.

My relationship with Gazza was not the sort of friendship that would lead you to talk on the phone as pals, but we did get on. When he was at Everton a few years later he called me out of the blue to ask me if I could help with his daughter's birthday. He told me I was her favourite player, and then turned up on my drive to give her a birthday surprise. He'd told her they were going out on an errand but had pointed his car in the direction of my house. Their visit was a huge success. We finished up playing snooker upstairs and taking pictures of each other so his daughter could preserve her memory of the day. My lasting impression of Gazza is that he's a really nice fella who could talk to anyone. There's a kindness about him that not everyone gets to see.

As a player, he had a profound impact on me. Italia 90 was the first major international tournament I studied as a professional footballer in the making. By then I understood the game a fair bit, and I took to Gazza straight away. I wish I'd been able to play with him for England when he was in his prime. As a striker, you dream of playing with mid-fielders who are blessed with his kind of skill. The one regret in Gazza's career is that we all wanted his incredible talent to last a bit longer. I suppose he applied his gift for as long as he could, but by the time I came on the scene he was no longer the force he once was.

To this day, though, I feel privileged to have been in the same England camp as him. In 10 years' time I'm going to be able to say, 'I played for England with Gazza,' and that's something special to have on your CV. I'll say the same about playing for Liverpool with John Barnes or Stan Collymore. It makes me feel old to reminisce like this, but playing for England with Gazza is right up there on my list of personal honours. When I'm 30 and one of the senior pros, the younger players will be impressed to learn that I shared time on the field with one of English football's finest artists. All footballers understand how special he was.

It helped that Gazza was matey with the Liverpool contingent – Robbie, Macca and Incey. The first time I went down to join the camp we had just played Chelsea on the Sunday. We didn't reach our base until the early hours of the morning. As I'd never been there before, Robbie and Macca showed me round the hotel. Robbie took me through a door to show me the video room – where we found Gazza, at two a.m., playing on some computer game. He was waiting for his pals to show up. In those days, on the night we assembled we were allowed to have a drink and a chat with our friends. So there he was. That was the first time I ever met him. I could see straight away that he danced to his own tune.

The England squad for France 98 was full of strong characters and was a fine blend of youth and experience. La Baule, our base in France, was a fantastic setting for a training camp, but the one problem with actually taking part in a World Cup, as opposed to following it as a spectator, is that you become detached from the drama of the tournament. Hoddle was meticulous in keeping the camp closed: no disturbances, no distractions, no one allowed into the hotel. If you're away for a month or two, the siege mentality can give rise to terrible boredom. Not meeting and mixing with people is definitely the hardest part. But in 1998 I thought the situation was normal as it was the only World Cup camp I'd ever known. Sven-Goran Eriksson is much more relaxed, and wants players to enjoy their time away. In France, though, boredom set in because we weren't allowed to see anyone, but I don't think it harmed us in any way. I've always struggled with being stuck in a hotel. For the first couple of days I like it, because it gives you a chance to clear your head and think. Soon, though, I do need to break out of the room, which can become oppressive. It's become much harder since my children were born. I get much more home-sick these days. Still, nowadays I feel a bigger part of the squad and I'm more central to the action, the card games, the conversations. After a few trips round the international circuit you move towards the front row of the social life. And in football, you have to earn the right to be there. If you demand a seat as an 18-year-old, new to the team, it really doesn't go down too well.

There's a hierarchy in international teams and it's not a good idea to ignore it. In France, Rio Ferdinand and I were new recruits, which is probably why we were joined at the hip. Nowadays, I'd hate to think of any new England player saying to himself, 'I can't talk to Michael Owen because he's too senior.' But, at the same time, it's still assumed that a youngster will start from a position of respect for those further up the line. Let me offer an example. It's not a good idea to plonk your meal down on the table on your first evening and announce, 'Here, listen, lads, I've got a great story which will amuse you.' The response to that kind of declaration is going to be, 'Who's this flash Harry?'

Believe me, players do make that mistake, more so than ever these days.

I say this with a grin because I'm making myself sound ancient, but there is a noticeable difference between 1997, when I was coming through, and the current Premiership culture. At the beginning of my England career I wouldn't start conversations; I certainly wouldn't try to dominate them once they had begun. Now, a lot of youngsters think they've made it to the big time before they're even established in the youth team. There's a certain strutting around, and that gets a few of the older pros' backs up. I wouldn't intervene, though. Even though I've played a lot of games, I often still feel like a kid myself. I'll voice a heartfelt opinion to a manager now, but I wouldn't impose myself on a fellow player. I'd have to be in my late twenties to take someone aside and offer serious advice. Even then, I'm not, by nature, the confrontational type. If I saw a young team-mate throwing his weight around I'd be more likely to stew about it, thinking, 'What a big-headed lad this one is.' Even though I was cheeky as a kid, I'm quite shy, and Dad has instilled into me a strong sense of respect. In the early days I would never have dreamed of walking into the pool room and saying, ''Ere, do you fancy a game, Shearer?' You wait to be asked.

The first instalment of our World Cup was against Tunisia in Marseille on Monday, 15 June. That day, Sky brought us news of rioting by England fans. We didn't realize how bad it was until we saw the TV pictures and then examined the newspapers. Nowadays I would think more about something like that, worry more about our reputation and, I suppose, fret more about us being thrown out of games or even a whole tournament, but in 1998 I just thought it was a few stupid drunk fans. There's a stronger fear among the England players these days that bad behaviour by the supporters could get the team banned from a competition. My response to hooliganism is more disbelief than embarrassment. I wouldn't associate myself in any way with people who cause violence and disorder. We come from the same country, but there the connection ends.

In the Tunisia game itself, Alan Shearer was the number-one striker and was accompanied by Teddy Sheringham, who had done wonders for England in the preceding years. Being so young and inexperienced, I was in no position to start insisting that it was between me and Teddy for the second starting place. Now that I'm a regular, I'd resent some young whipper-snapper coming in and saying he was fighting me for my shirt. If I'd been Teddy, I'd have said, 'Hang on, don't you remember Euro 96?' Nevertheless, Shearer was the number-one goalscorer, so the only way I could have played was if Teddy's position slipped.

We beat Tunisia comfortably, 2–0, and I got on for six minutes. I knew that wasn't going to be my best chance to impress. The moment Teddy was withdrawn in Marseille, I knew it was to save him for the next match. I didn't need to waste time wondering whether I would be starting against Romania the following Monday. Besides, I was too busy trying to live down the embarrassment of a partially televised golf day during which, on the first tee, I hit my opening drive about 10 yards and had to put up with everyone falling about laughing. What they didn't show was my second shot, which landed about six feet from the pin.

After the comforting win in Marseille came a hard landing in Toulouse. When we were losing against the Romanians in our second Group G match, the logic of Marseille was reversed. I knew my chance had come: 17 minutes to contribute, to prove my worth. When the team is trailing, a back-up striker is offered a chance to fundamentally alter the game he's been studying from his position on the bench. Against Tunisia, when I came on we were two goals up and simply keeping possession. I was unlikely to score in those circumstances. It was simply my welcome to the World Cup. But sometimes, coming on as substitute in a game in which your team is behind is a no-lose bet, because you're sent on more in hope than expectation. Similarly, if you are winning it can be a no-win scenario, because the manager doesn't require anything from you beyond ball retention and basic discipline. Not so against Romania. That night we were in trouble. A goal under those circumstances, I knew, would carry extra weight.

We'd gone one down shortly after the break to a goal by Viorel Moldovan, and I can remember warming up behind the goal, gazing up at the clock and thinking, 'There's half an hour to go, maybe he's going to bring me on.' I was concentrating on the game in front of me and thinking about what I might do to change its course. I couldn't stop looking at the bench. I was waiting for the wave. But the clock kept ticking, and the thought took hold of me, 'He's not going to bring me on here!' Then, 'He's not going to give me enough time!' As a striker, you want at least 15 minutes to make your mark. Time crawled on until there were 20 minutes left and I started to think I'd missed the boat. Then I saw a hand go up from the bench and I was rushing back to the dug-out to take my chance.

My first goal in a World Cup has a special place in my heart. When Alan Shearer crossed the ball, it took a little bounce off a Romanian defender and sat up as if on a golf tee. Lovely. As soon as I struck it there was no possibility of the goalkeeper forcing it out. Take it from me, it's an astounding sensation to score in a World Cup. A while later, I hit the post from 25 yards. Shooting from that far out isn't

Sisterly love. An early cuddle from Karen. With fists clenched, I'm ready for my two-fight boxing career.

Me at five months, with a mischievous grin. Not everyone sees my fun-loving side.

Blonde hair. Where did that go? A playschool boy, aged three.

No prizes for guessing how I passed my time on a caravan break at Colwyn Bay. It wasn't always glamorous foreign holidays.

Sisters Karen and Lesley with our pet rabbit, Carrot. I've always loved animals.

The caravan. Me, Karen and Lesley on the North Wales Coast. Can't remember why I'm doing the Winston Churchill victory signs.

Nicely turned out. Aged seven, I looked like the school swot. I'm sure I wasn't.

Donkey riding in Ibiza, aged eight. I fancied myself as a jockey, but I hope I never breed a racehorse this slow.

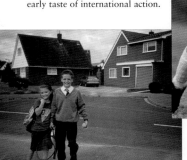

Fifty-fifty ball. Playing for Mid-Wales Celtics U-12s against Venezuela in the Dallas Cup. An early taste of international action.

Me and Lesley outside the family house in Cromwell Close, Hawarden.

Joining the jet set. Off to Jersey for a tournament with Deeside Schools. Dad raided the piggy bank to make sure he was there.

Here comes trouble. Deeside Schools touch down in Jersey. We look like proper tearaways, but we were choirboys, really. Honestly.

It may not look much, but Mold Alexander's grandstand seemed like Wembley to a seven-year-old.

Hawarden High School, where I studied before being fast-tracked into Lilleshall.

England, my England. I've been through the ranks in that famous white shirt. Here, I'm with the England U-15 squad, along with Wes Brown and Michael Ball.

Cover story: England schoolboys versus Spain. A little more than two years before my World Cup debut. My goal celebration hasn't changed much.

Riding the waves. An early taste of the rapids, on a family outing at Alton Towers.

Liverpool boy. Joy after the Ian Rush Tournament. Notice Steven Gerrard in the top row, third from the right, and sister Lesley as mascot.

Graduation day. My Lilleshall cap, after some of the happiest times of my life.

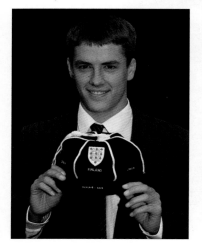

The start of good times with Liverpool FC.

Football crazy. Fourteen, and learning the finer points of the game.

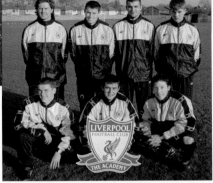

A golden age. Liverpool lads Steve McManaman, Jamie Carragher, Dominic Matteo, Steven Gerrard, me, David Thompson and Robbie Fowler.

The ultimate test. England U-15s against Brazil U-15s, 11 March 1995.

Healthy glow. The clean-cut image just seemed to stick.
But I can be a devil on the pitch.

something I normally do; it frustrates me when team-mates shoot from an impossible range. But by then I felt I could beat the world. I thought I could go on and win the game on my own. I was wrong. I assumed we had secured a draw, so the winning goal from Dan Petrescu in the final minute gave us a mighty shock.

Four members of my family were there to see my first World Cup goal: Mum, Dad, Andy and Lesley. It sounds incredible, but I didn't get to see them, even after the game. They made the effort to come and support me but there was no face-to-face contact for us all to remember. Security is always the main issue. A World Cup really is a long stint without seeing those you're closest to. It was only when we were no longer in the tournament that families were reunited, so you can imagine how closely the players are bound together. They only have one another. And, as I said, the 1998 World Cup came too soon for me to feel part of the hierarchy, so the sense of isolation was especially sharp. Still, better, maybe, to have confronted those feelings of homesickness early in my career.

In his book, the controversial World Cup diaries, Hoddle wrote that he'd always planned to start me against Colombia in the last group game, on the basis that their defence was vulnerable to pace. This was not something he confided to me at the time. Even after my goal against Romania I considered myself only fifty-fifty to make the starting line-up for our final group game. He certainly never gave me the nod in advance.

Still, true to his word, the Colombia game in Lens on Friday, 26 June was my first full 90 minutes in an international tournament. I played adequately but didn't get many chances to score. Having opened the door against Romania, my intention was to stay on the right side of it for the rest of the competition. When we came off the pitch I was flying because we'd qualified, but I still hadn't made sure of my place for the much tougher games ahead. The first time I felt 'Right, I'm part of this starting eleven' was when I scored against Argentina in the second round. From that moment on I felt as though I was an integral part of the England team. I wonder how many other people can trace such a huge breakthrough in their lives to a single act.

The other big story before the showdown with Argentina was, of course, David Beckham being left out for the games against Tunisia and Romania. The difference between David and me was that I didn't go into the tournament expecting to be in the first eleven, whereas it was a shock for him not to be picked. His club career was more developed than mine, though England were blessed with a strong, settled midfield. Darren Anderton was coming off a big tournament in 1996, and it was a tough part of the team to break into. Nevertheless, when Beckham didn't make it you could tell he was angry and resentful. I could see from his face that he wasn't happy. In contrast, I didn't have that same sense of deflation.

I never developed the impression that Beckham disliked Hoddle, I just thought he was annoyed at being left out of the side. In fact, as it turned out he was fuming, but there seemed no reason to suspect that there was any deeper personality clash. I'm no longer sure my limited interpretation was accurate, but this is how it seemed to me at the time. Hoddle used the word 'focus' a lot in relation to the way David applied himself to training and to games. Plainly that phrase had negative connotations. The manager didn't like us reading newspapers, so I had to rely on Mum and Dad to tell me what was being said in the press. The bulletins about me were good and my parents were always cheerful. 'You should see what people are saying and writing,' they would say. 'They're all saying you should be in the team.' I couldn't make myself believe it.

Where David was concerned, I just thought it was the old chestnut of a player being upset at being ignored. At that point in his career he was a much quieter and more private lad. He was already going out with Victoria, or Posh Spice, and a lot of the time he was on the phone to her, or retreating to his room so he could talk to her in private. He was never one to be seen in the pool room, in a card school or watching every game on TV. He was especially close to Gary Neville. But my earliest image was of him being in his room, talking to Victoria, who was jetting all over the world pursuing her Spice Girls career.

Our lives were taking shape. For both David and me, that World Cup was the start of a whole new story. We now have very different lives, but with England we've travelled a single road and been through plenty of dramas together. And at the end of June 1998 we were about to be pushed into the roles of hero and villain, however misleading those labels were.

6

Wonder Goal

My story should probably have a line down the middle, drawn on 30 June 1998, the night England played Argentina in St Etienne in my first World Cup. Before that day I was an 18-year-old striker trying to establish himself for club and country; after that date I couldn't play a round of golf or get into my own home without it being a public event.

I can trace much of my good fortune in football to the evening when I lined up in one of the best England teams I've represented. And I will always be grateful for the praise and the warmth of the English public when I returned home to a new life. It's a fallacy to think you can build a career around one goal, and I like to think I've achieved a few things before and since. But that Argentina game taught me something about myself and started a process that has given me and my family financial security for life.

In the camp, we knew throughout the group stage that we had a good chance of running into Argentina in the next round – which was frustrating, because no World Cup contender wants to be playing the really big opponents as early as the last 16. Not that we'd been in a position to be choosy: after losing to Romania, we had to beat Colombia just to be sure of going through. Equally, we knew we could beat them. We weren't remotely scared of them or their reputation. I don't think there was any team in France that caused us to be afraid, because we had a really good team that summer. We had a stronger sense of identity than in any year I've known, though we really fancied our chances in Japan and South Korea four years on. At Euro 2000, in contrast, there was no buzz and no confidence in the team – nor in my own heart.

In 1998 I felt we had a real beast of a team – mature, talented and robust – so we didn't shrink in the face of Argentina, even though they were able to call on such talents as Ariel Ortega, Juan Sebastian Veron, Gabriel Batistuta and Claudio Lopez. We just wanted to bring them on. For the second game in a row I was named in the starting eleven, which Glenn Hoddle announced as follows: Seaman, Gary Neville, Adams, Campbell, Anderton, Beckham, Ince, Le Saux, Scholes, Owen and Shearer.

In St Etienne in southern France that night there was an explosive start to the most dramatic match of the tournament. Very early on in the game I remember noticing how deep Argentina were defending. They were sitting way back, as if they were petrified of our pace up front. 'Tactically,' I thought, 'there's something wrong here.' Every time I received the ball I fancied my chances of causing havoc. They were giving me so much room between the midfield and defence that I had lots of time to crank up my runs. I also felt they were scared to throw in a proper tackle.

They went 1–0 up with a penalty from Batistuta after Diego Simeone had tripped over David Seaman's outstretched hands. Penalties are one of the touchiest subjects in modern football. It's hard to discuss them sensibly because the slightest ambiguity in the words you use will have people looking for sinister motives. Being awarded a penalty is an art, but not in the sense that you have to 'win' them dishonestly. The English are only just learning that you can force defenders to make incorrect or inaccurate tackles, which you can then exploit. You have to make the other team make mistakes and capitalize on them. That's not the same as simulation or deception, which I despise.

Let me explain. For Batistuta's penalty, nobody will ever convince me that he was incapable of staying on his feet. The truth is that he was waiting for Seaman to dive at his legs before he made his downward move. As soon as our goalkeeper slid in, Batistuta toe-poked it past him, caught Seaman with his foot and then went down. But I'm not denying that it was a penalty; neither am I saying that I wouldn't have done the same. If the keeper or a defender is going to be enticed into throwing himself at you, you have to be saying, 'Come on, I'm in your penalty area, come and kick me if you think you can do it within the laws. Kick me at your own risk.' Batistuta was well within his rights, but there's no doubt in my mind that he was playing for the penalty.

When I was running into their box around four minutes later, I was more checked than kicked, which is probably why people questioned the referee's decision to award a penalty. If that foul had been committed outside the area, nine times out of ten you'd have been given a free-kick; in the area, it has to be a stone-cold certainty for the referee to point to the spot. So I'm still not certain mine was a penalty. It remains one of those contentious ones. But what I will say is that if you are racing into a penalty area, especially with the light frame I had back then, then you can't keep your balance if you are kicked or checked when you are moving at breakneck speed. In those situations, every muscle in my body is being propelled in one direction, and there is only one aim in my head: to score. As much as I was waiting for someone to throw himself at me in St Etienne, if no one had gone near me I would have carried on running and then tried to score.

I've been taught this from my earliest days as a kid and as a footballer. If you're galloping 20 yards from the box and bearing down on goal, don't run alongside the opponent. If two players are running straight, like Olympic sprinters sharing a lane, it's easy for the defender to flick out a boot and knock the ball away. If you knock it across their path diagonally, they've either got to slow down to let you through, time their tackle perfectly or bring you down. It's a simple lesson that every forward is taught. If strikers didn't entice their opponents into kicking them in the wrong areas of the field it would be easy to be a defender. We would all be one.

Contrary to the speculation at the time, Hoddle did not tell me to go down if I was nudged in the penalty area. A theory grew up that the England manager was telling his players to fall over at the slightest provocation. There was no such instruction to me. I like to maintain that on a football pitch I'm as honest as they come. But I still insist that forcing a penalty is a skill, distinct from cheating. If you asked him privately, Hoddle might say that he developed a more complex view of the issue when he was playing abroad with Monaco. There aren't many people who would fly into the penalty area, absorb a daft challenge from a defender and then struggle to remain upright against all the physical odds. The alternative is to be the beneficiary of the defender's error. You've got to win games. This is our living. If you asked 98 per cent of the English population, they would say I was right to go down in St Etienne. They might modify that opinion long after the game is over, but at the time you can bet they were screaming for the penalty.

So where does the line fall between cheating and the legitimate exploitation of a defensive error? If you don't get touched – if a defender goes to make a challenge, then pulls out, but you still go down – then that's plainly unacceptable. I've never done that. I would never dive. I've seen penalties awarded that have disgusted me. I went through a patch of being called a diver and a cheat, and my dad was absolutely bloody livid. He could have killed anyone who called me that. I was upset too, because I've never been a cheat and I would never be dishonest on the field. What I am is an attacker who might try to make a defender make a bad decision. If that means someone diving in at you in the box, then that's the defender's lack of judgement, not yours.

People will of course make their own minds up, but the result of Roberto Ayala's bodycheck in the Argentina match was that Alan Shearer equalized from the penalty spot and set in motion a chain of events that was to launch me into a totally new life. The game raged on for another six minutes until I made my second major intervention of the evening – the so-called 'wonder goal'.

If I close my eyes, I replay it like this. I see David Beckham pick up the ball and I'm in a space between Argentina's defenders and their midfield, closer to their midfield line than to their centre-halves. David plays the ball to me, but there is a hostile presence at my side. The start of it all is a good first touch, because the initial movement is all in my natural stride. David's ball is quite high, just below hip height as it arrives, and I take it with the outside of my foot to get it in position to start my run. When you receive a pass like that, your first thought is not to give it away. If you get the ball beyond the defender in one movement, so much the better. As soon as I took the touch I knew I wasn't going to be caught. As I lifted my head, I got one of those pleasant surprises. To my disbelief, the main Argentine defender, Ayala, was retreating. Jose Chamot, his team-mate, was also in the vicinity, but I knew I had the beating of him. Here, our earlier penalty played a role. The reason they were back-pedalling, I believe, is that they didn't want me to run at them again from deep.

By the time I got to the point where I let rip, I'd run a good 20 or 30 yards. When a striker runs that far at full pace, a defender has no chance. Anxiety and confusion were telling Ayala to continue to fall back. By the time I pushed the ball across him, I was in full flight. From a standing start, it was impossible for him to do anything to stop me. Just then I saw Paul Scholes appear on my right-hand side, shouting 'Leave it!' or 'Scholesy's!', I can't recall which. Either way, as you can imagine, I wasn't tempted to respond to the call. If I'd left the ball for him it would have seemed incredibly odd. If Paul had taken control and tried to pounce on the moving ball, I still would have got to it first. Let's just say I was perfectly within my rights to complete the move.

When I finally struck it, the goalkeeper, Carlos Roa, had raced off his line, so there wasn't much space in which to work, but I managed to clip it hard and fast towards the far corner. On a run of that distance, it's rare for you to lift your whole head. You have this peripheral vision; you register things in the corners of your eyes. I never look at the ball when I'm running and I never look at the keeper when I'm about to finish. Since St Etienne I've developed the knack of chipping it over an advancing keeper, but I didn't do much of that then, so it was more of a sharp clip than a dink.

People may not realize this, but most of us don't analyse what we're doing in games. If you're a dreamer, you might come out for the warm-up counting the TV cameras, spotting members of your family in the crowd. But in the game itself you're not constantly thinking about individual moments. It's an instinctive sport; every decision is split-second. It's not golf, where you can plot your way round. I'm a quick thinker, a spontaneous creature, so I suppose the most famous goal of my England career was borne of me following an urge that I struggle to put into words.

If I had the same goalscoring chance tomorrow, maybe the execution would be slightly different. Maybe there wouldn't be a touch here or there. Perhaps I'd do individual elements of it better. But my mind wouldn't tell me to have a different intention, or to think any differently about the possibility of it coming off, even though I'm older and maybe more thoughtful now. There's one thing I can say forever without fear of contradiction: I know I couldn't have buried it any better.

The moments after a goal – any goal, really – are strange. When I say that scoring takes the pressure off, it implies that I go into a game experiencing pressure as an unpleasant sensation. I don't. It's just that when you've put that ball away you feel you've accomplished something that can't be taken away from you, however the game unfolds. You feel more relaxed, free to go on and impose yourself on the opposition. Before the goal, a voice says, *I've got to do something, contribute in some way*. In France, scoring against Argentina just made me feel that the possibilities for me in that game were endless.

For England, however, as we all know, it was a false high, because just as I was flying David Beckham was about to hit the ground extremely hard. The first bump, for all of us, was Javier Zanetti's equalizer from a free-kick on the stroke of half-time, though we still came into the dressing room feeling buoyant with the score at 2–2. Imagine telling us, as

96

we sucked on drinks and listened to the manager, that the second half was about to turn into one of the great football melodramas.

For setback number two was on its way: down went Simeone, felled, supposedly, by a flick from David as our future captain was lying on the ground. Up went the red card, courtesy of Kim Nielsen, the Danish referee. In my shock, I was looking for guidance from the bench on what we should do next. I was only 18 and I needed help. It felt like a calamity, but I didn't share that with anyone while David was walking off. I kept my mouth shut.

If Simeone had been the one doing the flicking and David had received the kick, I'm sure there would have been no dismissal, for the simple reason that David wouldn't have rolled around on the ground and put pressure on the referee to take such drastic action. The mentality of our players is that if we are not seriously hurt it's objectionable to go down in such a theatrical way. I honestly don't think any of our players would have behaved like Simeone did that night. What do we want from our football? We don't want cheats to prosper, surely. I think it's reasonable to argue that the incident with Simeone cost us the game. Nobody could dispute that David made a mistake in kicking him from the floor, but he didn't do so with sufficient force to bring him down or cause him pain. The letter of the law was that David should be sent off. It's incredible, though, to think that we were knocked out of a World Cup as a consequence of something so trivial. In essence, Argentina went through because they were more street-wise than us.

In the tactical reshuffle, both Alan Shearer and I managed to stay on the field, and we took turns playing right midfield, which I'd never done before. I'm sure it was new to Alan as well. Paul Scholes was sent over to the left and Darren

Anderton joined Paul Ince in the centre. In those situations, good players find the same wavelength, and our hope was that we could drag the game into a penalty shoot-out. I'm sure we all asked ourselves privately, 'How can we expect to beat a team like Argentina with ten men?' We defended as if our lives depended on it to get to penalties. It felt like a minor victory to reach that point after the exhausting ordeal of extra-time. A full hour of being bombarded by Argentina was about as much as we could stand. After Sol Campbell's headed goal was disallowed for a foul on the goalkeeper, I was in a trance. When the ball went in I was jumping all over him. David's red card has clouded people's memories of the match, but the fact is that we were unlucky not to have Sol's goal to see us through. I still can't see what was wrong with his header.

So we staggered on to penalties, and here I will make a declaration: there is nothing so nerve-racking as a penalty shoot-out, except maybe stepping into a boxing ring, which I did twice as a boy. Fighting for your life, one on one, or taking a penalty in a big game – in both instances your body simply doesn't belong to you. I can remember us forming a kind of huddle, and the manager asking, 'Do you want to take one?' No one wants to take one, not really, but you can't be seen not to. There have to be five takers. There is no choice but to volunteer. Nobody wants to be the fall guy, and the cold reality is that you don't get any credit for putting one away. It's a kind of duty to score; you just get blasted if you miss. Think of the names: Stuart Pearce, Chris Waddle, Gareth Southgate – all gallant Englishmen who had to cope with that humiliation. David Batty was about to join them.

I was asked, and I said yes. Then I remember Alan Shearer stepping up. Bang. That man defies belief. To smack the ball in the top corner as often as he does tells you everything about his character. In a World Cup, with that much stress! People don't realize how mind-blowing that is. And Shearer does it too consistently for it to be any kind of fluke. I also hit mine in the top corner, but more by luck than judgement. It could have gone anywhere for all I knew. To take a penalty you need a good finish and a decent pair of 'spuds', as we call them in the dressing room. Shearer must have the biggest in the world. As he walked back, mind you, I could see the relief in his eyes. He's a legend, no doubt about it, but even Alan Shearer is capable of experiencing stress.

I still don't know why, but I was laughing when I took my turn. Even now I look at it on TV and think, *Why am I laughing?* The answer is that I was absolutely crapping myself. I asked Shearer, 'What shall I do, where shall I put it?' I can vividly remember him saying, 'Just do what you normally do and stick it in the back of the effing net. Anywhere.' To this day I get butterflies thinking about the split second when I struck that ball. From the start I was hoping I wasn't going to have to take one to keep us in the game. I've seen what it does to people when they miss, the hell they tumble into. My dread, when extra-time ended, was being the final player on that pitch to miss. I remember noticing, though, that their keeper went the right way every time; it was only the quality of the strike that kept beating him. Paul Ince's was saved, but Incey wasn't the one who ended up taking the blame.

You can play the game for 20 years and practise endlessly, but it's what you're thinking in the final moments before you let fly that dictates what you do. In my case, I was fixated with this notion that Roa had gone the right way for Shearer (score), Ince (miss) and Paul Merson (score). I decided that I would have to pretend I was going one way but then shoot the other, which isn't the right way to approach the job. In a World Cup, there's just too much pressure for you to think normally. My body had detached itself from my brain, and I'd forgotten that it's extremely hard to shape your body to go one way when you're intending to shoot the other. As I walked up, I thought, *I've really got to open up my body*. Bingo. The keeper went the wrong way. You could have put four goalies in Roa's space and none of them would have stopped that ball. I just wanted to hit it anywhere on that side of the goal. To see it going high made my stomach lurch again, but it struck the woodwork and went in.

This is the incredible bit: after my goal I ran towards the crowd and ended up on the halfway line. The other players jumped on me, then slowly climbed off. In that moment I looked at the crowd, into a mass of eyes, and found myself staring straight into a group of faces from my own family. I had a sense of where they were in the ground, but somehow my eyes picked them out with amazing precision the very moment I looked up from the pitch. I punched the air again and again and again.

I feel guilty confessing this now, but the rest of the penalty shoot-out went by in a haze because I was so overcome by relief. For two minutes you are consumed by your own private ordeal – your own requirement to score, and all the fear and expectation that come with it. With my own little bit of the job done, I slid away, thinking, *Thank God it's over. If we qualify, wonderful. If we don't, at least I did my bit.* The last thing I wanted was to be hated by millions of people. I was 18, and I had scored a good goal in regular time, so maybe I'd have been spared the backlash. But I wasn't looking to test that theory. 'Thank God,' I kept on saying to myself, trying to refocus on the rest of that awful lottery.

Ayala stepped forward for Argentina. Goal. Now my

proper senses were returning, just in time to have reality hit me like a bucket of ice. David Batty was preparing to take his penalty, and as he placed the ball I felt optimistic again, thinking, 'Right, let's get through. Let's get the hell out of here.' I'm no clairvoyant, obviously, because a couple of seconds later I was studying Batts as he traipsed away from the goal with Argentina going berserk. Batty was that year's penalty shoot-out victim, and I felt his sorrow. Felt it, but didn't try to ease his suffering with empty words. I didn't see it as my duty or my right to console him. He had played hundreds of games for Newcastle and Blackburn; he didn't need a kid like me telling him how to feel. Nowadays I would walk over to the player and say, 'Don't worry.' No matter what anyone says, though, if it was me who had missed the decisive penalty I wouldn't want anyone talking to me. I'd just want to be left alone.

There were plenty of tears in the dressing room afterwards, even from senior players. In that environment you can look at a stricken team-mate in one of two ways – and we had three who were struggling, of course, because Batty, Incey and Beckham all felt as if the sky had fallen in. You can either say, 'You idiot, you've just cost us a place in the quarter-finals,' or you can extend a bit of sympathy and suppress the urge to blame. Fortunately for Batts and Incey, in the newspapers and in the court of public opinion, Beckham took most of the heat.

There might have been three devastated people in that dressing room, but there were also 15 or 16 who weren't far behind. If I hadn't taken a penalty myself I might have been feeling less sympathetic, but because I had been through that hell and experienced all the tension I knew that someone out on that pitch was bound to miss. Someone had to make the mistake that sent one of the teams through and the other one home. In a strange and doubtless selfish way, I was still just glad it wasn't me.

For me, though, it wasn't quite the catastrophe it was for some of the more senior players – and there was some real grief in that England dressing room. If you're lucky, you might get to two World Cups in your career; if I'm fortunate, I might make it to three or four. But for some of those England players in St Etienne it was the last World Cup match they would ever play. I felt more for them than anyone. I was young enough to leave those memories behind and create fresh ones to take their place.

Again, it sounds awful, but when I went out of the dressing room and we met our families for the first time I was smiling, even though we'd just been knocked out. Dad was eager to hug me, and Mum wanted to wrap me in an embrace, as if I, in the strictly personal sense, had emerged from the night a winner. It shouldn't really be like that, but there were echoes of it on my debut for Liverpool. We lost 2–1 that day which meant that we couldn't go on to win the League, yet I got on the bus absolutely buzzing. I'd scored a goal for Liverpool and was overwhelmed by that thought. It was the same in St Etienne. I had scored for England against Argentina in the last 16 of a World Cup. This is so hard to admit, but I'm sure most people will forgive me. In all these dramas, there is the team and there are individuals. I came off the pitch thinking, *I've done well here*, and at the same time, *I shouldn't be feeling this*. Even today I become uncomfortable when I recall my state of mind at the end of that night. But it's how I felt, and nothing can change that now.

We had one bad game out of the three in the group and then played exceptionally well against the odds in our showdown with Argentina, which was the game of the 1998

World Cup. I know we were better than them, and I'll believe that until the day I die. If we'd had 11 men throughout, there's no doubt in my mind we would have got through to the quarter-finals. That sounds as if I'm blaming David, but I'm not, because these disastrous moments affect us all in football. If we'd played Argentina again the next day, we'd have beaten them, no problem. They were scared of us. They were so relieved to have scraped past us to meet Holland in the next round. You could see it in their faces. The evidence was there as we walked on to the bus after the game. They couldn't quite believe they had beaten us. They were all dancing on their coach. In victory, they weren't exactly magnanimous. But a lack of grace always comes back to haunt you in the end, doesn't it?

Heartbroken, we flew home on Concorde. The pilot asked me if I would join him in the cockpit for the landing. The crew told me that when we landed they would open the window and hang out an England flag, so when you see those pictures of the cross of St George flapping below the pilot's window on the world's fastest passenger plane, it's my hand on the other end.

I was dumbstruck by the number of people who gathered to welcome us home. Some people thought this was absurd and made a point of arguing that it was inappropriate to give a heroes' welcome to a team that had been knocked out in the second round, and which had lost yet another penalty shoot-out. I understand that view, but I also think I know why there was so much warmth at the airport. It's because we were very, very unlucky. There are too many sob stories with England, I know, but I genuinely think we excelled at that World Cup.

I know my own life was unrecognizable from the moment the camera crews began camping outside my house. My goal against Argentina did far more than just help to make me wealthy or famous; it set me up for life to score important goals when my team needed them most. For some reason, I seem to be at my best when the stakes are highest. I had one of the best experiences of my life in my first really big game, and maybe I was never scared from that moment on.

7

Proving a Point: 1998/99

My feet were barely back on English soil when it was announced that a notable Frenchman would be following me across the Channel. On 17 July 1998, Gérard Houllier, the former coach of France, was appointed joint Liverpool manager alongside Roy Evans. The age of the Anfield boot room was coming to a close.

But first I had to get used to being famous, if you define fame as receiving constant attention. After the World Cup, interest in me grew by the day. There was an intense spotlight focused on my every move. Honestly, I hate the idea of myself as a celebrity. I don't mind cameras when I'm on the pitch, but immediately after France 98 there were 20 TV crews hampering my progress into the house. All my neighbours came out of their homes to congratulate me. Inside, I shrank from it all.

When the new domestic season opened I started to feel the heat. It was as if every eye was on me. I set myself a mission. *Nobody is ever going to call me a flash in the pan.* In the first game of our League programme, on 16 August, we played Southampton away. I put in the cross for Karlheinz Riedle to score our first goal and I got the second myself after half-time in a 2–1 win. I went home content because I thought everyone would have been studying me in that game. After a 0–0 draw against Arsenal at home, the next job was a trip to Newcastle for a game that was live on Sky. This time I scored a hat-trick and celebrated with the famous hand-rubbing routine. We won 4–1. Amazingly, it was already 4–1 at the break – a game of one half.

That match was one of my real career highs. Scoring three in 15 minutes at St James's Park would give any striker a thrill. But there was more to it than that. My anxiety in those opening weeks of the 1998/99 season was that people were watching me to find out whether I was going to be a one-hit wonder. Not just supporters, but fellow players as well. I had my achievements at schoolboy level to sustain me, but it was still possible that the Argentina goal would turn out to be a kind of curse. Maybe everything I did was going to be judged against that single act. Not just now, but for ever. I simply couldn't know. Some of my opponents were shrewd enough to recognize my insecurity. Some tried to exploit it, in the best possible taste. When the game against Newcastle kicked off, Stuart Pearce, that great England defender, turned to me and warned, 'You're playing against me today, boy. Just you be careful.' Notice the 'boy'. People are always asking me what we say to each other on the pitch. 'Nothing much,' is the usual answer, especially when there are so many languages competing to be heard. But that day I thought, *Oh Christ, this is serious. I'm a marked man now. This is what they warned me about.* I kept my mouth shut, but answered him as best as I could with the hat-trick, which meant that I had scored four times in my first three games.

When I got home I watched the replay of the match on Sky and heard Andy Gray remark, 'I've run out of things to say about this guy.' I sat there on my own feeling so proud, and so relieved that nobody would be able to point to the

World Cup and describe it as a fleeting moment for a lucky kid. It may seem odd to imagine me being so tortured so soon after that night in St Etienne, but I just wanted to kill the idea that I was a precocious boy who would fade. I had played a whole season for Liverpool before France 98, yet it would be an exaggeration to say I'd set the world alight. I had good stats, given my age, but I'd only done one big thing in my career. I felt I needed to achieve something fresh to convince people I was here to stay.

In those first few weeks, about the only thing people wanted to talk to me about was the World Cup, which was starting to wear me down. You can only churn over one memory for so long and then you want to move on. Around this time I started thinking more and more about my relationship with the Liverpool fans, who are among the most knowledgeable in the game. A strange feature of my career is that I made my name with England rather than with my club, so I was constantly wondering whether they would think of me as one of their own. Michael Owen the England player or Michael Owen the Liverpool striker? They won't mind me saying that they didn't warm to me the way they did to Robbie Fowler, and I've often regretted the fact that I made my initial impact for my country and not my club. At that time Liverpool supporters saw me as an England player. It was only after Liverpool's Treble-winning season that the perception changed.

But back to Gérard Houllier's arrival, which, plainly, was a turning point in the history of Liverpool FC. At 18 years old, you don't question decisions made at boardroom level. You assume everything is being done for the best. In hindsight, you can conclude that the club must have been easing Roy towards the door. Maybe they were just trying to do it nicely. Roy had done a decent job, but when Gérard became available the club evidently felt they couldn't turn him down. They had no reason to sack Roy, but nor did they want to miss out on the chance to sign Houllier.

I had never heard of Gérard, but from the moment of his appointment the papers were full of background pieces explaining who he was, so we got a measure of his achievements. The first thing to strike us was the role he played in developing France's World Cup-winning squad in his time as both national team coach and technical director with the French federation. That earned him instant respect from the players. He was from the same stable of French excellence as the Arsenal manager, Arsène Wenger. Days earlier, France had lifted the World Cup in Paris, and, rightly so, French coaches and French thinking were in fashion. If Spain win the 2006 World Cup, a lot of Spanish coaches and players will probably rise on a similar tide, though the Champions League has already had an impact there.

The first day I came back into Liverpool training, after being given an extra week off to recover from the World Cup, I expected it to be very relaxed, with players coming up to me to shake hands and offer their congratulations. I was in for a shock. There, before me, was someone called Patrice Bergues, who had joined the club alongside the new manager. He sent me straight out on to the pitch to begin pre-season running. I assumed I would be doing a light jog, but Patrice had me running lap after lap at a decent pace. 'What's happening here?' I thought. There was no hint of a smile from Patrice. By the end of his time with us, the summer of 2001, he was a highly respected figure and great company, always smiling, but obviously he and Houllier had decided that Liverpool were a club lacking discipline and so set about hammering it into us straight away.

The likes of Neil 'Razor' Ruddock got the biggest shock.

Razor was such a kind man – the gentle giant, and incredibly funny. He would look after the young players. When I first came into the team he was one of the people who made the dressing room tick. I felt very relaxed around him. But Razor wasn't one to bow down before a name or a reputation. When Gérard and Patrice asked all the players their names, Razor's reply was, 'Bloody 'ell, haven't you watched the telly for the last three years?' That kind of joke wasn't appreciated. Immediately the players knew a big, big change was on the way, though we did still manage to get ourselves in trouble at the Christmas party we organized for that year.

We started in a hotel in Liverpool, where everyone came downstairs in fancy dress. My two brothers and I went as scousers. At that time, because of the Harry Enfield sketch, there was this stereotype doing the rounds of argumentative Liverpudlians with perms, and we went along with it – not to take the mickey out of Liverpool people but almost to take the sting out of the joke. I had a big curly mop, a moustache and a shell suit. We had a couple of drinks at the hotel and then went on to the club we had lined up. Everything went quite smoothly at the start. Everyone was calm and enjoying a good night out. The first sign of trouble was when a couple of guys from security came rushing past and grabbed a fella and a lady because they were acting suspiciously. They ran, but left a bag behind, which turned out to contain a camera. They had been filming the whole night. At first there was a sense of relief because we felt we'd caught people who were trying to set us up. But they must have had two sets of equipment, because pictures still found their way into the newspapers. It was really no more than a typical Christmas session of the sort people in offices and factories go in for up and down the land, but it ended with eight players being asked to explain to the club why pictures from our party were appearing in newspapers. It was totally harmless, but it didn't look good. We haven't had a party like that since.

Back at the training ground, they were scary days. Suddenly training was physical torture, and the laughter on the training ground began to ebb. Under a new rule we were banned from talking while we stretched. We went from one extreme to the other very quickly, and some of the lads were worried about whether they could survive the new regime. Gradually, though, we came round to it, and this more serious approach to training and preparation became the norm instead of a huge culture shock.

The manager didn't like our established pre-season routine of going to Norway and Ireland either. We stuck with it for that first summer, but you could tell the new boss wasn't a fan of the idea and it's no coincidence that we didn't go back to any of those places once he assumed sole command. It was a tradition within the club that you would play a couple of games in Norway and then have a night out on the last day of the tour. Up to that point we didn't touch a drop of drink, but when the work was done after that final game there was a legendary nightclub in Oslo where we would assemble. But Houllier was having none of it. 'No, no, you'll ruin all the work we've done,' he told us. Roy tried to explain that it was a club tradition, but Houllier stuck to his guns. You could tell there was a clash between the way we used to do things and how it would be from now on. We were becoming more and more professional.

For matches, when the League season began, the players weren't sure who was in charge or who was having the greater say in team selection. Under Roy, the team would be announced verbally: 'Right, Jame-o in goal,' and so on.

When Roy and Gérard were in joint control, they would write the team on a flipchart, suddenly turn it over at the pre-match meeting and then both do their team talks. So you never knew what had gone on behind the scenes or who had picked the 11 names. Generally we assumed that the new manager was making more and more of the decisions.

To have a fifty-fifty share in team management doesn't work, in my opinion, though I can understand why the board tried the experiment. If I was a manager myself, I wouldn't know how to react if my partner's views were radically different to my own. Who has the right to win the argument? If things go wrong, who's blaming who? If things go right, who's taking the credit? And who decides on transfer policy and which players to buy? If I was the manager I couldn't have someone else interfering. Those guys live and die by results. If you're dying, imagine not having any input into the manner of your death. It's better to be your own man, and if you need help or advice, that's what the assistant manager and the coaches are for.

While Houllier was beginning to make his mark on the squad, I signed a new five-year contract. I was 18, and leaving the club seemed like a ridiculous idea. The only issue that August was how long I should sign for. The more years you sign for, the more they offer you. If you sign for a shorter period, you have more room for manoeuvre but a lower wage and less security. So it's a balancing act. Anyway, I was just delighted to sign that five-year deal. At 17 I had been on £500 a week; the new contract gave me a decent rise.

Up to that point, I had never needed money. I lived in the 'trackies' my sponsors Umbro gave me and probably spent about £20 a week. An extravagance, to me, was the odd bar of chocolate. Money just didn't interest me. It was only when I began wanting to look as smart as the rest of the players, and to look after my family, that I started to take more of an interest in the figures on the page. Helping my brothers and sisters became a priority.

At club level, I flew through that autumn, scoring four in a 5–1 win against Nottingham Forest in October. But two big managerial changes, with Liverpool and England, were on the way. In early November, Roy Evans seemed to be defending himself too much against criticism from ex-Liverpool players, and on the 12th the club announced that Houllier would be taking sole charge. The media had been full of speculation about the joint-manager experiment ending, and by the time Roy left I considered it to be inevitable. It was a poignant day, though. My main memory of it is seeing the gaffer in tears when he came out of his press conference. To this day I think he was harshly treated. He got us into the top three after all, and nowadays that would be regarded as solid Champions League form; then, however, it wasn't considered good enough. It was unfortunate for him that a top manager the club desperately wanted happened to become available.

It was a sad end for Roy, because we all wanted him to go out on a high. I had a lot to thank him for. He made me feel so important to the club at a time when I was a boy riddled with anxiety about the jump to first-team action. I have nothing but good memories of Roy Evans. To this day, when I see him, I say, 'All right, gaffer?' He was my first, and I'll probably always call him gaffer when our paths cross.

The club knew they were breaking a tradition by asking Roy to leave. At the press conference, it was noticeable that they emphasized Houllier's Liverpool connections – the time he had spent in the city and his close knowledge of the club. They were conscious of the size of the change so they tried to plant the seed in everybody's mind that it was something close to an in-house appointment. The message was that Gérard wasn't a total outsider.

France 98 had one more treat in store for me that year. On 13 December, a BBC car drew up outside Selhurst Park, where we had just played Wimbledon and I had picked up a black eye from Chris Perry's elbow. That was my main worry on the car journey to the London studio. Naturally, the penalty I'd just missed was bothering me too. Up to that point it hadn't been a great day, but it was about to get a lot better. It was the night of the BBC Sports Personality of the Year awards, and on the drive through the city I couldn't stop myself asking the BBC people whether or not I'd won. 'I can't say,' replied the presenter Ray Stubbs, 'because there's a vote on the night, but you're in with a shout.' Right up to the moment my name was announced the votes were still pouring in, so I had no idea whether or not I was about to win. I sat next to Glenn Hoddle, who was still the England manager. My only concern was rehearsing the speech I was going to make if I won. I had this dread of sounding inarticulate. I couldn't think beyond the speech. What if I left people with the impression that I wasn't good at communicating? My eyes wandered throughout the audience, to Nick Faldo, to Nigel Mansell and beyond. The odd thing is that I felt I belonged in that kind of company. I did go to the BBC party afterwards, but I only stayed for half an hour as I had training the next day. So, as the new BBC Sports Personality of the Year, I climbed back into the car with the rest of the family and arrived home in the early hours of the morning.

The next day at training I was teased something rotten. The fact that my mum had cried seemed to give the lads plenty of ammunition. At the time I couldn't quite understand myself why Mum was crying. It couldn't have been a sudden burst of elation because deep down most of us thought I would win. She'd had lots of time to prepare for it. Since that night I've come to understand that it was a case of her little baby boy standing up in front of all those important people and millions and millions of viewers at the age of 18. Seeing me make a speech in that context was, for her, the most touching part. She was proud of me for winning the award, but I suspect she was even more proud of me as a person.

On the international front, the memories of France 98 were quickly replaced by a gruelling qualifying campaign for Euro 2000, with Sweden and Poland our main obstacles in Group 5. We started badly, losing 2–1 in Stockholm on 5 September and then, at Wembley on 10 October, drawing 0–0 with Bulgaria in what was an especially tedious match. At least a 3–0 win in Luxembourg put three points on the board before the winter break. I played all 90 minutes in each of those three games, so it was reasonable to believe that I had established myself in Hoddle's first eleven. But a jolt was heading our way, and I was about to enter the most unhappy phase of my international career.

On 2 February 1999, Hoddle lost the England manager's job after making controversial religious remarks about the disabled. It was said that he had already lost the confidence of the players on account of his decision to publish his World Cup diaries, and personality clashes with David Beckham and others. Many assumed that this was the real reason he was sacked by the FA. I had no opinion on Hoddle's World Cup diaries at the time, but I can understand now why they created tension. If you're living with people for four or five weeks, you need to avoid doing anything that is going to create distractions or friction. I certainly didn't feel that the players had turned against him, but then Glenn Hoddle's England was all I knew so I had nothing to compare him with. To me, he was synonymous with England and every-thing it represented.

When he made his infamous remark about me not being, in his opinion, a natural goalscorer, he rang me straight afterwards and asked, 'Have you seen what's in all the papers?' I told him I had. I've never been a confrontational person, and as a teenager I certainly wasn't looking for an argument with an England manager who had selected me for a World Cup. I wouldn't describe my feelings towards him as awe, but my instinct was to respect the authority of the manager. He assured me that his remarks had been taken the wrong way, and that there were people at the press brief-ing who would back him up if I wasn't satisfied with what he was saying. He had been trying, he explained over the phone, to express the opinion that I wasn't just a goalscorer at the expense of every other aspect of my game. He said he could think of lots of strikers – Ian Rush was one he mentioned – who only scored goals. My recollection of what he said to me is this: 'I've tried to explain to the media that you're not just a natural finisher. You create chances for others. To me, a natural finisher is someone who stands in the box and waits for the ball. But you can link play.' He mentioned the goal against Argentina and pointed out, 'A natural finisher doesn't pick up the ball and run with it from inside his own half.' He insisted the media had got it wrong.

People have held those comments against him ever since; it still crops up in interviews even now. Whenever I read an article about Hoddle it reminds the reader that he was the England manager who left Beckham out at the World Cup and who said that Michael Owen wasn't a natural-born finisher. I always feel a bit sorry for him. I'd like to think he wasn't lying to me when he called me to offer reassurance. I'd also like to think that he really did regard me as an all-round forward. Mum and Dad certainly took what he said about me as a compliment.

Now, when I look back, I can see that there was tension between him and some of the big names. David Beckham may not have been his number-one fan, but I personally didn't harbour any grudges against him; nor did I feel he had a record of making bad decisions. Quite the opposite, in fact. Tactically, I thought he was fantastic. The one thing that let him down was that he struggled to communicate to the players what he was thinking. His words didn't always tally with his thoughts. John Gorman did most of the communicating for him. Hoddle, for instance, was capable of dropping David Beckham and not saying a word to him; then David would read the manager's explanation in the newspapers. Now that I'm older I can understand why a player would resent being dropped without being told why, but then, I couldn't. But strictly as a football manager, in terms of tactics, training and preparation, everything with Hoddle was spot on. He brought so much in in terms of diet and vitamins and scientific thinking. Historically, our natural mentality has been too closed, and there's no doubt that 99 per cent of the innovations you see in the Premiership these days come from abroad. Hoddle taught us a lot and helped to put a generation of England players on a new path.

We didn't like eating boiled pasta, boiled rice, boiled chicken and fish three times a day for a month, of course, and before France 98 we consumed a lot of pills and supplements. It was a killer, but he made sure it was all explained. Trying to smuggle chocolate bars into the camp was impossible. When you're away for that long, you look forward to going down to dinner to chat with everyone. But when we found ourselves eating boiled food with no sauces it was tempting to stay locked in the room. It's funny now to think of it, but at the time we found the dietary changes really hard work, even though they were doing us good.

Looking back, with the benefit of a good few years' experience of the England camp, I realize that Hoddle didn't speak to me much, but I don't hold that against him. He was the one who made me England's youngest player of the twentieth century, and he guided me into a starting place at the World Cup in time for the game against Argentina, which helped transform my life and the lives of those around me. He didn't say 'well done' the way some managers do, or try to cultivate our relationship, but when you're 18 and you're wearing a full England shirt you take what you are given. You assume it's the norm. This is England, so it must be right.

I've seen one or two England managers leave in my time, but none in such strange circumstances. Before we could blink, Howard Wilkinson was holding a press conference and recalling Arsenal's Lee Dixon (35) for a friendly against France, which we lost 2–0. Lee had last played for England in November 1993, against San Marino, so you can imagine his delight at being chosen to play right-back. The result increased public pressure for Kevin Keegan, the chief operating officer at Fulham, to be given the job, and in mid-February he signed up for our next four games, against Poland, Hungary, Sweden and Bulgaria. It wasn't until mid-May that he agreed to manage England full-time.

Passion was a big theme in the early days of Keegan's reign. At his first press conference, in February, he told the country that there would be a passionate approach to winning games from now on. I gather that all 75,000 tickets for his opening match, against Poland at Wembley in March, sold within 36 hours. Paul Scholes scored a hat-trick in a 3–1 win which I missed through injury, and the fans chanted Keegan's name. I was also absent for the June games against Sweden (0–0) and Bulgaria (1–1), though in the autumn I came on as a substitute both against Luxembourg (6–0) and Poland (0–0 away). We just about scraped into the play-offs, in second place, ahead of the Poles, which left us needing to beat Scotland to qualify for Euro 2000.

Keegan was the people's choice. It happens that way sometimes with managerial appointments. Everyone backs one candidate. Keegan had that luxury, and the players were overwhelmingly in favour. He had a good record at Newcastle and Fulham, and in his playing days, of course, he had been a star for Liverpool and England. So he seemed the complete package. But if it was for some players, it wasn't for me. Still, I wasn't to know that until we reached our camp in the Belgian forests in June 2000.

Before Keegan was appointed full-time, I had an eventful second half to the 1998/99 season. Disaster struck at Elland Road on 12 April when I ruptured one of my hamstrings against Leeds and was off for three months. Up to the start of the 2002/03 season, when I finally managed to take control of the problem, my hamstrings gave me so much trouble that I decided to set aside a separate chapter in this book to reveal how the problem started and why it took so long to overcome. Though three months sounds a long time, there were only seven League games left after my accident against Leeds, yet I still managed to finish joint-top scorer in the Premiership with 18 goals, sharing the golden boot with Dwight Yorke and Jimmy Floyd Hasselbaink. I scored 23 in all, which was a satisfying end to a season in which I had been desperate to prove myself in domestic football following France 98. But Liverpool finished seventh in the

Premiership, and it was obvious there would be heavy traffic in the transfer market.

The first sign of major change was when Macca passed his medical at Real Madrid in March. He carried on playing for Liverpool until the end of that season, but the old Roy Evans team was breaking up. By May 1999, Houllier had been around for a whole season to make decisions about who would stay and who would go. Among those who left, in addition to Macca (who went of his own accord), were David James (to Aston Villa), Paul Ince (Middlesbrough), Oyvind Leonhardsen (Spurs), Tony Warner (Millwall) and Karlheinz Riedle (Fulham). To us, at the time, it felt as if some of the heart and soul had been torn out of the team. Ince and James were the two big shocks. Houllier was starting the big dispersal, and four seasons later only me, Jamie Carragher and Steven Gerrard were left from those years.

Houllier's effect on the club really hit home when I turned up for pre-season training and saw about eight faces I didn't recognize. I was familiar with Stéphane Henchoz and Didi Hamann, but not Sami Hyypia, Titi Camara or Erik Meijer. I was already playing regularly in the first team so the new emphasis in the club's transfer policy didn't affect me much, but I did think some of our homegrown players could have done as well as some of the foreign players that were initially brought in – and I emphasize the 'some'. Had I been a young local lad coming through, I would have felt frustrated, for sure. I don't care where quality comes from, but, for me, all players should be real quality to justify their presence in the team. If a manager brings in foreign players who are good, everyone applauds. But if there's a flow of players who don't quite reach the required standard, that's when you get problems with the homegrown contingent.

Didi Hamann was one of the good signings, and he and

I just instantly hit it off. With all new signings, you make a fuss of them to make them feel at home and then gradually find out what they're like as a person. On his second day at the club, Didi walked in with the *Racing Post* under his arm and I thought, 'That's enough for me. He's one of my clan!' Then I found out that he loved golf too, and we arranged to play 18 holes. Every single thing I enjoy, Didi seemed to like too. He's the double of me, and he's probably the most genuine and honest person I've ever met. He seems totally English. He's got a German passport, but that's the only German thing about him. Talk about loving a pint, loving the lads and loving a day out. There's no question of him coming in for training, drawing his wages and then disappearing home. He lives for new experiences. He's constantly off on day trips around the country: visiting different theatres and cinemas, taking his kids to Chester zoo, going to explore the castles in North Wales. He loves life and gets on with it, always with a smile and a positive attitude. I hope to be friends with him for the rest of my life. Football takes you down different paths, but I hope we'll always be mates because we've got so much in common. Didi's a top man.

8

Hamstrings: Fact and Fiction

There is a false idea in some minds that I'm injury prone. In case anyone thinks I've been on the sidelines half my life, I should point out that I played over 300 games for club and country in my first six years as a professional footballer. An average of 50 games a year isn't bad. It's also worth reminding myself that I reached 50 caps for England by the time I was 23.

It's not hard to trace the origin of my one big injury problem, which I finally got to grips with after the 2002 World Cup. The key date I've already mentioned: 12 April 1999, at Elland Road. Every other setback to do with my hamstrings stemmed from the accident I had that day. I ruptured one of my three hamstring muscles – completely tore it, in fact – and was ruled out for three months. But this was just the start of my problems.

When I was confronted by serious injury for the first time, I was devastated because I was having a great season and was in line for the Golden Boot, which I eventually shared but would have won outright had my hamstring not ripped at Leeds. The rupture also put paid to my summer plans as I knew I was going to have to spend most of the holiday period in rehab. This is where the story takes an unfortunate twist.

When I came back for pre-season training there was a fall-out between Gérard Houllier and the Liverpool physio, Mark Leather, over how we should proceed with my recovery. The physio thought I needed to do strengthening work to restore my hamstrings to peak condition but the manager didn't want me to be off for too long without touching a ball or getting involved in training. My hamstring was healed by this time, but I still wasn't ready to take part in the sessions or play football in the normal way. Houllier was insistent that at the end of a long jog for rehab purposes I should be the joker in a five-a-side rather than head off to the gym to do strengthening exercises. He didn't want me to exert myself in training, but he did want me to get a feel for the ball again. The problem was that these were the critical points in my recovery. As much as the physio wanted to whip me off to do the rehab programme, the manager wanted to keep me with the other players, so there was a growing conflict of opinion between the two.

Mark Leather eventually left the club by mutual consent. When he did so we were halfway through pre-season. He wasn't replaced immediately so I went quite a long time without having a physio to consult. That made matters worse. Mark was a strong character who was very clear with the manager about what he wanted to do. As the two disagreed more and more about striking the balance between playing and rehab they drifted further and further apart.

My later problems, I believe, developed from there. I was missing out on rehab with weights because I was training with the team instead. After that injury at Elland Road I simply wasn't strong enough to run with my usual power or to do all the things I wanted to do. My hamstrings were never up to it. I half realized it at the time – and the physio was constantly telling me I needed to do more strengthening work – but at the same time I thought I could just play in games and get by. Every now and then I would pull up in matches with a slight pull here and a faint pull there. Then it started to affect my other leg, because an imbalance began to develop.

When the original injury struck, the club did take the best available medical advice. Karlheinz Riedle, our German striker, recommended Dr Hans-Muller Wohlfahrt, a re-nowned German specialist, and suggested I go over to Munich to see him. Dr Wohlfahrt had worked with Linford Christie, Boris Becker, Steffi Graf, José-María Olázabal and Jurgen Klinsmann. The press was full of stories about him injecting weird substances into the body, but that was never the case. The Liverpool club doctor, Mark Waller, had read the newspaper articles and he came over with me just to make sure there was nothing unusual about Dr Wohlfahrt's methods. All those scare stories were totally false.

But when the problem recurred, I started to ask myself, 'What on earth is wrong with me?' I had all my nerves checked and tried every kind of specialist to find the root of the problem. I went to Munich. I went to Harley Street. I went to Oswestry to do a gait analysis to see which parts of my feet I was using and how. I did isokinetic tests to deter-mine which sections of my hamstrings were working and how. Every time I got injured the question was, *Right, where can I go next?* But all the medical authorities told me the same thing: there was nothing wrong. Finally it clicked in my head that there was no structural fault, and that I just needed to work hard at strengthening a muscle that had been badly damaged during a specific accident. It was simply a question of balancing that need against my duty to play. Dr

Wohlfahrt was among those who told me that there was nothing inherently wrong with me. In a sense I was hoping they would find a specific fault – like a malfunction in a car engine – so they could fix it. But the cure turned out to be sheer hard work in the gym.

With the expert help of Dr Waller and the physios Dave Galley and Dave Browes, I finally took control and embarked on a special programme using leg-pulls, squats and gym balls, working the muscles inside you don't normally use. It wasn't to add muscle bulk, but to strengthen the muscles that were already there. Frankly, the medical staff were relieved, because it tallied with what they had been saying all along. They knew I had been ducking the issue, and had been telling me that as nicely as they could. I spoke to the manager before the start of the 2002/03 season and told him, 'I've got to get myself fit. I don't want to be injured any more.' He gave me his approval.

If I was due a bad injury in my early Liverpool career, the hamstrings were the obvious source because I was such a quick runner. The bottom line is that I tore my hamstring at Leeds and didn't recover properly until after the 2002 World Cup, when I launched into that special training programme designed to put all the frustration behind me once and for all.

It's difficult to play competitively while also doing strengthening work with weights, because if you spend too long in the gym doing leg exercises you can be stiff the next day. Ideally you do one or the other. If you play on Wednesday night, for instance, you're stiff on Thursday, and then Friday is the day before the Saturday game, so there's never enough time to devote to an individual rehab schedule. You're constantly putting it off. Hence I was getting weaker and weaker every time I was aggravating the original problem.

The 2002 World Cup, and our second-round match against Denmark, was the turning point. After coming off at half-time and then struggling through the quarter-final against Brazil, I told myself that I couldn't let myself be in that situation again. I didn't want to play through pain any more. I didn't want ever again to play below my full capacity. I didn't want to be incapable of sprinting flat out. I didn't want to play while I was worrying about my hamstrings. It was time to change.

After we lost to Brazil I told myself that I would have to put strengthening before everything else. I made it my absolute priority to get myself right in the 2002/03 season – to take the whole year, if necessary, to conquer the problem once and for all. From the day of the Brazil game onwards I went in early an hour before training to start my new regime. If it took some of the sharpness off me by making me tired, so be it. I was balancing a year of extra hard work against my need to stay injury free.

It worked. After we started on the new system I didn't have a single hamstring problem. The next part of the plan was to restore my speed and sharpness, because the strengthening exercises were designed to improve the reliability of my hamstrings rather than my speed of movement. I just felt I had to do it, otherwise my whole career was going to be stop-start, as it had been for the previous three seasons. I had never been able to get into a rhythm of playing.

I probably haven't sprinted as fast as I used to in the years before April 1999 – that's how serious the long-term effect has been. But I've been steadily working my way back up the speedometer ever since. To put it differently, you need to build a foundation before you can construct a house. For three seasons I was trying to build a house on no foundations, and I paid the price. I don't know how I coped, actually. Every time I pulled the hamstring I thought, *Here we go again.* I developed a very refined sense of how long each mishap would keep me out. If a team-mate pulls a hamstring they should call me because I can tell them absolutely everything they need to know. It was getting boring by the end. The trouble is, I was continually looking for answers or excuses in my own mind. *I've got to go and see him, or him, or him. They'll find something.* I must have known deep down, but couldn't admit it to myself, that I simply wasn't strong enough. I had been sprinting in football matches all my life, and I couldn't comprehend how one bad injury could sap so much of my strength in that area.

My injury scare before the Brazil game was deeply disturbing. I felt that was my stage, a quarter-final of a World Cup, and I may never play on one like it again. But if I do, I'm going to be 100 per cent. That's the promise I made to myself in those dark days after we were knocked out by Brazil. No more stop-start. No more waiting for the next twinge to come along.

I'm a great reader of the match stats in the Liverpool programme, and it was studying the number of games I played in my first six seasons that persuaded me I wasn't really injury-prone. There has been the odd nightmare, though. Missing the final World Cup qualifier against Greece in October 2001 was hell, as was having to sit out the Euro 2004 qualifier against Turkey in Istanbul. I'll never forget how bad those feelings were. I put the 2002 World Cup quarter-final against Brazil in the same category, because even though I played, part of the real me wasn't there.

I've always been in double figures in the goalscoring charts, even when I missed a lot of games with hamstring-related trouble. I've been fit for all the major finals and most of the really important Premiership games. If I get injured, though, it makes the back pages of the newspapers, which brings it to everybody's attention. But I'm not fragile or fatally flawed in one part of my body. My bones and my joints are all fine. It's just that I had one injury that took a long time to get right. The original hamstring tear started a process that took me a long time to understand. But it's over now. I'm no longer reliving that painful day at Leeds.

9

All the Pretty Horses

Shortly after my return from the 1998 World Cup, my agent Tony Stephens took a call from Coolmore, the powerful Irish racehorse owners and breeders who later fell out so spectacularly with Sir Alex Ferguson over the stud rights to Rock of Gibraltar. They wanted to discuss the possibility of me joining them in a joint-ownership exercise that would provide publicity for Coolmore and fun for me. I still have the fax with which they made their initial approach. Our arrangement would be similar to the one under which Sir Alex later raced Coolmore's Rock of Gibraltar in his own colours, after striking up a friendship with John Magnier and J. P. McManus, the two main players at one of the world's most successful studs. The deal was that Coolmore would retain ownership of the horse but it would race in my colours and I would be given a share of the prize-money. I would go racing when it ran and watch the horse work on the gallops – the full package. We would be transparent about how the arrangement was set up: I would get to race a Coolmore horse in my colours and they would get the publicity. It would be like a sponsorship deal in which I got paid not in money but through the pleasure of 'owning' a good horse.

I was only 18 but my interest in racing was blossoming. Despite this, Tony wasn't keen for me to rush down the path of being a high-profile racehorse owner. He thought I was too young and Coolmore too big a concern, so he politely declined their offer and suggested they come back in a couple of years. I've never been keen on the idea of sharing the ownership of a horse because it can get messy, but for me to be attached to such a huge bloodstock operation might have worked out well for both parties. A couple of years later, of course, Sir Alex Ferguson was the proud owner of Rock of Gibraltar who won seven consecutive Group One races. You never know, that privilege might have been mine. I'll say one big thing in favour of Tony's decision, though: it might have saved me a fortune in legal fees.

Tony has shaped my career like nobody else. I can't speak highly enough of him. In moderating my passion for horses he was merely protecting me, as he always does. But now I have a laugh with him about that day when he told Coolmore to 'come back in a couple of years'. But I've always respected Tony's decisions. Ninety-nine per cent of them are correct, and in hindsight this was another one he got right.

In my own career as a racehorse owner, I can't compete with Coolmore or the Maktoum family of Dubai, but already I've drawn an immense amount of pleasure from racing and breeding thoroughbreds – which is the other great passion of my life besides football. Here is a memory that conveys my love of the sport – not the betting, but the horses, and the thrill of the racecourse and the morning gallops.

Four of us – me, Louise, my dad and my sister Lesley – have travelled to Manton in Wiltshire to stay with John Gosden, who trains my horses, in the run-up to Royal Ascot.

John is putting the finishing touches to his runners for the big meeting, and we rise early to join him at dawn on the Wiltshire downs. Standing on the gallops at first light is magical. It's the sound of the horses coming towards you – the snorting, the beat of the hooves and the bird song. At that time of the morning it's generally misty, but you pick up a dot in the distance, which is the face of the lead horse, and your ears start to register the pounding of the hooves. The trainer can tell you when the horses are as far as a mile away which one is which. His knowledge is mind-blowing. We spend the whole morning with our spines tingling. And I think, *I fancy a bit of this for the rest of my life.*

Louise shrinks to about two feet tall when I'm around anyone from the horse racing community. If I end up sitting down to eat after a game with someone I haven't met before, the last thing I want is to be bombarded with questions about the match. But in racing company I just can't help myself asking. I'm OK with the jockeys. With them, I tend to confine myself to the odd question. John Gosden, though, must dread me coming down, because I don't give him a moment's peace. One night when the Gosdens looked after us, I kept John and his wife, Rachel Hood, up until about one o'clock in the morning; poor Rachel was falling asleep at the table. I just wouldn't take the hint. I can't stop asking questions. I want to learn. I want to know everything about the game. I regard it as a world I want to dive into when my football career is over. But in those situations I can see Louise in the corner of my eye shaking her head and thinking, 'Stop pounding them with questions.' The trouble is, I'm fascinated by the process of training racehorses. And it's such a vast subject. One week's worth of knowledge is only a drop in the ocean.

John has so much time for all of us. I have a big family,

but it doesn't stop him insisting that we all stay with him on the rare occasions I'm able to get down to Manton to see my horses. He wouldn't hear of us staying in a hotel. I usually keep the visiting party down to four; if I turned up in a group of 10 we might be stretching even John's hospitality. Given that he has over a hundred horses, it's amazing that he's able to make each owner feel so special. He calls me regularly with bulletins about my two. He doesn't come to Anfield, but he does follow my career. When we speak he always seems to know the details of what happened in the last game I played. He's too nice to say whether he minds me pummelling him with questions, but I can imagine him thinking, 'Shut up, please, I need to go to bed.'

As a boy I liked animals, but I wasn't madly in love with horses, though I had a year or two of riding lessons when I was eight and nine. On caravan holidays with my mum I would compete in donkey races. Sending me down to the stables in Ewloe on a Sunday afternoon was a good way for Mum and Dad to get rid of me for a couple of hours. I enjoyed the work that went with it – the mucking out. We went out for hacks through the countryside round Hawarden. Great fun. The two horses I rode were called Sunny and Major, who had a particularly lively attitude. If you turned up last, you got stuck with Major. He used to amuse himself by trying to unload you. Thinking I was a big, brave lad, I spent plenty of time hanging off him, determined not to fall.

I hardly ever ride now, but when I do I model my riding style on professional flat jockeys, which horrifies Louise. I refuse to have the stirrups at normal length; I set them the way Frankie Dettori would have them. Louise goes crackers and tries to persuade me that it's harder to balance riding that way, but she can never quite put me off. It looks so simple on the telly. But then, most things do. A game of football looks easy from the stands.

The main culprit for getting me involved in ownership is David Platt, the former England captain. Sitting next to him at the PFA Awards in 1998 changed my life. The conversation soon drifted round to racing. David had owned a couple of decent horses, including Handsome Ridge, who won him a couple of Group races. I was enthralled by what he had to say, but I didn't have a clue where or how to start owning my own thoroughbred. It was when David asked 'Why don't you own a horse?' that my mind began spinning. I was still 18, and I still had Tony Stephens' cautionary advice ringing in my ears, but this was a foot in the door on a more discreet level, and David made it sound easy. 'Speak to my trainer, John Gosden,' he suggested, 'and see which horses he's got available. It's sales time in a month or so. Have a look.'

So I contacted John, who called me subsequently to say he'd picked up two horses, a filly and a colt. 'Come and have a look at them and decide which one you want,' John said. After examining them both, I said to my mum, 'Which one, Mum, which one?' Because I'm stupid, I ended up buying them both. My mum's response was, 'Oh, go on, then,' because she loves horses and was an equally soft touch.

The horses had only just turned two and weren't fully developed. Etienne Lady, who I named in honour of my goal against Argentina in St Etienne at France 98, was a grey with plenty of spirit. When we first saw her she reared up on both legs. John assured us that was a good sign. After weeks and weeks of trying to come up with a name for the colt, we settled on Talk to Mojo. The 'Talk' stands for Terry, Andrew, Lesley and Karen – all my brothers and sisters; the 'to' forms the initials of Terry Owen; and 'Mojo' represents the initials of Michael Owen and Janette Owen. I was quite proud to have come up with such an elaborate name.

Talk to Mojo gave us our first winner – a moment I'll never live down. The theory, at first, was that Etienne Lady would be appearing on racecourses sooner than Talk to Mojo, who was a more 'backward' type. He was meant to reach his peak at three. As it turned out neither ran as a two-year-old because Etienne Lady had a slight problem in her first season in training. So Mojo was the first to make his debut, on 16 July 2000 at Newbury. Now, I'm a proud man, and even though you expect these things in racing, I didn't really want to go to Newbury to see him finish way down the field. John Gosden said he thought our horse was in decent shape, but he also pointed out that Newbury is a top track where it's hard to win a race first time out. Moreover, John likes to give horses a gentle introduction to racing. He always told me that he wouldn't let a jockey get stuck into a horse on his first run. 'If we trot in third or fourth, you should be happy,' he said. 'I don't think he'll win.' My dad was adamant we should go, but the rest of us were saying, 'No, come on, Dad, he's not going to win.' The logistics of getting everyone down to Berkshire were also becoming a bit complicated, so we twisted his arm not to go and decided to settle for watching the race on TV.

Fifteen of us set up camp in Mum and Dad's living room, and I spent the minutes before the race trying to calm everyone down and assuring them our horse wasn't going to win. Even the odds told us Mojo wasn't fancied: he went off at 10–1. The stalls cracked open for the race over a mile and a half and Mojo was out the back. But there were only eight runners, so he was in touch at the rear of the field. After a mile, we noticed that our horse was still 'on the bit' (or coasting, for the benefit of non-racing fans). 'Hey, we could finish third or fourth here,' I announced to the room. From an aerial shot, the camera angle changed to a side-on view, but ours wasn't among the three or four faces being tracked by the lens. Suddenly, though, we saw another nose poke into the picture. We all jerked to attention.

'Is it him, is it him?'

Then we saw my blue colours, and the whole room erupted. The jockey was still pulling his head off trying to preserve him for the finish, and by now my restraining influence on the family had disappeared. I'd lost control and was off my chair like a rocket. I wasn't the only one. Mojo eased into third, and the jockey still hadn't picked up his whip. Then he ranged up alongside the two leaders and swept into the lead with the help of one back-hander from the jockey. The next thing we knew he was scooting into a two-length lead and the living room was going berserk, so much so that our two Staffordshire bull terriers lost the plot. When we all jumped on one another they must have thought we were fighting.

Nobody had a penny on the horse that day because John plainly hadn't been confident he'd win first time out. Not long after Mojo crossed the line, the phone started ringing. My friends were calling to say, 'Thanks for the tip, mate!' But when your horse wins you couldn't care less whether or not you backed it, and within a month of our horses starting to run we had two big-priced winners. But I wasn't there to roar either of them home. Naturally, we did conduct a little inquest into why we hadn't made that first trip to Newbury. 'What were we doing?' I asked. 'We bought a horse and we weren't there to see it run!'

After the Newbury race, Talk to Mojo suffered a tendon problem and didn't run again until he was five. I had an opportunity to send him over jumps but turned it down. We also had Bonnie Lad, who was trained by Alan Berry, but was no good. He's nice to stroke, but that's about it. All he does now is live like a king in our yard.

It's only in the last few years that I've learned to enjoy the horses and the sport, as opposed to the betting side of racing. Flat racing is my first love. I don't mind jump racing, but I don't like the idea of one of my horses falling and injuring itself. I'm a bit soft like that. I'm only just starting to alter my thinking about the economics of racing, too. I can see, now, that horses have to earn their keep and am a touch less sentimental. Having said that, I can't stand the idea of casting one of my ex-racehorses into the wilderness. We've got 15 boxes at home, and the intention is to have them full of good mares so I can improve my stock and breed decent animals. If you look at my yard now, it's full of old racehorses – mostly 'boys' who aren't there to breed. If I'm going to be serious about being a breeder I'm going to have to weed out quite a few. I'll need my fillies and mares in the boxes to get them pregnant and maintain my string of active runners. As things stand, any horse who runs in my colours ends up living the life of Reilly. That will have to change. In future, Louise will re-school them as riding horses and re-home them. But it will still be sad when I have to start sending them on their way.

We've got two mares at stud who, if we do as we plan to once I retire, would be back with us at home, foaling in our own yard. Etienne Lady foaled to a stallion called Vettori in January 2004. As a racehorse she finished sixth at Yarmouth and then won a maiden at Newmarket before cracking a bone in her knee. That was the end of her racing career, but she's already given birth to a colt, and a yearling by Dansili. He's called Top Man T. Every horse we breed is going to have a family name, with everyone taking their pick. My dad always calls himself Top Man T whenever he does anything good. My mum's choice was Private Soldier, after 'Tommy' Atkins, her father. Etienne Lady is going next to a stallion called Zamindar, who raced for Sheikh Mohammed of Dubai.

The best horse I've owned is Treble Heights, who recently retired and was sent to Pivotal, who put her in foal. I bought her as a two-year-old from Germany for £110,000 on the recommendation of a friend of Didi Hamann's. John Gosden put her away for the winter to strengthen up and brought her out at the end of August 2002 for a maiden race at Chester, which none of the Owen family will ever forget. Under the jockey John Carroll, who is a friend of mine, she came swinging round that home turn on the bridle, with a couple of furlongs to go. She romped home by seven lengths. Even after the finishing post John had to fight to pull her up. She went off 4–1, and this time we all had our money on. It was one of the most exciting moments of my life. We all went out for a drink in Chester afterwards, and before we went home we walked back to the racecourse stables where she was staying overnight, to give her a pat and a cuddle. Not many owners would do that, I imagine, but we're happy to be thought of as sad like that! Given how effortlessly she had won, it was the least we could do.

The trainer was sufficiently pleased that the Group 3 Park Hill Stakes was picked out as her next target. She had only run once and was coming up against more experienced horses, but she finished second at 10–1 with John Carroll in the saddle again. We were delighted with that, and gave her one more run in a Listed race at Ascot – this time with Frankie Dettori on board. On TV – I was playing the next day so I couldn't attend – I watched her hit the front a couple of furlongs out, but a horse called Love Everlasting came out of the pack and collared her. This was her third race in five weeks, so we decided to pack her away for the winter.

As a four-year-old she went for the Lancashire Oaks at Haydock, where she wasn't fully tuned up and was last by about five lengths with two furlongs to go. 'No chance,' we thought. But then John Carroll gave her a crack with the whip and she absolutely motored through the field to finish fourth. So we went for an easier race called the Aphrodite Stakes at Newmarket to get another win under her belt, but the ground was quite hard and it didn't suit her. Ridden by Jimmy Fortune, she won by a short head – a real gutsy performance.

Then, in the second week of August 2003, off we went to Deauville in France for the biggest test of her career. What a day, what a place. We chartered our own private jet, walked round the harbour and took a look at the beach. The only problems were the heat, which was blistering, and the interest we attracted from the French media, who stuck a lot of microphones in my face. It felt like 120 degrees out there and we were all dressed up. I've never been so uncomfortable. We had a meal with Frankie beforehand – though, being a flat-race jockey, of course he couldn't eat much.

Treble Heights ran her heart out and stuck on gamely in second place in a Group Two race. In the paddock afterwards she really brought a tear to my eye. She was panting like a lion and her veins were bulging. She must have lost loads of weight. I'm always conscious of the effort my horses make on my behalf. I find it incredibly moving. I like to think we appreciate our horses as living things. We were so proud of her. We didn't mind that she was the beaten favourite, behind a filly called Vallée Enchantée. In her box we spent an hour giving her a pat and a cuddle before we got back on the plane. It was special to be part of such a prestigious event in France, where racing is so much more relaxed.

Treble Heights signed off in the Park Hill Stakes at Doncaster again. Frankie was on board once more and this time we really fancied her. But she laboured home and Frankie told us he knew it was over two furlongs into the race. He said she just didn't feel right. Back at John's yard we discovered that she had gone 'tight', or pulled something in her hindquarters. She was four and had done a grand job for us, so we elected to retire her and send her off to Pivotal. She carried the Owen Promotions Ltd colours with the most distinction of any of my horses so far.

I don't have a master plan at the start of each season. Instead, I tend to respond to events and advice from John. If he calls to say he's found a nice horse, I'll judge the situation on its merits. Generally, though, we've raced two or three horses per season. I don't spend silly money, though. Like all owners, I've bought one or two horses that turned out to be not much good, but you have to take those risks. In racing there's more rough than there is smooth. If Treble Heights breeds good foals, she will cover some of the losses in other areas.

My plan, when I'm 40 or 50, is to have 15 boxes at home full of good mares. If I get 10 foals a year, I'll probably race half and sell half. Louise will do the daily work, supervising the upkeep of the mares and foals, while I organize the matings. At the moment I take advice on which stallions to use for our mares, but I want to have more and more input in that respect. For me, that would be heaven. So Louise will get all the dirty work – pulling the babies out – while I'm in the kitchen poring over the stud books. When I look at the day's results in the *Racing Post* I always look at the sires and dams of the winners to see who's hot on the breeding front. I'm building up quite a mental log.

It's not about making a fortune, because breeding is a highly competitive business. The purpose of it will be personal enjoyment. The challenge will be to make the business at least break even. I don't see myself as a racehorse trainer, though I wouldn't completely rule it out. Several ex-footballers, Mick Channon especially, have successfully made the leap from the pitch to the gallops. Being a trainer, though, is like being a football manager: you have so many people to please and so many responsibilities to owners and your staff. Every day starts at dawn.

My passion is for horses and breeding, which gives me a heck of an advantage in the sense that I already know one of the things I want to be doing when I'm no longer playing football. It's a passion based on the prospect of me breeding my own winners. That's preferable to buying a horse out of a sales ring. I like the horse to have been mine from when it was a baby. Imagine owing a winning racehorse that you yourself pulled out of the mare's womb at two o'clock one morning. For me, that feeling connects to how I experience football. I love seeing foreign footballers in the Premiership, but the biggest thrill is winning a trophy with homegrown players. Think of the Manchester United team of Beckham, Scholes, Giggs, Butt and the Neville brothers.

As a person, I need a buzz. I need something to get my adrenalin flowing. In the summer, after a couple of months without competitive football and goals, I'm hell to live with. It's the same when I'm injured. I'm just crazy – very on edge. I can easily fly off the handle. After two weeks out I'm like a bottle of bubbly ready to explode. I just need something to give me a rush. I just hope being a breeder and going racing is going to give me that buzz. If it doesn't, I don't know what on earth I'll do. I would have to find something else – be a football manager, perhaps. Or maybe I'll try and take Gary Lineker's TV presenting job. (Only joking.)

If there was one race I would love to win as an owner, it would be the Derby, though I've never made it to Epsom for the race on account of my football commitments – mainly international matches with England. I tend to make it to the same meetings every year. We get to Newmarket for the 1,000 Guineas, and we've been to Ascot for the Festival meeting in September. Often we fly from our local airport, Hawarden, with all seats full. It's not hard to fill the cabin. By the time we've included the five Owen boys and girls, plus partners, my mate Mike Jones, my dad's friends Barry Elvstone and Gilly Griffiths, who are real characters, and maybe Didi Hamann, there's not a place to be had. I just love to see everyone enjoying themselves. For Newmarket meetings we land at Cambridge and pile into a mini-bus for a stop-off at the New England Stud where Etienne Lady and Treble Heights are among dozens of broodmares looked after by Peter Stanley, the stud manager, who is one of the nicest people in the world and advises us on which stallions to use. Then it's off to the races before the flight back home.

There is no better day out than that. Louise and I live for those days. We have two or three of them a year. All the girls get dressed up and the family have a drink on the plane on the way home and a good chat about the day's events. After Frankie Dettori won the 2002 1,000 Guineas on Kazzia he gave us a tour of the Newmarket weighing room and then took us back to his house for a spontaneous party. We couldn't stay long because the airport was shutting, but it was another of those days that fired my imagination. In retirement, I'll be able to go to any race I want.

Racing and horses are my escape, and I try my best to preserve our privacy when we're at a track. It's a feature of my personality that I hate being stared at. I like the feeling of giving someone an autograph, and seeing their appreciation, but I have to be honest and confess that I shy away from situations in which people chase me for my signature. I don't want that to sound nasty; it's just that I don't respond well to being the centre of attention. If I can't book a private box, we won't go racing. You can't understand what it's like unless you've been famous. To most people, the thought of signing a hundred autographs might sound appealing. At the start of my career I used to hope people would come up to me and ask me to sign. You think you're the king of the world. But that changes. For me, racing is my day off, my private world, and it's harder to enjoy that free time if I'm being swamped and reminded of my footballing celebrity. If I'm standing in an open area watching my horse there will probably be 10 photo lenses fixed on me, and I feel constrained. I don't feel I can shout or jump around. I know I shouldn't feel that way; I know I should just let my emotions go. I sometimes beat myself up about it. At Chester with Treble Heights, for example, I had all my family there and plenty of my friends, but the joy I felt when she won was all inside. I couldn't let it out. Maybe it's just a hatred of being watched.

I don't have to be in a plush executive box, though. I would settle for a cubicle, as long as it had a telly and it was private. I need to be in my own cocoon. Louise has become the same. She hates the hassle of being spotted, and all the attention that invariably follows. We want to be normal. In a perfect world we wouldn't be recognized at all. I know this sounds awful, but it's just the way we are as people. We're not drawn to the light. We accept it in the professional sphere, but we need our space to live and think normally away from the job.

From family days out, I have at least two unpleasant

memories. The first happened during a visit to Belle Vue greyhound track after I had been sent off for tackling Manchester United's Ronny Johnsen with both feet. Greyhound racing is a great laugh. You sit down, have a meal and a bet, and scream the dogs home. Because Belle Vue is a Manchester track, though, we try to find a table in a discreet location. Liverpool players aren't too popular in that part of the world. That particular night I was approached to present a trophy after a race. I said no on the grounds that I didn't want to be recognized in such a potentially hostile environment. However, by then the word was already getting round. While we were having dinner, a group of three United fans trundled up the stairs waving fists and shouting, 'If you ever touch Ronny Johnsen again we're going to kill you.' They were obviously drunk. And it wasn't as if they threatened us and then walked away: they stayed, waiting for us to leave. There was enough of a male presence on our table to have enabled us to battle through, but we decided to leave early and make our exit through the back.

The other bad memory is from a day at Haydock for the Lancashire Oaks. Again we were having a meal before racing, with John Carroll and a few other guests, when my dad slipped out to the toilet. He's such a nice man that if anyone asks him to get my autograph he finds it really hard to say no. On the way back, a Scouse fella stopped him and said, 'You're Michael Owen's dad, aren't you? Do us a favour and get his autograph.' My dad said, 'He's on a day out, with a room full of guests, so would it be OK if we waited until the end of the day?' To which the guy replied, 'My son's got cancer, and Michael signed a shirt for him a while back. I just want to go in and say thank you.' So Dad ushered him into the box, at which point our visitor started chanting 'Rooney, Rooney!' and 'Everton, Everton!' He used his son supposedly having cancer as an excuse to abuse a room full of people. Is that the lowest of the low? My dad was horrified, and of course I had a go at him. He'd done nothing wrong, but because of how it made us all feel Dad bore the brunt of my frustration. It spoilt an otherwise good day.

The advantages of being a high-profile footballer, of course, far outweigh the disadvantages. And for some footballers there are no disadvantages, because they love fame and everything that goes with it. I only love the football; the rest I can live without, but only because I'm a shy person who wants to live in his own world. The best activities, for me, are the ones that anyone can do. For example, going racing with my girlfriend, my children and my family; having a bet and watching the horses. Going to the zoo with Gemma will be another. I can't think of anything worse than flying to Milan to do my clothes shopping, or attending a film première in London. None of that interests me. I suppose the downside of fame is that it's the simple things that get taken away from you rather than the glamorous ones.

But nothing will ever undermine my love of horses and breeding. Golf was my first big non-footballing obsession, but racing is a stronger passion now. All I need, when my career is over, is for Louise to do all the dirty jobs while I'm inside in the warm with the stud books, trying to arrange the right romances!

10

Dark Clouds: 1999/2000

I was an accident waiting to happen. At the start of the 1999/2000 season, my worst in football, I was fully fit, as in healed, but not strong enough to be the player I knew I was. I was lucky just to be playing, really. Every game I managed to make it through without injuring my hamstrings was down to pure good luck. With club and country, this was my darkest period.

I made my comeback from a three-month lay-off in a 2–0 win against Arsenal at Anfield on 28 August and got off the mark for the season with two against Leicester City three weeks after that. The first hint of the conflict to come was when John Gregory, the Aston Villa manager, called me 'a baby-faced assassin'. We had lost to Everton the week before and had just drawn 0–0 with Villa at their ground when Gregory mentioned my horrific tackle on David Weir in the Merseyside derby. John liked to make controversial comments. He had a history of trying to get under people's skin. Knowing that, I wasn't offended by being referred to as an assassin. In fact, I thought he was right.

I was a tough little sod who wanted to mix it with who-ever crossed my path, no matter how big. That's something I've lost out of my game, though I wouldn't mind putting it back. Not the recklessness, but the controlled aggression. I worry that opponents playing against me nowadays think they can kick me without fear of getting one back. In those days I was shown more respect by defenders. If they hurt me, they did so knowing I had it in me to take revenge.

The source of the bad feeling in that Villa–Liverpool match on 2 October was a clash between Steve Harkness and our old team-mate Stan Collymore. With a brutal tackle, Stan went straight through Harkey, whose leg was a gashed mess, and really Stan ought to have been sent off. In the second half I went in on Stan, half protecting myself with a foot raised in case he was going to kick me first. Unfortunately he didn't go in for the tackle fully and so was caught by my studs, for which I should probably have been booked. It wasn't intentional on my part; I was just scared of Stan kicking me. But he took exception to the challenge and pushed me in the head as he was climbing back to his feet. Result: a second yellow card, and off he went.

I felt bad about that. I liked Stan, and I didn't want to be responsible for getting him dismissed. I hate red cards at the best of times. But there was a lot of bad blood in the game on account of whatever had been said between Collymore and Harkness. Stan later claimed that Harky had said something racial. Whatever it was, it caused Stan to go after him in the tunnel when the final whistle had blown. When I saw Stan rampaging in our direction, I assumed he was coming after me!

Before I played football properly that season, I played the English diplomat, travelling to Zurich with the MP Tony Banks and Geoff Hurst to help the Football Association present the 2006 World Cup bid. They asked me to say a few words in front of the committee, so I stood up and declared, 'In my lifetime, I've been to Euro 96 and it was a great tournament, well organized. I'd love the World Cup to be in my own country. I had such a great experience at France 98. It's a burning ambition of mine to play in a World Cup final in my own land.' Later, I found myself struggling to answer awkward technical questions about the English bid. But it was an honour to be asked. If we'd been successful, it would have been nice for me to feel I'd played a part in bringing a World Cup to England.

We weren't to know it in Zurich, but this was to be one of the country's barren spells on and off the pitch. In the autumn of 1999 we were still trying to rescue our Euro 2000 qualifying campaign, with Kevin Keegan now in full charge. We beat Luxembourg 6–0 and drew 0–0 in Poland, but then needed Sweden to beat the Poles for us to finish runners-up in Group 5. Their 2–0 win in Stockholm must be one of the biggest presents English football has had. Later, the Swedes gave us Sven-Goran Eriksson too, but for now we were just happy to be given a second chance of qualifying via the play-offs.

When we drew Scotland, it just seemed to come out in the press one day. I don't remember there being an actual draw. I did notice that all the big countries missed one another, which always seems to happen in play-off draws. Scotland weren't a great side, but they hadn't yet started their rapid downward slide, so it was no easy tie.

I've never bought in to the old hostility to the Scots, mainly on account of my dad's Tartan ancestry. Though England–Scotland is an ancient rivalry, it doesn't match up to the struggles we've had against Germany over the years. The Anglo-German duel is easily England's biggest. Besides, there was no need for Kevin Keegan to stoke the fire prior to the Scotland ties: from the outset people jumped on the idea that it was 'the Battle of Britain'. In any event, Keegan wouldn't have called them 'Sweaty Socks' or been rude about them in any way. He wasn't one of those managers who go in for cheap shots.

From the way the first leg at Hampden Park on 13 November was hyped, we expected to walk into the hottest cauldron of our lives. That's not the way it turned out. I've experienced much greater hostility than the Scots directed at us that day. At the hotel there were bagpipes on the morning of the game, either for a wedding or maybe to intimidate us. It didn't disturb our stomachs. There was a cracking atmosphere inside the stadium and we were surprisingly relaxed. Paul Scholes did the trick with two first-half goals and we flew back south with a comfortable win.

I love playing in games where you feel everyone's against you. I'm sure the Turkey–England World Cup qualifier in the autumn of 2003 was one of those, though I missed that trip with a shin injury. In those environments the players don't have to say anything to one another. Eleven men will look into one another's eyes and just know they have to stick together. It's you against 80,000 people, baying for blood. That draws something from very deep inside.

The return leg at Wembley was just four days later, but the manager let some of the players go home after the first leg. I remained in the camp because it would have been impractical for me to get to North Wales and back in the time allowed. Alan Shearer stayed too. We sat up late to watch Lennox Lewis fight Evander Holyfield and then played golf round Sunningdale the next day. On the night of the boxing we had a couple of drinks, with the inevitable result that the newspapers were full of stories about a mammoth drinking session. I wouldn't say we were exactly knocking it back, and it wasn't as if we had gone behind the manager's back. He'd given us permission to unwind. Of course we had a few glasses, but we were sensible about it and didn't abuse the privilege. It was laughable to claim we were out for the count. The last thing you would want to do as an England player is make a fool of yourself in front of hotel staff. When a manager gives me permission to relax in that way I never want to betray his trust. One of Sven-Goran Eriksson's great strengths, for example, is that he has faith in his players. If you're there, it's because he believes in you. The basis of our relationship with him is respect, and it flows both ways. If you asked to go on a marathon shopping trip the day before a game, Eriksson would probably say no. But it would hurt him to turn down the request. The benefit, of course, is that the players don't want to let him down. Repaying his faith becomes a mission.

Back in 1999, there was no chance that our evening off would affect our performance in the home game against the Scots, though there's something unnerving about going into a second leg 2–0 up. Deep down you're assuming you're through unless there is a miracle. No England team would ever contemplate surrendering a two-goal lead at Wembley, our old fortress. But, strangely, those games are hard to play in. I remember, with Liverpool, beating Roma 2–0 in their Olympic Stadium and then struggling desperately when we took them back to Anfield, where they beat us 1–0.

But a 2–0 lead is nevertheless a comfort zone, and recent history teaches us that England are at their best when the world is against them. For some reason we relish being under the cosh. At Wembley that night, Don Hutchison put Scotland in front after 39 minutes, and we didn't manage to respond, despite being able to call upon, at various stages of the game, Alan Shearer, Emile Heskey, Paul Scholes and me. If Scotland had scored again I'd have been deeply alarmed, because we wouldn't have had much time to shake ourselves up. Though we eventually limped into Euro 2000, we did so with a strong spine to our starting line-up comprising Seaman, Campbell, Ince, Adams, Beckham, Shearer and Scholes. What we needed to do was put the awful qualifying campaign behind us and start acknowledging our many strengths.

On the home front, Liverpool went out of both cup competitions early – in the League Cup to Southampton and in the FA Cup to Blackburn – and we struggled along in fourth, fifth and sixth positions in the League, though we did climb to second in April before losing three of our last five games and drawing the other two. In that late-season collapse we didn't score a single goal against Everton, Chelsea, Leicester, Southampton or Bradford.

The big news that season had been Emile Heskey joining from Leicester for £11 million, and Gérard Houllier dismissing the idea that either I or Robbie Fowler would be leaving as a result. I certainly didn't feel my position was under threat. From what the manager was saying, it just seemed that there would now be three of us competing for two starting positions. At that time squads were getting bigger, and the word 'rotation' was entering everyone's vocabulary. All the players knew Emile was joining long before he actually signed the forms. As time wore on, it became apparent that he was a very different kind of player to me and Robbie, so from then on it was going to be Emile in the team and us two competing for the other striker's shirt. That change of emphasis wasn't obvious at first, but it became so during 2000/01 when I had to fight harder to keep my starting place.

Against Bradford on the final day of the season we had needed to win to make the Champions League, while our hosts required three points to have any chance of staying in the Premiership. Leeds were on our shoulder, chasing that same last bus to Europe. Then Bradford's David Wetherall forced a header past us in what turned out to be one of the great relegation escapes. When the inevitable pitch invasion came, we couldn't wait to get down that tunnel and away from Valley Parade.

The whole Champions League obsession is strange. When you don't quite make it into the following year's competition, you don't feel the way you would if you'd lost an FA Cup final. There are no medals for qualifying. In our subsequent Treble-winning season, if you had offered me the chance to reach the Champions League but lose the FA Cup final I know what I would have said. Give me the silverware every time. Give me the sensation of actually winning something. A manager, mind you, would probably say the opposite. Of course I was sad that we hadn't made it into the Champions League, and those feelings followed me through the summer, but the sense of loss wasn't comparable to a big defeat in a match where there is a trophy on the line.

In League goals and appearances, 1999/2000 was the worst season of my Liverpool career. But then I was absent for 11 of our 38 Premiership games. I finished with 11 goals in 27 matches, and Liverpool finished 24 points behind the champions, Manchester United. We clung to the hope that this had been the first full season for a new-look team, and that things were bound to improve next term. Against that, there was the nagging realization that we had failed to beat Bradford City when all we needed was a scrappy victory against a relegation-threatened team to get us into the Champions League. On that basis there was no reason to expect such a dramatic improvement in form a few months on.

Nor did I expect that summer's European Championship

to be such an unhappy time for me and the England team. If losing at Bradford damaged my morale, much worse was to come under Kevin Keegan.

11

Euro 2000 – the Low Countries

The goal I scored against Brazil in a 1–1 draw at Wembley
in May tricked me into thinking I had established myself as
Alan Shearer's partner in attack for Euro 2000. What a false
hope that was.

My problems with Kevin Keegan's management hadn't
emerged by the time we scraped through in the two qualifiers
against Scotland. I had no problem with the fact that Andy
Cole and Emile Heskey had also been involved alongside
Alan in the qualifying campaign. They were playing well and
deserved their chances, though Andy missed the tournament
through injury. It was only at the championship itself that
my relationship with the England manager deteriorated.

Quite rightly, Shearer was still the main man, but I was
certain I could nail down the other starting place by the
time we arrived in Belgium. There is a difference, though,
between knowing you're going to be on the team-sheet and
feeling that the manager has total faith in you, that you're
'his man'. Keegan's attitude, I believe, was that Shearer was
the number one, while I was the best of the bunch chasing
the other shirt. To be accurate, none of us was really impos-
ing himself on the other candidates. In the build-up I missed
the prep game against Malta but had started against Brazil

and had scored a decent goal. That was what made me assume I'd be Alan's partner up front. I went to Belgium thinking, 'Right, the manager must fancy me after the goal against Brazil, so it's going to be me and Shearer from here on in.' I hit the tournament with high expectations. But I was deluding myself.

Keegan is an exceptionally positive man, and we all went off to the tournament thinking we had a pretty formidable team. On the training ground the manager had recruited a few ex-players who were old friends, Nigel Spackman and Peter Beardsley among them, though they didn't supervise the sessions. Derek Fazackerly and Keegan did most of the coaching. Kevin tried to make it fun, with lots of shooting practice and small-sided games, but I didn't enjoy England training while he was in charge. I liked Arthur Cox, Keegan's old ally, but the chemistry between Fazackerly and me wasn't good. His attitude towards me was negative throughout, so there was bound to be trouble.

For me, the warning signs were all there on the training pitch. I assume the manager had conveyed to his staff what he thought of me, and plainly it wasn't complimentary. I felt I was being singled out, not just by the manager but by the whole coaching team. Fazackerly was pulling me up a lot in training. If I did one tiny thing wrong there would be a rush of critical comment. He didn't shout, but he was constantly intervening, stressing the importance of holding the ball up and becoming a link player. I thought, *The whole staff have got it in for me here*. If you're not satisfying the manager or his coaches, your confidence will quickly slip down the drain.

Keegan was certainly 'one of the lads', which made him the direct opposite of his successor, Sven-Goran Eriksson. If Keegan came across players dealing cards he would join in for maybe 20 minutes and sometimes get more heavily involved. He would organize a race night once a week and take the bets himself. His instincts told him to have a laugh with us, not to be some remote authority figure. Sometimes it's hard being confined day after day, even in a five-star hotel, where you can run out of things to do. You need to escape from your room. To Keegan, being active around the hotel improved team spirit. There was a lot written in newspapers about the alleged gambling culture in the squad, and Keegan probably left himself open to criticism in some respects, but we were never betting in thousands of pounds. Ridiculous figures were being bandied around. Yes, the papers got half the story right in the sense that we did play cards, with the gaffer as one of the contestants. If there was a group of us all trying to outdo one another we would probably play three-card brag; with three or four players we might plump for hearts, which lasts a long time, for a penny a point. It passed the time and brought us together. Only half a dozen of us played regularly, though. I found it therapeutic. We were very angry about the figures being splashed across the papers.

With me carrying bad vibes from the training sessions, we travelled to Eindhoven in Holland to face Portugal on 12 June. It wasn't a good start for me because I boarded the bus after the game with my confidence totally drained. The reason was simple: I had been substituted at half-time. More seriously, we had been 2–0 up after 18 minutes but had somehow managed to lose the match 3–2.

For our first goal, I went wide in a nice phase of link play and found David Beckham, who crossed the ball for Scholes. I was involved throughout the first half and was playing well, or so I thought. With a 2–0 lead, we carried on attacking. In retrospect, I can see there was no need for us to continue pouring forward so early in the game. All of a sudden, from having them pinned back in their own half, we seemed stretched. I can remember Figo collecting the ball and running with it, seemingly forever, and then crashing it into our net. As things began to deteriorate, we weren't making individual errors, it was just that we were being pulled across the pitch. Huge gaps were opening up. Before we could adjust, we conceded a second inside 16 minutes. By the time we got back to the dressing room we were in a terrible state.

My job in those situations is to think about goals: how to score, how to create. I was satisfied with my own first-half performance and certain that I could contribute more after the break. But when we sat down, Keegan made an announcement. He said he was going to change the team. Then I heard my name. I raised my eyes and saw the manager looking at me. He said, 'I'm going to bring you off.' I went numb. Sometimes you come into the dressing room thinking, *Bloody hell, I was awful out there, and I know there's an alternative sitting on the bench*. Hard though it is, you accept the need for change. But I never thought for a second, against Portugal, that I was about to be withdrawn. I was baffled. Then really hurt.

I imagine that people back home were in heaven after Scholes and McManaman had blitzed the Portuguese, and then in hell when Luis Figo, João Pinto and Nuno Gomes (in the second half) embarrassed us with three unanswered goals. My first impulse was to be deflated for the whole team, but I also felt deep resentment against Keegan himself. I felt that his mistake in changing the team unnecessarily contributed to the result. Obviously no slight is intended against Emile Heskey, who took my place. It's just that there was simply no need to bring me off. Keegan tried to explain himself. He told me not to worry and said I had played well. His explanation was that he had wanted to try a different type of striker to restore our control of the game. 'Oh, right, OK,' I said, trying to understand, and traipsed back to the hotel.

The next day on the training pitch, Keegan came over to me and said, 'Don't worry, I've every confidence in you. You're starting the next game, against Germany.' But actions speak louder than words. I know 100 per cent that if Emile had played well and scored against Portugal then he would have kept his place. I felt the manager was trying to pull the wool over my eyes, and that scarred me for the whole tournament. It was just getting worse and worse. I was happy to be starting the next game, but I knew Keegan didn't have much confidence in me.

So on we went to Charleroi, five days later, to face Germany. Martin Keown came in for Tony Adams, who was injured, and Dennis Wise replaced Steve McManaman on the left. Up front it was Alan and me again. It was a fairly dull first half, which ended goalless. We were doing OK, though. Eight minutes after the restart, David Beckham clipped in a cross which skimmed my head and then bounced to Shearer, who put it away. Grand. I was fizzing. For eight minutes, anyway. With half an hour left, Keegan brought me off again. I was disappointed, but I could understand the logic. In my place he sent on Steven Gerrard to strengthen the midfield. This was a tactical change to help defend the 1–0 lead – the manager's prerogative. Naturally I accepted it.

Romania, who had given us so much bother at France 98, came next. In training all week Keegan had kept me behind, playing balls into me and telling me what he wanted me to do. His lectures were based on the idea that he wanted me to hold the ball up and link the play more, with Alan Shearer staying on the shoulder of the last defender to 'keep the length' of the attacking formation. I didn't feel able to object out loud; I was still a young lad. So I was phoning my dad every night, telling him, 'He's getting me to do this, that and the other, and I don't know what to do.'

Getting off the bus back in Charleroi, I was still really low on confidence, having been substituted twice already and then picked to bits on the training ground. Before we departed, a team meeting was called to enable us to discuss the Romanians. A pattern was developing in the way Keegan spoke to me at these gatherings. In all the post-match debriefs he made a point of saying that I needed to improve this or that aspect of my game. Suddenly, at the pre-Romania meeting, he set off on a 20-minute lecture, just on me: 'Michael, if I was any other manager, you would not be playing tomorrow. You've not shown enough yet, and you've got to improve or we'll have to change. The only reason I'm keeping faith is that I know you can do better. Spinning and trying to get in behind defenders is Premier League stuff. It won't work in international football. You've got to hold the ball up better . . .' And so on.

I came out of the meeting – I came out of the whole three weeks – thinking, *Is it me? Am I the problem?* In fact, I was thinking too much. Maybe it wasn't just me he was having a go at; maybe he was having a go at everybody, just using me as the vehicle for his thoughts. But I can vividly remember us going on a walk the day after that particular meeting and Gary Neville and David Beckham approaching me with some comforting words. 'Don't worry about what he's saying to you,' they said. 'He thinks you're a good player; we know you're a good player. Just do what you normally do.' That told me that everyone else was aware of what was happening. I could sense in their voices that they shared my disbelief. They weren't having a go at the manager, but their message seemed to be, 'Don't listen to him.' But by then I already had a mass of unhelpful thoughts racing around my head. And that's the last thing you need when you're preparing for a big match. My head was in orbit.

When the game kicked off, I felt a level of tension I hadn't experienced before and haven't felt since. Fifteen seconds in, the ball went back to Gary Neville who played a relatively easy ball forward along the floor to me. I had a defender reasonably close to me, but not worryingly so; he was just close enough to steal the ball if I happened to take a bad touch. I was so tense that I completely missed the ball. I'd never done that before. It just doesn't happen. And it wasn't as if I missed it by a few inches: my foot went nowhere near the damn thing.

As I turned to retrieve the ball from the defender who had pinched it, I shot a glance at the bench. A terrible thought filled my head: *That's exactly what he wants me to do, because it confirms what he's been saying all week.* Guess what. When I caught sight of the manager he was throwing up his arms, shaking his head and gesticulating at the other coaches as if to say, 'Did you see that?' That, I can assure you, is one of the worst feelings in the world.

In the next five minutes I managed to get in another couple of touches, but at the same time I couldn't stop looking over towards the bench. Ten minutes in and I could see the three substitute strikers warming up. Just the strikers – no other players. My desperation to impress the manager was turning to anger. In those moments I really resented him – not as a man, I should stress, but as a manager. With a quarter of an hour gone, I thought, *Sod him, I'm playing my own game. I've played in a World Cup, I've played for Liverpool, I've done well in my career so far. I know I'm a good player.*

I don't need his advice if it's going to make me feel like this.
So I spent the last half an hour of the first half trying to get
in behind defenders as I would for Liverpool, trying to take
people on.

Just before the break, the ball came in to me and I steered
it round the keeper and scored. Up went the linesman's
flag, though it was shown subsequently on the replays to be
onside. A few minutes later I scored a proper goal. The relief
was immense. I just wanted to make a gesture to the manager that said 'I told you so', even though I had not discussed
my feelings with him before the match.

Going into the dressing room at half-time, of course, I felt
vindicated. One of Keegan's strengths was that he would go
round the players individually. That was a bad thing from
my point of view because I was so worn down by everything
he'd said to me that I was incapable of interpreting anything
he said in a positive way. I can remember him coming up to
me and saying, 'Well done, good goal, but I still want you
to do this and that.'

At 2–2, he brought me off. The Romanians scored again
while I was off the field. The two facts weren't related, but
again I couldn't help thinking, 'It's his own fault.' I'm
not sure whether he thought the way he played was the only
way for a person of limited size to operate. Maybe he was
trying to recreate me in his own image. My dad had read
Les Ferdinand's book, and there were echoes of what he
was attempting to do to me in what Keegan had tried to
do to Les at Newcastle. He was trying to make both of us
something we were not.

Holding the ball up? Yes. But I was playing with Alan
Shearer, who was arguably the best in the world at doing
that – an iron striker who almost never surrendered possession. My idea was that I could make runs off him the way

Craig Bellamy subsequently did at Newcastle. I couldn't understand why I was being expected to drop off and show for the ball in positions where I couldn't employ my natural abilities. My dad, who was naturally supportive, couldn't understand it either. Whether he meant to or not, it was as if Keegan wanted to take away everything I could do well and force me to do things I'm only now learning how to do. If he had said, 'Your pace scares everyone to death and you're a terrific finisher, so if you can just do these things as well . . .' then I would have loved the man.

He certainly didn't apply the same mindset to Alan, but I had no problem with that. I wouldn't have expected him to pick holes in Shearer. It comes back to the question of hierarchies. The most senior players don't need to be told they've made a mistake. I would bet that Arsène Wenger never had to tell Tony Adams he'd done something wrong. They both would have known, so the words would have been wasted. With me, though, all the England coaches were on the same bandwagon.

In the build-up to the Germany game I suspect Keegan had been stung by the criticism from the Portugal match, when he was accused of playing too openly and not protecting a 2–0 lead. When we went 1–0 up against Germany he responded to that criticism by dropping our traditional 4–4–2 formation and bringing on an extra midfielder to tighten things up. Fair enough, but half an hour was too long, too conservative. I think he feared the press a lot. So it was no surprise when I was taken off. When we scored against the Germans, I think he had it in the back of his mind that he didn't want to be savaged again for surrendering a lead. Keegan didn't like the media, especially after the defeat against Portugal. After the Germany game his attitude was, 'If we beat Romania,

I've got the power to go to my bosses at the FA and say we don't want to do the press any more.'

I think often about what happened to me on those training fields in the Belgian town of Spa. I have a responsibility to try to see it from their point of view so I've retraced my steps to see whether or not there is some basis to their opinion of me that wasn't apparent at the time. During the 1999/2000 League season I had been injured a lot – one serious problem and a lot of subsequent niggles. So plainly I wasn't at the peak of my physical powers. That might have instilled some doubt in their minds about my ability to use my pace. But I still think they handled it badly. Even if I wasn't playing unbelievably well, I felt I was worthy of a place in the team. From the start it would have helped if Keegan had done more to encourage me and keep my confidence up. Instead, he substituted me early in games throughout the tournament and forced me to do things on the training ground that I wasn't capable of doing. I'm fierce about wanting to improve, and if anyone can refine my game I will listen, but he wanted me to do things I didn't want to do and will never do again, because I'm not the type of player he was wanting me to be.

I don't think Keegan had any sort of a personal agenda against me, I just think that as the England manager at a major tournament he felt under enormous pressure and he needed something or someone to blame. I was an easy target. I wasn't 100 per cent on top of my game. I take my share of responsibility, because maybe I wasn't at my absolute best. Maybe I should have been grateful that he was picking me every time. I respected him as a man and I'm sure he liked me as a lad, but when it came down to business there was so much pressure on him that he needed a scapegoat. As soon as he said one negative thing about me it led to another one, and then it became a habit.

It was all so bewildering for me because I'd had no experience of being criticized in public, or of being singled out in front of other players. At times I didn't know where to put myself. It was only when other England players intervened and advised me not to let it damage my self-esteem that I began to achieve any kind of perspective on what Keegan was saying to me.

At that tournament we had good players, but I never felt we had a formula for how we wanted to play. I can recall a lot of the senior players contributing to the constant debate we were having about how we should organize ourselves on the pitch. Dennis Wise spoke a lot; Alan Shearer also contributed a great deal. I can remember having one of those sessions after the defeat against Portugal. As I listened, it seemed astonishing to me that here we were talking about how we ought to defend – the basic issues – when we had already played the game. I didn't feel there was any organization from minute one. If we'd had any nous we wouldn't have surrendered that 2–0 lead against Portugal. It wouldn't happen now, put it that way; Sven-Goran Eriksson wouldn't allow it. We had a good team in 2000, with great spirit, and we had a lot of fun inside the camp, but we had no organization. In major tournaments you need quality, team spirit and good organization. We had two of those, but we lacked the third.

Kevin Keegan's reign as England manager came to an unhappy end, of course, at Wembley on 7 October that year, after we lost 1–0 to Germany in the teeming rain. It was the first game of our 2002 World Cup qualifying campaign, and we had got off to the worst possible start. Didi Hamann's free-kick had broken through our defences while our concentration had lapsed. After the game we trooped into the dressing room and waited for what seemed a long time for Keegan to join us. When he finally appeared we were taking our boots and socks off to get in the shower. He announced, 'That's it, lads, I've had enough.' Arthur Cox and Derek Fazackerly jumped in and said, 'No, wait, just give yourself five minutes to think.' But Keegan was adamant. 'No, no, it's too late. I've made up my mind. It's definite. Thanks for your efforts. I've decided to call it a day.'

I was already down the tunnel by the time he left the pitch, but subsequently I've seen pictures of him stopping to respond to something that was shouted by someone in the crowd. There's obvious shock on his face. If he had any doubt in his mind, getting stick from the fans was likely to push him over the edge.

There's never a good time for an England manager to leave. Plenty of people thought he'd left the team in the lurch, but I'm not inclined to criticize him for quitting when he did. We'd just been beaten by Germany, and he was so deflated that it was hard to imagine him pulling himself round by the time we met Finland the following Wednesday night. He was on such a downer, and the team was so dispirited, that maybe we'd have lost again in Helsinki and therefore not even qualified. He probably did the team a favour. I certainly wouldn't accuse him of a lack of loyalty. I know how proud he was of being England manager.

Howard Wilkinson was rushed in to restore order. His methods were unusual, to say the least. For our first training session with him he walked us down to what felt like a local parks pitch, with lots of local people watching. There's nothing wrong with that, but it was a bit of a leap from Bisham Abbey, high security and being taken everywhere by coach.

Howard said, 'Right, we'll do a few set-pieces,' and we walked about a mile down the road with our boots on to what might have been a school. We were all looking at one another as if to say, 'What on earth is going on here?'

I'm not sure what Howard's thinking was. I'd never come across anyone like him before. Some of the things he said during team-talks made me think, 'Oh my word, this is new.' I can remember him naming the team for the match against Finland and saying to David Seaman and Nigel Martyn, 'I'm not sure which one of you to pick. I've got no feeling either way. I'm fifty-fifty. I could toss a coin, but I've decided to pick you, David, so you owe me a favour.' I thought, 'Aye-aye!' He also said to Emile Heskey before the game, 'I don't know your position. I don't think you know your position. But I'm going to play you on the left.' That was the position Emile had played for Leicester City before he joined Liverpool. Robbie Fowler was less than amused by his treatment, too. Robbie had been to see Howard to tell him he wasn't fully fit, and I think Robbie had it in mind to go home to get some treatment and work on his fitness. He wanted it kept quiet, but Howard announced it in a team meeting a few minutes later.

Then Howard called on Teddy Sheringham, who he picked alongside Andy Cole after deciding to leave me on the bench, which I couldn't really understand. Worse was to follow. The game was stuck at 0–0, and without blowing my own trumpet, what do you do when the game's frozen like that? You bring on a fresh striker with a bit of pace to cause a few rumblings in the last twenty minutes to half an hour. But the clock ticked away, and it stayed goalless. I don't think Howard changed anything at all in that game. He was quite pleased with the draw.

The Howard Wilkinson era was always going to be

shortlived. Looking back on the Keegan era, one main feature stands out for me. It made me question my footballing ability for the first time in my life. And yes, it scarred me. I used to go into games believing that the opposition was scared of me and that nothing could get in my way. That feeling, that belief, evaporated at times when I played under Keegan. Certainly it was a dark phase in my career. It made me more sensitive and self-protective.

12

The Treble: 2000/01

After the agonies of Euro 2000, I was ready for the good times to roll again. In June, Gérard Houllier signed a new five-year contract and continued to put his stamp on Liverpool's first-team squad. The main reinforcements for the 2000/01 campaign were Christian Ziege, Nick Barmby, Markus Babbel, Gary McAllister and, later, Jari Litmanen. The squad was bigger and stronger, and it needed to be because we found ourselves playing 25 cup-ties in what turned out to be a marathon season.

Houllier was a big fan of targets. During pre-season training he spent a couple of evenings reviewing the previous season and telling us what he expected of us in the coming campaign. He set out any new rules and regulations and then laid out the aims. Every few weeks he drew things to a halt and said, 'Right, this is where we are at this stage of the season, this is what I want us to get out of the next few games.' He had his major objectives and he broke down the season into phases as we went along. But that summer of 2000, I don't recall him telling us he expected us to win five trophies over the next year!

Our Treble-winning season got off to an explosive start: three players were sent off during our 2–0 defeat at

Highbury on 21 August, and then Southampton came back from 3–0 down to take a point off us at The Dell. They snatched two in the last 10 minutes, and that really rocked our manager. He had a proper blast at us after the game. My own form, though, was just taking off. I scored two against Southampton, a hat-trick against Villa a week later and two in our next three games. In between, I came off the bench to equalize for England against France in Paris. Having scored two against Southampton, I wasn't too happy to be left out of the starting line-up when Kevin Keegan decided to play Andy Cole alone up front, but it was reminiscent of how things had gone for me in Belgium. When the manager brought me on and I scored, a gesture to the dug-out was added to my goal celebration – a ten-second stare.

Looking back, I feel faintly embarrassed that I did that, even though it wasn't picked up on at the time. I must have been grumpy about a few issues that autumn. When I scored at The Dell, I pointed to my left foot both times. My left peg seemed to be a major talking point in those days. I remember, in one England game, trying to cross a ball with the outside of my right foot when I probably should have played it with my left, and hearing groans around the stadium. So pointing to my left boot that day was a swipe at my critics.

At the end of September, I came up with another pointed gesture. After scoring against Sunderland at Anfield from a cross whipped in by Ziege, I slapped my forehead to make a point to those who were questioning my heading ability. See? I can score with my left foot and my head as well. At that time I was working very hard on aspects of my game I needed to improve. I was practising an awful lot – left-foot shots, headers, holding up the ball – and suddenly it seemed it was all paying off. Later that season I began scoring regularly for England with my left. In the FA Cup final against Arsenal in May 2001 all the hard work paid spectacular dividends, but by then I'd stopped making dramatic gestures to critics up in the stands.

The problem with watching old tapes is that you can't believe some of the silly things you've done. One recording from that autumn I'm happy to avoid is the one of my shocking head injury at Derby on 15 October. This was my scariest moment in football. The chain of events started when a corner came in which Emile Heskey met first with his head. I happened to be going for the same ball, but I ended up on my knees and then felt an almighty bang from behind – Christian Dailly's knee cracking into my head. The first thing I remember is waking up in hospital, having been in an A & E room where an injured motorcyclist was lying on a bed next to me. The first words I heard were, 'I think he's gone, I think he's dead.' That's when I really panicked. I was asking the nursing staff why I was there and what had happened. I was hugging my mum and saying I wanted to see Louise and my brothers and sisters one last time. The story I got back later was that I had been stretchered off the pitch with blood all over me. Apparently you could see Emile looking at me and then turning away as if he was about to be sick. I needed 13 stitches in the back of my head. The gash had gone through the fatty tissue as well as the skin. Emile says there was a massive lump of skull showing through. The club doctor, Mark Waller, has since told me that I was shouting to the manager all the way down the tunnel: 'I'm coming back on, I'm coming back on!' Dr Waller assumed I was going to be OK because I was shouting so coherently. But as I was being stitched up I kept raising my head and seeing Veggard Heggem, who had just come off with a hamstring pull, and Veggard later told me he knew something was wrong when I kept asking him,

'What are you doing here? What's the score?' Veggard swears that in the 10 minutes it took for the ambulance to arrive I must have asked him the same questions 20 or 30 times. So the doctor got the message.

My mum and dad were at the game but the rest of my family were watching on Sky, and my brothers phoned my mum and told her I was being taken to hospital. She ran down and joined me in the ambulance while my dad got the car and followed. I ended up having two brain scans at a Liverpool hospital. After my initial treatment in Derby, I insisted on getting back to the ground and on to the team coach with the lads for the trip home. The doctor steered me on to the bus. I was still in my full Liverpool kit with blood all over it. At the front of the coach, for some reason, I was crying my eyes out. I kept lifting my head and asking myself, *What are you crying about?* Then my head went down and I sobbed for another 20 minutes. I was inconsolable for two hours, and I didn't have a clue why. The doctor later explained to me that the part of my brain that had been smashed was the bit that deals with your emotions. The other players still take the mickey out of me for being so distraught on the bus. When the manager came over to see me I was still crying, and I told him in a weepy voice, 'I was at the hospital, gaffer, and I thought I was going to die!' It was as if Houllier was the father figure and I was crying on his shoulder. So embarrassing. To this day, some of the players tease me with, 'Oh, gaffer, I thought I was going to die!' in the same teary voice.

At Liverpool, my agent, Tony, met me off the coach and we went on to hospital, where I had the scans and stayed overnight. Even a week later I was wobbly on my feet and kept forgetting things. I was a mess. I found out later that the motorcyclist had died just as I was waking up.

I missed the next three games, but the form of the team remained mostly good. To win things in English football nowadays you need every player to be performing consistently well. It's no good some players being good while others are off colour. When I cast an eye over the 2000/01 season, I understand why we were so solid across 60 or 70 games. We had a dependable back four for a start, in which Babbel, Hyypia, Henchoz and Carragher excelled. Up front, too, there was a constant flow of goals from me, Heskey, Fowler, Gerrard and McAllister. The team spirit was first rate, and we had a nucleus of good English players: me, Carragher, Redknapp, Barmby, Heskey, Murphy and Fowler, just off the top of my head. We hit it off as a group. Emile had his own goal celebration which he used all that season, an impersonation of a DJ spinning a record while holding a headphone to his ear. I believe it was a promise he'd made to a DJ he and some of the lads had met on holiday.

Although we were never higher than third in the League before the New Year, we won 1–0 at Manchester United and thrashed Arsenal 4–0 at home within seven days in the run-up to Christmas. We were developing a good record against the top clubs. We were criticized for being a counter-attacking team, but our strategy worked brilliantly against the very best sides. They would pour on to our excellent defence and we would retaliate with our pace up front. We were good at soaking up pressure and then hitting teams on the break. We'd honed it to perfection, and we hurt a lot of top opponents. The victory against United was their first home defeat in the League for a year and 363 days, and it was Houllier's hundredth match in charge.

Around this time, Robbie Fowler's position at the club began to deteriorate. Robbie wasn't in the team every week, and the relationship between him and the club was going stale. When that happens, the smallest disagreement gets turned into a huge argument with the staff. Robbie was really loved by the other players, and certainly by the fans, but the manager wanted to get rid of him. Once Robbie knew that, it was only a matter of time before the parting of the ways. The manager admitted publicly that he'd turned down a £12m offer from Chelsea for Robbie, and after that the speculation about his future just wouldn't go away. In January 2001, apparently, Aston Villa put an almost identical bid on the table.

Jari Litmanen, the Finland striker, joined us from Barcelona that winter, and the fans were especially keen to see him play a major role. It was a time when Liverpool were being characterized as a counter-attacking or even a long-ball team, and Litmanen was brought in to link the midfield and the attack to give us the option of stringing together more elaborate passing moves rather than mostly moving the ball to the strikers without passing it around in midfield. But, though he could unlock defences and was a class act, Jari had ankle problems which prevented him from being available every week. Every time you walked into the treatment room before training he would be strapping his ankles up quite heavily. If he played a full game he would hobble in the next day a bit stiff and a bit sore. Fans don't get those insights. The players train every day and they see their team-mates before and after games – see how they cope, physically. Some people just can't play too many games. Some people are so bad in training that you can't imagine them in the stadium, never mind on the pitch, yet in the game they emerge as top-class pros. Jari could have been used a bit more than he was, especially at home, but people need to understand that he was fragile. So we didn't see enough of him, which was a pity, because he was a great player, not least on the training ground. He could see everything in front of him and could always deliver the killer pass. By the time he got to Liverpool he'd lost a yard of pace, but he had adapted his game to make himself more effective outside the box. That was a measure of how good he was.

We entered 2001 in fifth place, with some good wins against big teams under our belt but with a less impressive record against the smaller clubs. Why? I think because our style of play hurt our more positive opponents but gave us problems when the other teams retreated and put 10 men behind the ball. We found it hard to unlock the lesser Premiership teams. We were probably short of width. Nick Barmby played wide midfield, but it wasn't as if he was standing on the touchline like a conventional winger. Teams were defending very narrowly against us and we didn't have the means to hurt them down the flanks.

In the cups, too, we were starting to build up steam. After beating Chelsea 2–1, Stoke 8–0 and Fulham 3–0, on 10 January we found ourselves at Selhurst Park for a Worthington Cup semi-final against Crystal Palace, a 2–1 defeat during which I missed a couple of chances. This seemed to excite Clinton Morrison, the Palace striker, because he was quoted in the newspapers as saying he would show me how to score when the teams met again in the second leg. Bearing in mind that the tie was only half over, it was a brave thing to say – or allegedly say – and The Kop gave him some stick when he came to Anfield. Clinton tried to get in touch with me through my agent, and left a message to say that his words had been twisted. Unfortunately for him, the Liverpool fans knew nothing of his attempt to apologize and tried to make him pay for the things he had said. I wasn't able to play in the game, much to my annoyance, because I wanted to rectify those missed chances in London, but we won 5–0 to reach our first cup final since 1996.

Our UEFA Cup run was proving far more tricky. To reach the final that May, in addition to Rapid Bucharest and Slovan Liberec in the earlier rounds we had to get past Olympiakos, Roma, Porto and Barcelona in a two-leg semi-final. In the first leg against Roma on 15 February I scored two in the Olympic Stadium – a steal for the first and a glancing header for the second. There had been some uncertainty about which two of the four strikers would be playing that night because Emile was carrying a slight injury. By the time we awoke from our afternoon sleep the manager had changed his mind, and I'm not sure I would have played had he not told me already that I was in the team. We thought it would be a much tougher game than it was, a real backs-to-the-wall night, but in the end we beat them comfortably.

I love those big European nights. From our hotel we could hear supporters on both sides singing all afternoon, and when we reached the stadium Roma's followers were absolutely fanatical. Those games really get my juices flowing, and the scene was set for a good performance, which managed to see us through despite our subsequent 1–0 defeat in the home leg (I missed a penalty). Barcelona, away, in the semi-final in April carried the same intensity. We defended for our lives and I barely got a touch, but to fight like that in the Nou Camp and come away with a 0–0 draw in front of 90,000 spectators was an achievement in itself.

In this country we underestimate our strengths. I talk to foreign players in the Premiership about how they see our game, and they tell me that teams on the continent dread being drawn against English clubs in European competitions. We haven't developed that reputation for nothing. We don't like being beaten and we're as tough as nails. No one would ever question our heart, and no one would ever steamroller an English team. One thing we have is courage. I like a player whose attitude makes him impossible to beat. If you think back to the two Euro 2004 qualifiers against Turkey, we gave them a good pasting at home and as a result they were fearful of us before we'd even kicked a ball in Istanbul. I watched it from home, injured. *Boy, I wish I was playing in this.* Ten minutes from time, away in Turkey, with them needing to win, you would expect an avalanche of pressure. But I wasn't worried for one minute. We were never going to concede a goal. We killed any hope they had by getting 'at them' from the moment the game kicked off. I think the overseas influence on our domestic game has helped us be smarter, more tactically aware. When you're a kid you think you just need youth, energy and enthusiasm; experience is a meaningless concept. But when you've been around a bit you realize you need to be clever and canny, to see things coming a bit more. The opening up of the Premiership to foreign thinking has had a huge effect.

The Roma game, I felt, was the turning point of my year. It was those two goals and my all-round performance which raised my confidence for the rest of the season, though 10 days later I was to suffer the terrible blow of not being selected for the Worthington Cup final in Cardiff against Birmingham, who were then a First Division side. That was exceptionally painful, and the memory still hurts me now.

Emile Heskey was the first-choice striker, and whoever was playing best between Robbie Fowler and me would get the nod for the other place up front. It was Robbie who got the call. And when he scored a terrific goal after half an hour his confidence was up for the rest of the match, which made it very unlikely that the manager would bring him off. Emile, as I've said, was a very different player to us, and because his place on the pitch was safe there wasn't an opportunity for me to come on. Birmingham's equalizer, a penalty by Darren Purse, sent the game into extra-time, and when our third substitute went on during those additional 30 minutes my chance had gone.

I did feel, and I still think, that I was entitled to be given a chance to play a part in that final. It wasn't as if we were demolishing Birmingham; in extra-time we were making heavy weather of it. It was a highly emotional occasion, of course, which ended with poor Andrew Johnson missing a penalty for Birmingham and Trevor Francis, their manager, crying on the pitch as he tried to console his players. We had luck on our side. I was desperate for us to win a cup for the first time in six years, but at the party afterwards I didn't feel as if I'd played a role. The manager tried to reassure me. 'Don't worry,' he said, 'there'll be other big games like this.' But to this day it's left a mark.

One of Houllier's big themes was always that we were 'all in it together'. Whenever he left you out, you could feel his eyes following you around to see how you were reacting. In this instance, after we had won 5–4 on penalties, I wanted him to see that I was fed up. Naturally I congratulated the lads as much as I could and was happy for the club and the fans, but I wasn't too bothered about my own medal. I could quite happily have thrown it to the supporters and left it in the crowd.

Three days later, on the last day of February, I had a more uplifting experience with England for Sven-Goran Eriksson's first game in charge, a 3–0 win against Spain in a friendly at Villa Park. The first big question that had followed Eriksson's appointment as England coach was whether I minded a foreign coach being given the job. As players we all said we weren't troubled by the thought of a non-Englishman taking over. In an ideal world, I suppose, an English coach would have got the call, but at the time there weren't many homegrown candidates. There were one or two long-term contenders, but none who was ready to take over quite yet. Terry Venables, who had been England coach before, was the only finished article, but political issues seemed to be ruling him out. The only option therefore was to look abroad. I had heard of Eriksson, but if you'd asked me to run through his CV I wouldn't have been able to start. Until the newspapers started carrying more details about his career all I knew was that he was a top-class coach on the continent who had won the Serie A title in Italy with Lazio. After the FA confirmed the deal, Lazio's results seemed to dip, so it spoke volumes for him that the fans and the directors in Rome gave him such a warm send-off.

The first time I encountered him was in the build-up to our friendly against Spain at Villa Park. I had missed the previous two England games – under Howard Wilkinson, and then Peter Taylor – but I was now in Eriksson's first starting eleven, and I set up Nick Barmby for our first goal. It was the start of a strong relationship with the new England manager, who I very quickly came to admire.

Despite my personal setback in Cardiff, my form wasn't affected, and I soon picked up from where I had left off in the Olympic Stadium in Rome. In May, for example, I scored seven times in our last four games, including a hat-trick against Newcastle. I was playing some of the best football of my Liverpool career that spring, but before we reached two more cup finals and chased the last Champions League place in the final game of our season, at Charlton, we had important international business to attend to.

For the first World Cup qualifier under the new manager, against Finland on 24 March, the Liverpool lads had the added comfort of playing at Anfield. But we got off to a bad start. We were 1–0 down to a Gary Neville own goal and weren't playing particularly well. A couple of minutes before half-time I swung my left leg at a loose ball and it took a deflection before finding the bottom corner. After that we were kicking into the Kop End, and I felt we were going to bombard the Finns, though David Seaman had to make a cracking save to stop them scoring again.

I felt comfortable under the new manager. A Sven-Goran Eriksson or a Glenn Hoddle will try to add to your repertoire while preserving what you already have, whereas Kevin Keegan never told me I was good at anything. In fact, the opposite was true: I felt he was taking things away and trying to force on me a new style of play. Eriksson and Houllier focused on the assets I already possessed while trying to add new capabilities wherever appropriate. I love linking the play and making a wider all-round contribution while remaining true to my basic job. In the early days of his managership, Eriksson didn't tell me I was going to be his number-one striker or an automatic choice. I can't speak for other players, but I wouldn't be fooled if a manager made me promises he might not be able to keep, if he called me into his office and told me I was 'his man'. It might be true at the time, but a manager lives or dies by results, and if you haven't scored for 10 games and your two rivals are scoring every time they come off the bench he's got to pick his best team to protect his own position. Words don't matter; it's actions that count. Since Eriksson became manager he hasn't had to speak to me on the subject because he has picked me for every game. I feel he rates me as a player. It's liberating to have the confidence of the manager. You're free to concentrate all your thoughts on the job without worrying about your place in the team.

After our victory by two goals to one over Finland – David Beckham scored the winner – we set off on a tremendous run, beating Albania, Greece and Germany away – the latter an historic victory which I've written about in a later chapter – and then the Albanians again before the David Beckham free-kick moment against the Greeks at Old Trafford in the last of our eight qualifying games. We got on a good roll right from the start which gave us the sense that we were becoming invincible and working under a very accomplished manager. In qualifying, a single defeat can take the edge off a team, but with us in 2001, the players started looking forward to England trips.

In fairness to Kevin Keegan, he did make England get-togethers fun. Glenn Hoddle had felt that, because the clubs had us most of the time, international week should be long and intense. We were told to join the camp as soon as our club matches were over, and often, by the time the game came round, there was an air of staleness about the squad. Keegan changed that, but Eriksson took it on to another level, so that we were all relaxed and enjoying everything that went with playing for England.

With the Finland (home) and Albania (away) games behind me – I scored in both – I rejoined the Liverpool squad for a storming end to the best season I have known. Having completed the League double over Manchester United for the first time in 22 years, on 8 April we worked our way past Wycombe Wanderers to reach the FA Cup final. As the occasions grew in scale, we seemed to get better and better at overcoming them.

Not that we were being universally praised. After the goalless draw in Barcelona three days before that Wycombe game we'd taken a lot of stick for being too cautious and conservative. That didn't trouble me because it kept up the pressure on us to be more adventurous, and to involve the strikers more. The issue of the lack of goals in that first leg faded anyway when Gary McAllister's penalty saw us through in the home leg. Liverpool were on their way to a European final for the first time since 1985. The season was becoming a dream.

Winning is the best defence against exhaustion, and we seemed not to notice the fact that in April, for example, we squeezed three important matches into six days. Our squad was a bit bigger, and we were starting to rotate a bit more. Anyway, we were too overjoyed to be tired. On 5 May, in the League, I scored my tenth, eleventh and twelfth goals against Newcastle inside six matches. I've no idea why I always seem to score against them. Against some teams, or on some pitches, you just get a particular tingle, and I love St James's Park. The ground and the support are just so fantastic, I always stand on their pitch feeling I'm going to score. Conversely, I never seem to get a look-in against Arsenal at Highbury. If you've had a good first experience of these places, often it sets you up for the future. The first time I played at St James's I scored a hat-trick, and I've loved it ever since.

But the highlights of the season were still to come. I was heading into the most productive seven days of my life in club football: an FA Cup final, a UEFA Cup final and Liverpool's last, crucial Premiership game – all between 12 and 19 May. This time I wouldn't be looking on from the bench.

13

My Greatest Day

For me, there's no debate. The greatest single moment of my career so far happened in the country where I've lived all my life – in Wales, at the Millennium Stadium in Cardiff, in the Liverpool away kit we wore to face an Arsenal side featuring the likes of Thierry Henry and Patrick Vieira in the 2001 FA Cup final.

The FA Cup is so much bigger than the League Cup, with so much more history and tradition, and I had more than a month's worth of anticipation to prepare me for our special day. It was 8 April when we beat Wycombe 2–1, and 12 May when we pulled into the FA Cup's temporary home on a blistering afternoon. I was on a hot streak and I knew the manager would pick me, so there was none of the anxiety I had felt about team selection before the Worthington Cup. I was also sure that if chances came my way I would bury them. That's the psychology when you're scoring regularly.

Before Cardiff, I had been wearing my normal Umbro boots and was banging goals in. On the Thursday, I came out wearing the special new boots Umbro had created for me for the final, to showcase their new line. I was trying to break them in for Saturday when Phil Thompson noticed that I wasn't wearing my normal boots. 'You're not planning on wearing them against Arsenal, are you?' Thommo asked. 'You're on fire with the old ones – don't tempt fate.' It was a sufficiently big issue for Thommo to bring the manager in on the debate. The tone was only half-jokey. Neither of them was happy with the idea of me abandoning the boots that had brought me so many goals in the preceding weeks. In the end they suggested I call Umbro and ask them to hold off until after the final. And it wasn't blisters the manager and Thommo were worried about; it was more to do with superstition. Naturally I did as they asked, and Simon Marsh, my main contact at Umbro, was very understanding. Two FA Cup final goals turned out to be a good advert for superstition.

It was so hot that we were almost fainting during the national anthem. Equally suffocating was the pressure Arsenal subjected us to for 80 or so minutes of the game. They battered us. It was one of those games in which you're constantly clearing shots off your own line. It took them 72 minutes to score, through Freddie Ljungberg, but I sensed that they were becoming frustrated by their inability to make the game safe. It was as if they had burned up all their nervous energy trying to score a second goal, and when we struck back 11 minutes after Ljungberg's goal their morale seemed to collapse.

Once we'd equalized, I was absolutely certain we would win. If you believed in fate, you would say our win was meant to be, because all the time Arsenal were failing to kill us off they were storing up trouble for themselves. We might have been dead and buried by half-time. My basis for saying I knew we'd win once we had equalized is that Arsenal were utterly deflated after my first goal. You could see their bodies sag. They had thrown everything at us but had only the one goal to show for it, and suddenly we were level, with seven minutes to go and with a fresh bounce in our stride. When the momentum switches so violently in a big game everything that went before becomes irrelevant. As soon as I scored my first I knew the game was over.

For my first with seven minutes left, Gary McAllister sent in a free-kick which Markus Babbel knocked into my path. I beat Martin Keown to the ball and Robbie Fowler did well to hold off Patrick Vieira, who was about to descend on me. A swing of the leg, and the ball was in the bottom corner. Never mind what happened later; just to score one in an FA Cup final sent a surge through me. I wanted to go on and win the game, but I also wanted to savour the moment of scoring against a great team in such a cracking stadium.

I have to search for the right words to describe what happened five minutes later, because the memory is so special to me. It started with an Arsenal corner, which was cleared to Patrik Berger, who played a long ball down the side of Lee Dixon, the Arsenal right-back. I managed to sprint past Lee and take it to the side of Tony Adams, who was racing across to intercept. In the first half I had run at Tony and pushed the ball past him, but I'd felt him stop me with one of those brilliant pieces of obstruction that are so subtle referees cannot spot them. That was Tony bringing all his years of experience to bear. *If he does that to me all afternoon, how the hell am I going to get past?* This time I had first run on him, and all I needed to do then was strike the ball well at precisely the right moment. Ever since that day, whenever we've played Arsenal they've left Keown back for their own corners to give them an extra yard of pace. I think they learned their lesson. As the ball left my foot I could see it heading towards the corner. Looking back now, I was slightly lucky it went over David Seaman's hand.

And so to the famous somersault, which I'm embarrassed about to this day. As a kid I used to try handsprings in the garden, but I hadn't attempted one in a big match. I hadn't tried one for perhaps 10 years. When the ball came to rest in the net, I was so excited I didn't quite know what to do. I needed an outlet for the incredible joy inside. Something possessed me to recreate the Owen family garden on the Millennium Stadium pitch. It wasn't the prettiest celebration but at least I landed on my feet. My family were dispersed all round the stadium, but I managed to point to one group straight after the goal and seemed to pick them all out on the lap of honour. Half of them were in tears.

For the ceremony, Robbie and Sami told Jamie Redknapp, our injured captain, that the players wanted him to collect the trophy. Jamie was embarrassed, because he's a very proud man who didn't want to take any of the glory, but the players were adamant that they wanted the club captain up there receiving the prize. Jamie is an extremely nice guy and a cracking player, and was an England first choice for a while. He can talk to anyone. He is so genuine. If a young player came into the camp Jamie would put an arm round him and offer him encouragement. He was someone I felt at ease with. It was such a shame that injuries took their toll on him. He's had terrible luck, but always fights back. Once you have one injury then it can escalate. If, for example, you damage your knee in the way that Jamie did, you are immobilized for two or three months and your muscles totally waste away. If every part of your body isn't hardened again when you come back, other muscles are susceptible. There is an imbalance. Hamstrings, quads and calves can be undermined on the side where the original injury occurred. It can trigger a run of setbacks. The greatest tribute I can pay Jamie is that when he walks into a training ground, no matter how many problems he's had he's the one smiling the most.

Anyway, Jamie finally went up after a lot of persuasion. You could see the discomfort in his face as he lifted the cup, but to have all the players celebrating together on that podium seemed to symbolize our year.

The one thing the Millennium Stadium lacks is the long walk up the steps to receive the trophy. As a boy, you watch teams making that climb and dream of following the same steep route to the Royal Box. To receive a trophy down on the pitch isn't quite the same, but I suppose it's only a small blemish when you've just won an FA Cup.

On ITV, I gather, the commentator Clive Tyldesley announced, 'Michael Owen has won the FA Cup all by himself.' When I spoke to the press afterwards, they asked me, 'You've heard of the Stanley Matthews final. Do you think this will be the Michael Owen final in years to come?' I could see the angle, but no game can ever be simplified like that. Who gave credit to Sami Hyypia and Stéphane Henchoz for clearing endless balls off our line? To beat Arsenal, every single player has to play to the maximum. So it definitely wasn't a one-man show – even if, in the future, they will probably call it the FA Cup final in which Michael Owen scored twice in seven minutes. I won't object.

Though I've had special moments with England, this was the pure adrenalin of winning a major prize rather than scoring a hat-trick in a World Cup qualifier or having a good experience in the early rounds of a tournament. I had been to two World Cups but had come home empty-handed. My goal against Argentina at France 98 can only be seen in the context of us losing the penalty shoot-out. Likewise, my goal against Brazil four years later made for a fine memory but didn't lead us anywhere. Those two FA Cup final goals actually meant something, and we got something from them as a result. I'm very clear about that day being my all-time number one. On a one-off occasion, that Liverpool team of 2000/01 seemed to be able to beat just about anyone. This was our twenty-fourth cup-tie of the season and we'd come through them all.

My mum and dad watched the game as guests of Simon Marsh at Umbro, and I managed to buy tickets for my brothers and their mates. Fourteen of them sat in one long row. The girls in our party had my complimentary seats. The whole group wanted to be together but it just wasn't possible to seat them all in a block. Apparently the 14 lads, all grown men, looked along the line when I scored my second goal and noticed that they were all crying their eyes out. The girls, apparently, were just going ballistic.

Louise joined me for the post-match function, but it wasn't open to the whole family, so the rest of the Owens crawled home up the motorway. Nobody cared that the traffic was stationary for a large part of the way. My mum and dad listened to 'You'll Never Walk Alone' on the car stereo, and people began climbing out of their cars, singing 'There's only one Michael Owen'. It was a special day for my family and friends as much as it was for me.

In a normal year, the FA Cup final would have been the great climax to the season, but we had two more important dates to keep. There was no time to celebrate fully in Cardiff because we had to get ourselves off to Dortmund in Germany to face Alavès in the final of the UEFA Cup.

On paper, if you just looked at the names, we were the red-hot favourites, but in reality our Spanish opponents had built up an impressive record in the competition. They had beaten Inter Milan in the fourth round, Rayo Vallecano in the quarter-finals and then Kaiserslautern 5–1 and 4–1 in the semis. To win a European semi-final 9–2 on aggregate is pretty impressive. We'd watched a few short video clips to prepare us, but we didn't really know what to expect. It turned out to be a real ding-dong match, high-scoring and full of drama, like the Worthington Cup.

In Dortmund, we were a goal in front after four minutes from a glancing header by Markus Babbel, and then I helped to set up Steven Gerrard 12 minutes after that. They pulled one back before I was grabbed around the feet by the Alavès goalkeeper, Martin Herrera, as I was going round him in the box. It was a blatant attempt to stop me tapping in the ball, but somehow he stayed on the pitch with just a yellow card. Gary McAllister converted the penalty so we went in at half-time 3–1 up.

In the dressing room there was disbelief at how easy the game was for us. Nobody expressed that feeling, but inside I was imagining us winning 5–1. We were just not the type of team to suddenly concede a rash of goals. We were exceptionally tight at the back that year, so there was no reason to fear a big response from the Spaniards. Every time we went forward we'd cut them to bits, so the second half was going to be a stroll.

Or so I thought. Javi Moreno, the Alavès striker, scored twice within six minutes of the restart and it required a goal from Robbie Fowler to restore our lead going into the final quarter of an hour. To protect that narrow advantage, the manager took me off and sent on Patrik Berger – an extra midfielder to help keep them at bay. It didn't work. Incredibly, Jordi Cruyff, once of Manchester United, equalized with a glancing header with a minute to go, and for the second time in three cup finals that year we were heading into extra-time. How they got it back to 4–4 was just beyond me. At times in the game we'd been queuing up to score, and if we'd been more professional we would have killed the game off before extra-time.

I ought to point out here that Alavès managed to get two of their players sent off, just to add extra tension to a match that must have been giving our supporters panic attacks. This was a game with everything: eight goals, two red cards and bags of drama. And the gods weren't finished with us yet. We had kept the scoreboard rattling for 117 minutes when Gary McAllister chipped in a free-kick which Geli headed into his own goal. His own golden goal, in fact, because under the UEFA rules that night the first team to score in extra-time won the game.

When the season was over, it became apparent that for the manager and a lot of the foreign players that was the biggest victory of the three. For them, the UEFA Cup was a European competition so it carried greater weight. For me, though, there was no comparison with the FA Cup – and not just because I had scored two goals. I would have said the same thing before we took to the pitch in Cardiff. I was of course delighted to have won the UEFA Cup, but to me it was closer to the League Cup in stature, even though clubs such as Barcelona, Inter Milan and Porto had contested it in our year. It was by no means easy to win. Still, on my personal list I would place it second behind the FA Cup and ahead of the Worthington.

And there was still no time for rest, still no major celebration. From Germany we had to travel to London to play Charlton in the final Premiership game of the season, with a Champions League place on the line. There were parties, but we weren't allowed to drink. After the Worthington Cup we were permitted a glass or two, but having watched the whole event from the bench that day I had been in no mood to drink. In the wake of the FA and UEFA Cup finals there was no alcohol on show, for obvious reasons; it was only after the Charlton game that we arranged to have a few on the team coach and carry on to a nightclub in the city.

Our last challenge of a mammoth season, at The Valley on 19 May, was worth millions of pounds to the club. It was too important for us to surrender to the tiredness of the previous seven days. Oddly, given the eventual score, they besieged us for the first half, after which we could easily have gone in 4–0 down. A bollocking was delivered in the interval and normal service was resumed. We scored four times after the break. Robbie got two, and Danny Murphy and I got one each. In fact, I scored Liverpool's last goal of that momentous 2000/01 season – with my left foot. To stroll through that last half hour of the campaign was very pleasurable. We finished third, 11 points behind Manchester United (the champions again), and booked our place in the following season's Champions League qualifying round.

People ask me whether that was the best Liverpool side I've played in. As a team, it was the strongest, best organized club outfit I've represented. It was a side with a tough character and identity and no weak links. It wasn't spectacular, but it was impressively solid. It didn't have a Robbie Fowler or a Steve McManaman at his peak, or a John Barnes, but we all knew what we were doing, and the discipline was first-class. That counts for an awful lot in big games. I would always prefer to be part of an efficient team that wins things than an entertaining one that falls a bit short. We took a lot of stick in 2001 for having an unattractive style, but if someone asks to see my medals in 20 years' time I won't have to describe every game we played and tell them whether we were spectacular or just efficient. We won three trophies in four months. The method was bringing results. We were winning games 1–0 without playing particularly well.

Though the players mostly ignored it, the criticism did start to eat away at the coaching staff. They didn't like being told that counter-attacking was the wrong style, especially when United and Arsenal were also using that tactic to great effect. I couldn't have cared less what people were saying, but the manager did start to take offence.

But nobody at Liverpool was concerned with tactical debates when we boarded an open-top bus for a victory parade through the city. When we set off from our training ground at Melwood the streets were lined four or five deep, which was exciting enough in itself, but then we hit the Albert Dock and we had to edge our way through an ocean of bodies. I've never seen anything like it.

One of the people I was most pleased for was our chairman, David Moores, who travels with us on the bus to and from games and is a real supporter yet doesn't interfere one bit. Everybody I've ever played with at Liverpool has passed comment on David Moores. They all say, 'What a great chairman he is.' He's a supporter who just loves the club. He's not in it for the business or the money, he just wants Liverpool to do well. I've never heard a bad word about him.

The parade organizers announced later that there were hundreds of thousands of people on those streets. We toured for two hours. There was the odd quiet patch, but in the areas where fans had congregated we were stunned by the weight of bodies. From the parade, we went straight to our end-of-season party. It was a long and happy day.

On a personal level, the joys of 2001 continued through the summer into another big match in Germany, and a poll to determine the European Footballer of the Year.

14

Hat-trick!

Germany 1 England 5.

Even now I see T-shirts commemorating that improbable triumph, and people still ask me to sign them. If you displayed a picture of the electronic scoreboard from that night with the goals taken off, people would always know which game it was from. It's one of the great footballing images of modern times.

But I should start by putting my own contribution to the result in proportion. Not for a second would I compare my hat-trick in Munich on 1 September 2001 with what Sir Geoff Hurst achieved in a World Cup final between the two countries in 1966. OK, mine was on German soil, but for anyone to beat the German defence three times in the climax of a World Cup is beyond belief. What a sense of timing Sir Geoff had. His achievement will surely never be surpassed. One winter's night recently, I watched that Germany–England World Cup qualifier again. I hadn't seen the match in full before. It was our first win on German turf since 1965, and mine was the first hat-trick against Germany by an Englishman since Sir Geoff's. I wasn't, however, aware of any of these daunting statistics before we set off for Bavaria.

It had already been a memorable summer for me, of

course. I was coming off the back of a good season with Liverpool, we had five trophies in the cabinet, having added the Community Shield (as the Charity Shield was now called) and the UEFA Super Cup to the collection. I suppose our 3–2 victory over Bayern Munich was the start of a great week of victories at German football's expense. Moreover, come September I was fit and healthy. I'd finished the previous season well and I had begun the new campaign in decent form. When you're playing regularly it's as if you're building up the immune system. The Germany game came at a stage in my career when I wasn't picking up niggling injuries. In the period prior to that great summer my body hadn't been helping me – and it let me down again soon afterwards, against Spurs on 22 September.

Going into the Germany match, we were still six points behind our old rivals at the top of Group 9, and there was a widespread assumption that we were heading for the play-offs. We went there believing we could win but assuming we'd end up second in the group on account of our bad start to the campaign. In any competition, losing your first game is a bad blow. Being defeated at home by Germany, and then only drawing in Finland, knocked the air out of us. Munich turned that round. After the 5–1, as everyone now calls it, there was renewed confidence in the team. It was there right through the following summer's World Cup and beyond.

Despite all the statistical analysis of games between two countries, past results mean nothing. Nothing went right for us when we lost 1–0 to them in London in October 2000. But it wasn't as if they'd bullied us in the last game to be played at Wembley before the demolition crews took over. Still, nobody could have predicted that we would pummel them on their home ground.

For the really big England games, the atmosphere in the

camp shifts. It's more focused, and the preparation becomes even more precise. I don't know what the other players were doing in their rooms but I can remember what I was up to: I was trying to get as much sleep as possible, and making sure I was eating exactly the right food. Hot baths, lots of stretching. There was extra attention to detail.

Having played them so recently, we knew all about Germany's strengths and weaknesses. The general feeling was that a draw would be a good result, given that we were playing away from home. Looking at Germany now, I think they lacked a really top-class striker. They had some cracking midfield players – Didi Hamann, Michael Ballack and Sebastian Deisler – and a world-class keeper in Oliver Kahn. Deisler was a player we had our eyes on – skilful, young and naturally gifted. Steven Gerrard was asked to pick up Ballack's runs, and Emile and I were ordered to stop Hamann getting on the ball too often. Our concern was that Didi would start a lot of the German moves from his defensive midfield position just in front of the back three.

I did speak to Didi, my Liverpool team-mate and friend, four days before the game, but that was the end of it. Even though he's a close mate, I didn't feel comfortable with the idea of calling him every day for intimate chats about the match. I'd hate him to think I was just phoning to find out their team or to acquire classified information. So we kept it to a minimum and discussed other subjects. Nor did we converse at all during the game. I'm not a talker in matches; I'm too busy concentrating. Neither do I go in for rousing speeches before the first whistle, even in games of that magnitude. When the game's that big, nobody needs a head full of emotional speeches when they step out on to the pitch.

Though Didi was careful in what he said during the build-up, I seem to remember Oliver Kahn spouting about what the Germans might do to us. You never go into a game with the sole intention of shutting one individual up, but certainly afterwards it's nice to feel you've taught somebody a quiet lesson. The England players said nothing provocative in the run-up to the match. There was no need to. There's nothing to be gained from winding up the opposition. If you show them respect and say flattering things, words don't come back to haunt you. Five goals was a very good answer to anything Kahn might have said.

We read in the papers that we would be staying next to an incredibly noisy bierkeller, but I didn't hear a whisper all week. The hotel was exceptional. Unusually, we didn't have any injuries going into the game so the manager was able to pick his first-choice team: David Seaman in goal; Gary Neville, Sol Campbell, Rio Ferdinand and Ashley Cole at the back; David Beckham, Steven Gerrard, Paul Scholes and Nicky Barmby in midfield; and Emile Heskey and me up front.

When I prepare for games I normally concentrate on the opposition's defence, to pick out areas in which I might attack. Our own back four focused on the giant Carsten Jancker and wrestled with the problem of how to stop him exploiting long balls into our penalty area. Jancker is about as far from me on the physical spectrum as it's possible to go – a huge, old-fashioned centre-forward. The traditional image of the vast target man is dead now, and those who fit the bill are certainly a dying breed, because the emphasis nowadays is on agility and pace.

Germany lined up against us with a back three. If the wing-backs in that formation push up, they allow you extra space, but if they sit back you end up facing five defenders, so I have no firm preference about defensive formations.

When we started to dominate, they were forced out of their favoured shape. In those situations, players run out of position in an effort to change the course of the game, and the team who are on top are given even more opportunities to pounce. Watching the DVD now, you can see that a long diagonal ball from Beckham or Scholes hurt them every time, because their wing-backs were pushed so far forward. The harder they tried to come back at us, the more we found the holes they'd vacated and exploited those gaps.

It's possible that only an away game could have produced a performance of such quality. The key to it was the unity we felt after conceding a goal early in the game – by the giant Jancker. It was the opposite of what we'd been expecting. We'd visualized a long ball to Jancker which he would nod down for Oliver Neuville, his co-striker. Instead, Jancker got on the end of a pass coming in from Neuville, who wasn't marked, so the goal came as a tactical shock. There was no need to point out any positional errors to our defenders. In football, as in life, experienced people don't need to be confronted with the blindingly obvious. Also, at the start of the game you don't want to be rattling cages or messing with anyone's confidence. The team that keeps their heads up the longest is often the one that wins. My private thought was, 'Oh bloody hell, what's going on here?' When you play away in Germany, you assume you're going to need a clean sheet to win the game. It's not logical to believe you're going to score two or three goals in such an unpromising environment. Who would think such a thing, given Germany's formidable home record? So our immediate thought was, what would we give now to get out of here with a draw?

At 1–0 down against Germany with six minutes gone, a lot of countries would have thought, 'We're in trouble here. Let's try and keep it respectable.' But no English head went down. As soon as we equalized I knew we'd win, because we were threatening them every time we had the ball. It was one of those days when everything we touched turned to gold, though we mustn't forget that they had a cracking chance to score a second when Deisler was blessed with an easy chance but miscued in front of the posts. That was a bad miss, and a massive turning point. As John Motson said of Deisler's mistake in the BBC commentary, 'You don't see many missed like that at this level.' There was another decisive moment just before half-time when David Seaman made a first-rate save from Jorg Bohme, Germany's left-back.

After the Jancker goal, we recovered our composure quickly. Since March we had won three World Cup qualifiers in a row and there hadn't been much chopping and changing in selection. We felt we had become a settled side – young, but confident of our places in the team. At 1–0 up and with the game only 10 minutes old, the German fans were already chanting 'Ole, Ole' when their team were knocking the ball around. Premature, to say the least. I trust they learned their lesson.

Within seven minutes of Jancker's goal I got the first of my three. Watching it again sends a shiver down my spine. It was preceded by a fantastic piece of awareness by Nick Barmby, who could have tried to flick the incoming ball into the goal, or even attempted an overhead kick. But he seemed to catch sight of me in the corner of his eye. In moving the ball on to me, he might have been clattered by Oliver Kahn, who came running out thinking he could collect the ball but realized halfway there that he'd overcommitted himself. Nick was brave to keep his head. He did most of the work for that first goal. He was the provider. Though it looks a simple finish, I had to concentrate hard on keeping the ball down because it bounced above waist height. I had the whole goal to aim at but had to swivel and make sure I directed it downwards.

Look at the body language in the moments after that equalizer and you can see confidence returning to our team. At that point I just knew we were going to win. I had a buzz in my stomach. Every time we attacked from then onwards we looked dangerous. Our passing was fluent from the beginning. As ever, the support from England's fans was immense. When I speak to players from other countries who have played against us they simply can't believe how much encouragement we receive, whether we're playing badly or well. If you're an England international and you're accustomed to it, you probably take it for granted; it's only when someone from another country points it out to you that you realize how well supported you really are.

The referee that night was Pierluigi Collina, commonly regarded as the world's best. He spoke to me only once, after I'd had my shirt pulled as I was running into the penalty area when the score was still 1–1. When I turned to him and asked, 'Is that not a penalty, ref?' he replied, 'Well it would have been if you'd gone down.' I hadn't needed to go down. I felt it was a penalty without me being pulled all the way to the ground.

As the game sped towards half-time I was constantly sneaking into threatening positions. When that happens you start to sense fear in defenders. Maybe confusion more than fear, because their main concern is where they should be positioning themselves to smother the next attack. Whatever they did, we seemed to have an answer for it. It was a tough night for defenders. After the game, they were knackered. You could see it.

After Steven Gerrard's brilliant 30-yard drive just before half-time, we bounced into the dressing room, but not before

Stevie had escaped from a mound of bodies formed by his ecstatic team-mates. He has that capacity to rifle the ball in from long range. This one fell beautifully for him to strike and provided him with his first international goal. We sat down knowing that Germany would have to chase the game and therefore leave holes at the back. Myself, Emile, Scholesy and Stevie realized we could do some damage in those vacated areas. Picking holes is our speciality. We had a feeling by now that this was our night, though it was only when the fourth goal went in that we felt the game was over. That's when I really relaxed and started to enjoy the whole experience of being part of such a resounding victory.

I can't put my finger on why I tend to score in big games, though people are always pressing me for an explanation. One theory is that my first experiences of big games as a kid – for England against Argentina, or later against Brazil – taught me that I had the temperament to score when the pressure was really on. As a schoolboy, I always seemed to score in cup finals. Maybe I'm always falling back on that inner knowledge. Either I'm a lucky so-and-so or there's a deeper explanation. The most likely answer is that if you start doing it early in your career then the know-how and the self-assurance to keep on doing it stay with you. I never have a 'panic' before a game. The bigger the test, the more composed I have to be. The only time I might ever feel anxious is if I haven't scored for 10 games; then I might feel myself snatching at a chance. It wouldn't be a question of my 'bottle' or courage going; it's more about me being desperate to put the chance away – the intensity of what's inside.

My second goal arrived three minutes into the second half. Emile did well to keep the ball down as he chested it towards me but it was bouncing awkwardly and I couldn't really place my shot. I assumed Kahn would keep it out. I was just trying to hit it as hard as possible with the outside of my boot and then hope for a bit of luck. A moment later Didi hurt me, the sod. He left me with deep stud marks after we collided in midfield. As I rose, I wasn't thinking of hat-tricks. I was just flying because we'd put a two-goal cushion between us and Germany.

Sometimes such moments seem to acquire extra meaning, so it's with a smile, now, that I notice that the official time for the hat-trick goal was 66 minutes. I promise I didn't wait for 66 to come up on that famous electronic board. By that stage the game was like a chess match in which you've taken half their pieces and they have to grope for a way back into the contest. On the DVD I watched on that winter's evening, my third is heralded by John Motson shouting, 'This is getting better and better and better! One, two, three for Michael Owen!' What started the third was Stevie Gerrard's talent for interception. He's excellent at reading a pass and cutting it off. When he does that, he looks up straight away and lays the ball into my path. And so it was in Munich. I had only to touch his pass once to set up the shot. I saw Kahn go low so I decided to place the shot high.

Again I don't know where my subsequent goal celebration came from. It was a handspring – the sort I'd done as a kid. I hadn't done one for about 10 years when I brought the somersault back to life in May, in the FA Cup final against Arsenal. You only see them when I get over-excited. The one in Munich didn't look too pretty, but it sure as hell expressed how I felt. But if ever there was a time for having an elaborate goal celebration, this was it. My normal style is to thrust one hand up, though not in the classic Alan Shearer style. The only distinctive goal celebration I'm associated with is rubbing my hands together as if warming them by a fire, which I first did after scoring in a game against Newcastle. The background was that Jamie Carragher had provided some tickets for a friend, who came and knocked on our door to collect them and was so excited that he started rubbing his hands together in glee. For some reason I thought it would be a good idea to copy his reaction that day if I scored. As it turned out, I scored a hat-trick then as well. After the first goal I forgot to do the hand-rubbing routine, so 'Carra' reminded me. After the second I forgot again, and Carra was there once more to jog my memory. For the hat-trick I finally remembered. It was less elaborate than my handsprings in Cardiff and Munich but seemed to attract as much comment.

The hat-trick goal against Germany was the sweetest of the three, and the last 25 minutes of the game were just one long high. I started drinking in the atmosphere and the sense of occasion. I suppose it's the footballer's equivalent of booking half a day off work. My mind was racing. Suddenly I was noticing the fans and taking in their songs. Pure confidence was driving me along. In that mood you feel invincible. Emile, of course, added a fifth, and in the final 10 minutes German supporters began flooding out of the ground. Their players were in shreds, so many of the fans simply fled.

My mum and dad were at the game with Didi's wife and parents, who looked after them throughout the day. Afterwards they all shared a drink. Didi said much later that my mum and dad were as humble in victory as they would have been in defeat. They didn't insist on talking about the game. I was very proud of that. Not that I was surprised. I knew what kind of parents I had. There were livelihoods and World Cups at stake. It's not a laughing matter, beating a close friend 5–1.

The lasting effect of that amazing game was to show us

what we were capable of. The reference point will always be there for the players who were lucky enough to take part. It proved to us that we were able, on our day, to beat any international side. You need one of those results once in a while to re-ignite the flame. It's not stretching the point to ask whether the 5–1 win in Munich was the basis for our victory over Argentina at the subsequent World Cup. It provided the necessary self-belief.

Looking at it two years later, I noticed that my all-round play was much better than I remember it. I hadn't realized how much I was involved, or how dominant we were. There is a case for saying that the German team of September 2001 was not the best in their history, but Germany, as a nation, are always a global force, as they showed by reaching the final in Japan and South Korea. They went further than us in that competition, despite their 5–1 defeat that night in Munich.

Naturally, I took possession of the match ball, but there is a story attached to the shirt-swapping. Initially I exchanged jerseys with Bohme, but when I finally sat down by my locker I immediately regretted it. *What have I just done? I've scored a hat-trick in Germany and I've given my shirt away!* So I got in contact with Christian Ziege, a friend and team-mate from Liverpool, and implored him to find Bohme to ask whether he'd mind taking my replacement shirt instead. For England games you're always given two, and I was hoping he wouldn't mind having the second. Christian disappeared for a few moments and came back with my shirt. It could have been an expensive mistake, but thankfully Bohme took pity on me.

Of course, in one sense it was Germany 1 Liverpool 5, because all the England goalscorers were Anfield men. There must have been a glow of pride back at Liverpool. Poor Didi came back to work knowing that three of his training-ground colleagues had scored against him in a 5–1 win. If it had been a friendly we might have taken the mickey, but, as I said, there is less inclination to drive the joke home when the game is a big one and there's a lot of pain involved.

The reaction back home was overwhelming, and we had another game four days later, against Albania at St James's Park, which turned out to be a tough one, not least because people were expecting us to repeat our performance against Germany. We won 2–0 and I scored the first just before half-time, but Albania were better than they looked and gave us problems right up to the point when Robbie Fowler scored again to make it safe. The one I scored was quite hard to execute, and I probably wouldn't have tried it had my confidence not been so high after the hat-trick against Germany. That night in Newcastle I felt totally shattered, maybe as a result of all the running I'd done in Munich. It's rare for me to feel quite that drained.

To have another few days with England, though, soaking up the elation in the country and absorbing all the newspaper coverage, was a bonus. A large crowd was at Newcastle airport to greet our flight from Munich. The manager applied his usual rule to the team's celebrations. 'Common sense' is the phrase he uses. That covers everything. He likes good timekeeping, and that too comes under the banner of common sense. His attitude is that if you want a glass of wine or the odd game of cards at the right time it's fine so long as you don't abuse the privilege. If you get drunk or play cards for loads of money then that's a betrayal of him and your professional duties.

There's nothing like a big sporting occasion to get the whole country flying. Those are the days that make you feel privileged to be doing what we do for a living. We are such a sporty nation, and I can't think of anything that brings people together like a big World Cup showdown, as the England rugby team showed when they won the 2003 World Cup in Australia. The country is either in the front room or in the pub in front of the telly, and sometimes you can almost feel the vibrations from the whole nation as they bounce up and down. The Sunday after the Germany game was like a national holiday. Quite right, too.

I still have the match ball. I lent it initially to the People's History Museum in Manchester, together with my shirt and boots from the game. My intention is to put all three in a cabinet at home. I have loads of memorabilia, but you must reserve a special place on display for the really big memories, and be careful not to detract from them by having too much paraphernalia on show. On the A-list are my medals, my England debut shirt against Chile, the England Under-15 shirt I wore for a whole season and my jersey from the Argentina game at France 98 – not to mention my FA Cup winner's shirt from the Liverpool–Arsenal final in 2001. Come to think of it, I've got a fair amount on display.

After the game, Sven-Goran Eriksson described me as 'ice cold' and 'a killer'. In Munich that's exactly how I felt.

15
Houllier's Heart: 2001/02

One Saturday afternoon in October 2001, Liverpool Football Club went into shock. It was a day that almost cost our manager his life. For five months afterwards, every game we played, every goal we scored, was for Gérard Houllier.

Anfield, 13 October: Leeds United at home. It was a routine three o'clock kick-off, seven matches into our League campaign, and also the second of three games on the sidelines for me. When I poked my head round the dressing-room door to wish the lads good luck there was no hint of the trauma to come. I climbed the steps to my seat in the directors' box to watch Robbie Fowler and Emile Heskey try to get round the Leeds defence. We were 1–0 down to a goal by Harry Kewell at the break, but even when the teams came back on to the pitch there was no suggestion of a crisis below us in the club's medical room.

After about five minutes, though, it was evident to me that the manager wasn't in his usual position on the bench. I looked along the rows of directors' seats and noticed that Gérard's wife, Isabel, had also left her seat. I sensed then that there might be something wrong, but still it was a long time before the news filtered through. Much later that day, I heard that the manager had been rushed to the Royal

Liverpool Hospital, and then on to Broadgreen Hospital, after his half-time team talk. Though it was unsettling, I had no idea of how serious it was until we turned up at the training ground the following day.

My understanding was that the boss had told the club doctor, Mark Waller, that he felt light-headed and a bit odd. Before Dr Waller had taken a look, Dave Galley, the physio, had laid the manager out on a couch. The game had restarted with only the substitutes aware that the manager was unwell. Gérard credits our doctor with a big part in saving his life.

At training the next day the staff delivered the awful news that the gaffer's condition was 'very serious, and possibly life-threatening'. It was only then that the mood among the players went downhill. On the day the crisis broke, nobody entertained the idea that Gérard might lose his life – perhaps because the crisis was handled so well. From the first sign of trouble to the moment of operation itself, the medical staff seemed to take all the right decisions with the minimum of fuss.

Eventually, with the team preparing to fly to Kiev for a Champions League game, Phil Thompson told us of the 11-hour operation, and the complications that came with it. The diagnosis was a dissection of the aorta, which is worse and more dangerous than a heart attack. We were stunned. The day unfolded in virtual silence as each of us struggled with his own thoughts. One of the coaches organized a huge get-well card and asked us all to sign it, but that was as much as we could do. The manager was far too ill to take visitors, so Thommo, who had taken control of the team, stressed that the only way we could help was by getting on with our jobs and winning games. Before each game, he would pin a sheet to the noticeboard saying in block capitals

DO IT FOR THE BOSS. We always felt that the manager was watching and told ourselves not to let him down. In fact, we found out later that although he had missed the 2–1 win in Kiev, he had tuned in to the Champions League game against Boavista, just 11 days after his operation. We weren't at all surprised. At the end of October, the fans chanted his name as we beat Borussia Dortmund to join Arsenal and Manchester United in the last 16. Later, they unfurled a huge French flag on The Kop bearing his name, which really touched him. When we were summoned to his office, the first picture we saw was that French flag rippling across The Kop. He held that image very close to his heart. The way the club pulled together in his absence meant a lot to him.

After the operation there was no contact for a couple of months until, suddenly, we started hearing that familiar French accent on the phone. He would ring individual players from time to time and without warning. A few weeks after the calls began, he put his head round the door at Melwood, told us he was proud of us and urged us to keep up the good work. He said he would be back as soon as possible but couldn't rush it. In the weeks that followed he popped in at regular intervals but didn't do any work. He did look very frail and had lost a lot of weight. It was strange to see a man with such a strong character looking so weak. If there was any news on the manager's condition it would be delivered by Thommo. The last thing the manager needed was dozens of people descending on him, asking questions and making demands. He just needed his own time to get well, and he took a couple of holidays to re-evaluate how he should approach the job now. It was five months before he was restored to the Liverpool bench.

The temptation in those grim early weeks was to assume

he had been a victim of stress. At first the media ran away with the idea that his illness was purely stress related, and that all football managers now needed to get their hearts checked without delay. To this day I don't know whether the pressures of the job played a part in causing to explode whatever defect Gérard had. I don't have the necessary medical expertise. But the conclusion seemed to be that there was a fault around his heart that had been there all along. In November, Houllier admitted to knowing for two months prior to the attack that something wasn't quite right, though obviously he hadn't shared those suspicions with the players. Still, already he was planning his return.

I wasn't at all surprised that he wanted to get back to his job as soon as the doctors gave him permission. He's a strong man, with a great passion for football. He loved his job at Liverpool. Had you gone to the training ground at seven a.m. you would probably have found him there; likewise, the light in his office would still be on at seven p.m. He would be in there working away at something. If you take a man's passion from him, you take a large part of who he is. He wasn't a conventional football manager in the sense that English players expect a boss to be. He had his values and was very strict on discipline, team bonding and mutual respect among the players and staff. Other managers don't talk as much about unity and values; they take those issues for granted and concentrate more on the training ground and on the business of kicking the ball around. Houllier did a large proportion of his work in and around the facilities at Melwood rather than on the training pitch, though he did get involved in shaping the daily preparation of the team. He was a sharp observer, the kind of man who could manage any business. He knew how to organize things.

My relationship with him had its highs and lows, which is

hardly unusual. The two lows were being left out for the 2001 Worthington Cup final and for a Champions League game in Valencia in September 2002. I've been rested or not selected lots of times, but those were two games when, in my eyes, I shouldn't have been dropped. Those are two occasions I'll never forget. Sven-Goran Eriksson has picked me every time I've been available, but I won't fall into the trap of drawing a direct comparison between club and international football. A club manager has to deal with your injuries and your occasional dips in form. He has to protect you when you've been playing too often. He has to nurture you more.

Before Houllier's heart problem stopped us in our tracks, our season had started brightly. Within weeks of the FA Cup final I was back on that special Cardiff turf. I only have to put one foot on the Millennium Stadium pitch to love the feeling it gives me. When Wembley is reopened and English football's biggest occasions come home from Wales, I'll miss playing in that great Cardiff arena. And the Community Shield that summer carried extra significance, because there is no such thing as an exhibition match between Liverpool and Manchester United. We were beating United quite consistently in those days, and they fielded a full-strength side, which told us what their intentions were. I scored in a 2–1 win – our fourth trophy within six months.

We were still riding the wave from the previous season, so nobody should have been surprised that we went to Monaco for the UEFA Super Cup against Bayern Munich at the end of August determined to treat the game as much more than a ceremonial affair. The manager regarded it as a high-profile event, a European showcase, and we cruised into an early lead before Bayern realized they needed to shake themselves up. Whatever the experts think of the Super Cup, the fact is that we beat the winners of the Champions League and came home with a fifth trophy to complete our incredible sequence.

Before the season could get under way, the talk was of a bust-up on the training ground between Robbie Fowler and Phil Thompson. Thommo had been kicking out balls that had become tangled in the net. He was behind the goal, not looking, when Robbie took a penalty that caused the net to bulge near where Thommo was freeing the balls. It missed him, but only just. Thommo looked up and demanded, 'Who was that? That nearly hit me!' Robbie owned up to it, but didn't think it was a major crime because Thommo hadn't been hit. But Thommo came back with, 'I've told you before about doing that. Someone's going to get hit.' The discussion bounced back and forth and gradually turned into an argument. For a couple of weeks Robbie refused to apologize because he didn't think he had done anything wrong; Thommo also refused to back down. For a while, Robbie was left out of the team, until he apologized. Had it been me or Steven Gerrard, say, there would have been an argument followed by apologies and a handshake. But with Robbie, relations were already going downhill, so an incident of that nature was bound to escalate.

People ask me how I got on with Thommo, because it's obvious that he was a very vocal figure both in the dug-out and around our dressing room. I can see why he wasn't popular with opposing fans and players. He would be the first to admit that he's a bit biased. If we had an appeal inside the opposition's box, it was a definite penalty; if the other team had half a shout, it was never a penalty in a million years. Thommo wore red glasses, we all know that. But how can you have a bad word to say about someone who just loves the club and the lads? He's Liverpool through and through, and his enthusiasm was infectious. If we lost a game he got deeply upset, and if we win you've made his week. He stood in total contrast to Houllier, who was usually calm and collected. Thommo let you know what he felt. It was written all over him.

A couple of weeks after Robbie and Thommo clashed, the manager displayed his ability to make tough decisions. Good managers steer clear of sentiment, they say, and it was with a cold eye on the future that Sander Westerveld, our goalkeeper in the Treble-winning season, was replaced as number-one choice by Poland's Jerzy Dudek. Sander had made a few high-profile mistakes, but that wasn't the only reason he was demoted. He had been asked by the manager to stop writing so freely on websites and talking so much in newspapers but was reluctant to do as he was asked. The problems between them began to escalate, and when Sander began to go through a sticky patch on the pitch the manager decided to let him go. In December he was sold to Real Sociedad for £3.6m.

I was happy enough with my own early-season form, having scored three in the opening five games and that hat-trick against Germany in Munich before a hamstring injury forced me off against Spurs. This caused me to miss England's final World Cup qualifier against Greece on 6 October. I was sick with disappointment, but four days after the Tottenham game I signed a new four-year contract that took me up to the summer of 2005. I'm a lad who likes continuity; I don't go looking for change. Everything was going well at Liverpool and we were developing as a team, improving every year. I was still young, Liverpool were on the up and we'd just had a terrific season, winning three major prizes. There was never any question of me not signing. Again, the only issue was the length of the deal.

For that England–Greece game, which we needed to win to be certain of finishing top in Group 9, I agreed to be an analyst on Sky TV, so I had to go through all the nail-biting in a glass commentary box. They showed my wild reaction when Beckham scored the magical free-kick that sent us to the World Cup on the back of a 2–2 draw. For me, above all, that match confirmed that international football isn't as easy as it used to be. After our 5–1 win in Munich so much expectation and pressure was concentrated on our final qualifying game. I don't care if you're from San Marino or Greece or wherever; if you put 11 men behind the ball you're going to give even the best teams problems. Most countries, when they come to England, are realistic. They consider a draw to be a good result. If England don't score in the first 20 minutes the crowd get edgy and the players grow tense; if the opposition score, the anxiety deepens. The Greece tie was one of those games. Twice they were ahead before Beckham scored the free-kick that no Englishman or woman will ever forget.

As if to bring me back down to earth, at Anfield three days later Grimsby knocked us out in the third round of the Worthington Cup, so we lost one of our titles. I hate losing cup games because there's no opportunity to put things right. It's the end of the road. If the manager blamed himself for fielding a weakened team, winning and losing football matches was about to become a trivial issue, for it was only four days after the Grimsby defeat that Houllier found himself fighting for his life.

Thommo built up a terrific record during his time in charge, and that helped the manager with his recovery. On 4 November we beat Manchester United again to go top of the Premiership, where we stayed for six weeks until our 4–0 defeat at Chelsea in mid-December. The one setback during

that period was a heavy defeat against Barcelona in the Champions League. You get those games sometimes, and it's important not to let your confidence dip. It doesn't mean you are inferior. You might play the same opponents a week later and win. Moreover, with the team performing well overall there was less temptation for Gérard to rush back too soon. There was no need for him to place himself at risk.

As Christmas approached, the manager delivered one of the best pieces of news I've had in my career. On the day of our 0–0 draw against Roma in the Champions League, an hour before kick-off, he called our liaison officer, Norman, from his sick bed and told him to get me out of the dressing room. The gaffer made me swear not to tell anyone that I had been voted European Footballer of the Year. He said, 'I just wanted to give you a boost going into this big game.' I told my mum and dad but otherwise sat on the news for 12 days and waited for the announcement.

In terms of individual awards, it can't get much bigger than to be voted the number one footballer in Europe. I thought of my team-mates who'd helped me win all those cups with Liverpool, and to score the hat-trick against Germany. By and large I was fit and playing week in, week out. Everything seemed to go right for me in 2001. I don't think much about awards. They aren't personal targets for me, but that one did shake me to my bones. Apparently I was only the sixth Englishman to win the European award and the first since Kevin Keegan. What made it so exciting was the fact that I'm part of an amazing generation of European players. There are so many good footballers spread across the continent. If I'm honest, I'm not the best player in Europe. Zinedine Zidane's better than me; Thierry Henry's probably better than me. The award, as I understood it, was for my achievements in that particular year.

The trophy itself was housed in the Liverpool FC museum.

I didn't have to attend a ceremony, they came to me. They pulled up at the club and took photos and organized interviews. There was no real celebration at my house. I'm sufficiently shy not to be able to ring round my friends and announce, 'Hey, I've won the European Footballer of the Year award – let's have a party,' though I did play around with the trophy quite a bit. To be voted for by so many people was incredibly special. I gather the margin of victory was quite wide, so it can't have been a fluke. I think Patrick Vieira rang me to say well done. Or at least the caller said he was Patrick Vieira!

A few days later, just after Christmas, I scored my hundredth goal for Liverpool, in a 1–1 draw with West Ham. We were plugging away in the League, just dropping to fourth place as the New Year began. Our main focus had long been on the Premiership – hence, for instance, the manager playing a weakened side in that match against Grimsby in the Worthington Cup.

Before 2001 turned into 2002, I took a call from the manager informing me that he was thinking of taking Nicolas Anelka on loan from Paris St Germain and asking me for my thoughts. That may sound odd, but there's a lot more communication in modern football between players and managers, and managers feel a greater need to keep the main players happy and involved. If you're asked for your opinion, you feel part of the process. The message from above was, 'Don't worry, your place is safe, we just feel we need another quality striker.' That's why I was asked about Anelka. Even if I'd been sceptical, I assume the club would still have signed him. As it was, I was in favour. The day before Nicolas joined us the manager gave me his phone number and asked me to call him to welcome him to the

the match against Roma,' which we needed to win to be sure of going through. So there he was, taking the team talk, to the amazement of the players, who'd expected him to wait another couple of weeks. Plainly it was the importance of the game that drew him back. His character hadn't altered. He was just the same.

In the lead-up to that Roma match, in the late winter and early spring of 2002, we'd been in fantastic form. The 1–0 win at Old Trafford on 22 January revived our season and began a sequence of 11 victories and a draw in 12 League matches. We beat Leeds 4–0, Ipswich 6–0 and put three past Newcastle without reply. Our problem was that Arsenal, the eventual champions, were demolishing everything in their path. Incredibly, they won their last 13 Premiership games. Had they slipped up one little bit, we would have gone steaming past. I remember Freddie Ljungberg being a particular menace that spring. He seemed to score in every single game.

In the Champions League we beat Leverkusen 1–0 at home and were in an excellent position travelling to Germany for the second leg on 9 April, but then had one of those atrocious nights when everything goes wrong, and we finished up losing 4–2. That denied us a semi-final against United. To make it worse, Lucio, their Brazilian defender, stamped on my toe by accident and I could hardly walk as I left the ground. Dr Waller was a bit concerned that I had broken my foot, but the X-ray showed that there was no fracture, which was a relief. England already had a broken-foot drama with David Beckham and his metatarsal. With the World Cup so close, I don't suppose Sven-Goran Eriksson wanted to be worrying about me as well.

My England career was about to reach another high. In mid-April, at Anfield, I had the honour of being the club. I spoke to Nicolas for five minutes and said hello, see you in the morning at training. Whenever a big signing came the manager was always keen for him to feel at home. He regarded it as part of the team-building process. When Emile Heskey came, he asked a few of us to phone him straight away.

Anelka had a reputation for being moody and hard to work with, but I found him fine, as I did Stan Collymore. Neither of them was disruptive. Nicolas was very quiet, but at no time did he give us any problems. He didn't score a lot of goals for us – he joined on 21 December and didn't open his account in the League until 23 February – but you could see he was a class act with great ability. In training he showed that he had a lovely touch, could drop deep and link the play, and had pace as well. He put in a couple of breath-taking performances in the time he was with us, and the fans thought, 'Wow, we'll have a bit more of this.' Against Newcastle in March he was electric. The supporters were disappointed when we didn't sign him full time and went in search of other targets. I don't know the details of why he didn't stay with us, but I do know that El-Hadji Diouf was the big-money signing we made to fill the gap Anelka had left. Had we not made such an expensive signing, I assume the supporters would have been more upset about Nicolas moving on to Manchester City.

Not long after Nicolas dazzled Newcastle, Gérard Houllier resumed his place on the Anfield bench for the Champions League win against Roma, which gave us second place behind Barcelona in Group B and sent us through to a quarter-final against Leverkusen. I didn't play in the Roma game, but from what the lads tell me they were at the hotel getting ready when the manager turned up without warning. He had called Phil Thompson and said, 'I'm coming back for

A goal on my debut, as a 17-year-old substitute, against Wimbledon at Selhurst Park on 6 May 1997. In my own mind at that age, nothing less than a goal a game would do.

An England debutant in a friendly against Chile, at Wembley. At 18 years and 59 days, I was the youngest England international of the twentieth century.

Shame. An awful lunge at Manchester United's Ronny Johnsen, for which I was deservedly sent off.

Celebrating with Alan Shearer – an inspiration to me, on and off the pitch.

Glenn Hoddle sends me on against Tunisia late in our opening game at the 1998 World Cup.

That goal against Argentina in 1998. It changed my life for good.

Gérard Houllier brought big changes at Liverpool FC.

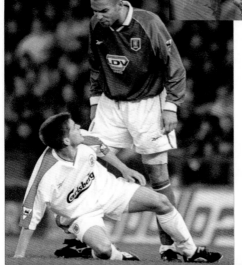

Stan Collymore takes offence after I catch him late in a Liverpool v Aston Villa match. Later, when Stan goes looking for Steve Harkness in the tunnel, I assume he's coming after me!

Warm all over. My famous hand-rubbing goal celebration after a hat-trick against Newcastle in August 1998.

A boy from the streets. Though many Merseyside folk assume I'm a Chester boy, members of my mum and dad's families are dotted all over Liverpool.

A classic Walker's Crisps advert, with Gary Lineker.

Summer holidays are brief, but I make sure I switch on when there's a jet ski around.

Can't claim I look comfortable with a gun-toting woman. Lara Croft, the cartoon character, at an Eidos launch.

Frankie Dettori, a top jockey and a good friend who's ridden for me. We're at Chester, my local track.

Another passion, golf, this time at Bearwood Lakes. As a teenager, I became so keen on the game that dad worried I might prefer it to football!

The new Jaguar X-Type, nicknamed the 'baby Jag', comes off the production line at Halewood, with me on the bonnet.

Phil Thompson gets me in a headlock. He always wore his heart on his sleeve.

The hand of 'God'. Robbie Fowler fell out of favour at Liverpool. But not with me.

Kevin Keegan studies my technique on the England training ground.

My mum's proudest moment. Her son receives the 1998 BBC Sports Personality of the Year Award.

Another trophy. Life's good. Carling Player of the Year 1997/98.

The start of a long nightmare with my hamstrings, as I limp off against Leeds on 12 April 1999.

Different paths, same joy. Celebrating an England goal with David Beckham.

Umbro Mach Speed Launch, North Weald, Essex, in April 2000. Speed has been the theme of my career.

Buckingham Palace, 19 November 2002, and a hand-shake with the Queen.

Talk To Mojo, the first racehorse I ever bought, now seven and retired to our paddocks back home. You can't beat the thrill of being on the gallops at dawn.

New life. A fresh addition to the Owen string. I'm learning fast about the art of breeding thoroughbreds.

country's youngest captain since Bobby Moore. It was a pre-World Cup friendly, and as Argentina were in our group Paraguay had been chosen to familiarize us with the South American style. My lasting memory of that match was all the physical testing we did at Carden Park, our base in Cheshire, near my home – blood samples, lactic acid and the like. Owen Hargreaves of Bayern Munich came out top by a wide margin, and I remember Sven-Goran Eriksson expressing his frustration with English football because the blood readings showed a lot of us to be run down. Exhausted, in some cases.

I was walking off the pitch one day, waiting for a car to take us back to base, when the manager came over and said to me, 'I haven't made up my mind yet, but I'm considering making you captain against Paraguay. What do you think?' It wasn't a hard question to answer. I told him, 'I'd love to be given that responsibility.' He told me not to assume I'd be wearing the armband because he needed to think on it some more. But he said I was 'in his plans'. Naturally, in my excitement I reached for the phone. 'Mum, Dad, I could be England captain.' I told them on the strict understanding that they wouldn't spread the news. A couple of hours later the manager knocked on my door. 'I've decided I want you to be captain,' he said, 'and there'll be a press conference in a couple of hours.' Paul Newman, the press officer at that time, ran me through what would happen next. So within an hour I was talking about it to the football correspondents. I had been captain of the England U-18s but had got myself sent off. I was sure I could do better this time. Within four minutes I scored with a glancing header right in front of The Kop, the first of England's four goals that night.

Before Liverpool's England contingent flew east, the team signed off with a 4–3 win against Blackburn and a 5–0 victory over Ipswich, who had therefore conceded 11 goals against us in two League games that season. The effect of that wonderful end to the year was that Liverpool finished second in the Premiership for the first time and pushed United down to third. That was a big stepping-stone. Still, the questions we were being asked were mostly negative in tone: 'Was this an anti-climax after the Treble-winning season?' There were no trophies in 2001/02, but we did do much better in the Premiership and achieved a points total that would have won us the League in other years. Reaching the quarter-finals of the Champions League also felt like progress of a sort, and we were still kicking ourselves over surrendering a 1–0 lead from the first leg against Leverkusen – especially considering that we scored first in the return, which left them needing to score three to reach the semi-finals with only an hour to play. It was sickening. Michael Ballack had inspired them with two goals and their fans had really got behind them. Ironically, when the quarter-final draw was made, we'd suspected that Leverkusen were the weakest team of the eight and fancied our chances. We had such a good recent record in knockout football that maybe we felt invincible.

Still, it was a mercy to me that I didn't have to miss too many games with injuries, and that I managed to put another 27 goals on my pile. In the Premiership, in three seasons, we had progressed from fourth to third to second, so headway was being made in the battle to regain the League title. With a few successful signings we felt we were ready to make the final push. Liverpool's biggest victory that year, though, was seeing Gérard Houllier come through his darkest hour.

16

Big in Japan: 2002 World Cup

Before we touched down in the Far East for my second World Cup, I was constantly being told that Liverpool and Manchester United were big in Japan and that David Beckham and I would be attracting endless attention from local fans. By the time the plane took off I was starting to convince myself that the interest would be split fifty-fifty between the two of us. Thankfully, it turned out to be 90 per cent David and 10 per cent me.

On Awaji Island, our main base for the tournament, there were Japanese people camped outside our hotel, which meant that our curtains had to remain permanently drawn. If you stepped out on to the balcony, you'd hear an almighty roar. We were so high – on the sixteenth or seventeenth floor – that you couldn't make out faces, but you could hear the chatter from our foreign supporters, who seemed to be keeping up this vigil morning, noon and night. Whenever we pulled out of the hotel for practice, the roads were lined with Japanese faces most of the way to our specially built training pitch. The journey took 20 minutes, which gives you some idea of how many people were strung out along those roads. Most of them were locals, though some had come from cities hundreds of miles away. That daily commute helped me understand the popularity of English football. I was aware that David had developed a high profile around the world but I wasn't prepared for the presence of thousands and thousands of Japanese people wherever we went. After the host nation, we were the 2002 World Cup's most supported team.

In fact, I was staggered by how much the Japanese idolized our captain. It was an eye-opener for the whole team. And no, I really didn't want it to be half and half. Of course it's satisfying to see people wearing your name on the backs of their shirts, and it would make anyone proud to discover that they had admirers in countries they had never visited before. But by nature I'm a quiet lad who isn't drawn to the idea of myself as a celebrity. David, on the other hand, had become expert at dealing with all the attention he was generating.

Of course, over the preceding six weeks or so England (and, no doubt, Japan) had been gripped by the question of whether or not David Beckham would actually make the trip after breaking a small bone in his foot during a Champions League game in April. Ironically, we lost Gary Neville, who is such a solid presence, to a similar injury not long after. All the players felt from the beginning that David would be fit in time for the opening World Cup game; the only doubt was whether he would aggravate the injury in training. It was already very late when David rejoined the full sessions. From personal experience, I know how hard it is not to play for a month and then throw yourself into a full training session two days before a match. Firstly, your touch is all over the place. By his own admission, David didn't have a great tournament, though he scored that vital penalty against Argentina. But he did as well as he could, given that he had only trained fully two days before the tournament. If he was struggling, it was wholly due to his injury and nothing else. It did occur to me that if David didn't make it I might be asked to captain the team. I assumed the role for a while when David went off in the opening game, against Sweden, having played for as long as he could, so I did manage to wear the armband at a World Cup. But all along I wanted David there, fit.

During the build-up back home, I didn't go to David and Victoria Beckham's pre-World Cup party. It was a tempting invitation, but I knew *OK* magazine had bought the rights to take photos, and at that stage of my life I decided to maintain my policy of not exposing Louise to that kind of publicity. We've always protected our privacy and I didn't want to jeopardize it just before going away, even though the party was bound to be fun and on a lavish scale. No offence was meant and none was taken.

The first of our major stops on the road to Japan was Dubai – a fantastic place with plenty to do as we tried to put a long and tiring domestic season behind us. The one surprise was how much physical work the coaching staff put us through. We were all aerobically fit after a full domestic campaign and assumed we were there for a week's holiday. When we arrived in the searing heat with families and girlfriends, everyone threw themselves into the social mix, and the chemistry around the hotel was excellent. In the meantime, though, we worked hard on the training ground. Baking sun combined with square bashing is bound to make footballers grumble. There weren't serious rumblings, but there was a good deal of banter with the staff along the lines of 'Why the bloody 'ell are we doing this?' There was plenty of hard running.

By the time we reached the Far East it was time to get down to the serious business of acclimatization. In our initial camp in South Korea, which was dull by comparison to Dubai, we trained in the evenings and early mornings to avoid the worst of the heat. The time there seemed to drag, though we did play one game, a 1–1 draw with South Korea in Seoguipo on 21 May. If you could have one magic wish as a player, it would be to dispense with all the preparations. They have to be done, but after a while you're champing at the bit to get on with the games. If you're not careful, a hotel room can turn into hell.

My fitness was fine, but I was aware that I'd be playing games intensively in hot conditions and in the back of my mind I felt I would do well to get to the end of the tournament. That feeling stemmed from all the problems I'd had for a year or two. Hope, more than expectation, was driving me on.

At least I made it to Japan. Steven Gerrard, of course, had to be left at home to undergo an operation. He was devastated. At Euro 2000 it had been in Kevin Keegan's mind to give him a starring role. Each time he was on the brink of being given that chance injury seemed to get in the way. It was savage for him to be missing the second tournament of his international career, and I knew how he must have been feeling. For months we had both faced the question 'Are Michael Owen and Steven Gerrard going to be able to make it through a World Cup without breaking down?'

Stevie and I have always been close because we were in the same age group as we worked our way through the Liverpool academy. We both joined the club at 10 or 11 and have always shared a bond. We're not best mates, but we're close. We played in virtually every team together, whether at Liverpool or with England. Whenever I was injured he seemed to be injured too, and we spent a lot of time jogging round pitches together, struggling to be fit, discussing medical issues and fantasizing about a life without lay-offs. As we set off for the World Cup, it hurt me to leave him behind.

Injury dramas aside, the manager had been splashed across the front pages on account of his relationship with Ulrika Jonsson. The players discussed what was being written about the boss and we all felt sorry for him. Most footballers will tell you that adversity brings teams together, and the manager's problems had that effect, because we didn't like to think of him suffering. Pressure imposed from the outside rarely splits a camp. Internal problems are what create disunity. We didn't hold specific meetings to discuss what was being said about his private life, but he did say during one of the team gatherings, 'You'll have noticed that I'm in the papers a lot at the moment. It wouldn't be like this in any other country.' He'd managed in Sweden and Italy, where, I gather, they leave private lives to be private. It was quite a shock to him that our press had got hold of the story so quickly and had run it wall to wall. But he didn't seem perturbed. He was angry at the press for raking over his personal affairs but there was no question of it affecting his or the team's morale. He didn't behave like a man who was under pressure or contemplating his future, though I will admit that we were afraid he might leave the job. If anyone in the press had asked me at the time, I would have said, 'He's not happy with the way we treat these issues in England, and if you don't stop hammering him he's going to walk out on us.'

Sven definitely has an aura about him. He commands respect. I've seen Eriksson disappointed, but I've never seen him lay into any one. If I was the England manager, I wouldn't use anger as a tool either. You have to remember that they're not your players, and you only see them maybe once a month. As England manager, you don't want to be losing any friends. It's also a joy to work for Eriksson because his ideas about the game are easy to understand. He doesn't over-complicate things to make himself sound clever, and I'm not one for over-elaboration. Football is a relatively straightforward game. As we prepared for our opening game, against Sweden on 2 June, he mostly stuck with the tried and tested 4–4–2 formation. Ninety per cent of teams at home played 4–4–2 and it is Eriksson's favourite system. Everyone knew his job.

I've never felt pessimistic in an England shirt. I've always been encouraged by the quality of the players around me. In an England press conference you can never say 'We're happy just to have qualified' because people expect a much greater level of ambition. But I try to be honest about the quality of the teams I'm in. I've played in Liverpool sides where I've thought we weren't good enough to win the Premiership. I'm a realist. Yet I've gone into every international tournament with England believing we could go all the way.

In that tense opening match in Saitama we went a goal in front from a header by Sol Campbell but then lost our way. The defence retreated so far downfield to protect the lead that the strikers ended up 60 yards from the ball – hence the growing number of punts upfield. We've never been a long-ball team; we've always been encouraged to pass it along the floor. Maybe the occasion – the first game of a World Cup, with us desperately wanting to do well – scrambled our thinking. As the game wore on the Swedes started to look more dangerous than us so were entitled to be satisfied, if not overjoyed, with a draw. I won't criticize our defenders. With a 5 on my back I would have adopted the same approach. At 1–0 up with our team under pressure, I wouldn't have risked short passes into dangerous areas where we were short on numbers. The manager told us exactly where we had gone wrong.

As an England player, you simply can't take everything that's written or said about you to heart, but the amount of stick we got did start to annoy some players, me included. We weren't a long-ball team; we just found ourselves in an awkward tactical position and didn't handle it well. That was no reason to start calling us cavemen who wanted to lump the ball into the sky. I was disheartened not to score, as well. As the striker everyone is looking to for goals, you feel a particularly acute sense of responsibility in an opening game. I felt really sharp against Sweden. Some of that might have been down to all the running I had done in Dubai, which I grumbled about at the time. I felt strong, but I didn't get many chances to open my account.

In between games our exposure to Japanese life and culture was, I admit, quite limited. For example, we took our own chef with us, but if we'd stayed on after the tournament a lot of us would have headed out to sample the local cooking. I enjoy being immersed in cultures that are unlike my own, but what people sometimes fail to realize is that we are professionals who are being paid to do a job. The idea of us eating sushi, say, is appealing, but a change of diet alters your metabolism and presents a new challenge to the body just when you need it least. Japanese cuisine would have been wonderful, but it was a question, as ever, of maintaining our routine. Even with Liverpool at European games we stick to the food we would have been eating in England. Routine is a big part of being a professional athlete, but with our camp being so tightly closed the manager could see there was a risk of us getting bored so we did break out when we were bursting to. There was a golf course 20 minutes away which we were allowed to use at appropriate times. Eriksson assumed we would act like adults and not abuse the privilege by messing about or staying on the course too long. We also had a night in the local Hard Rock Café, and a massive McDonald's consignment was brought in after one of the games. The 1998 World Cup had been the ultimate in healthy eating: lots of pills, fluids strictly monitored and a tight rein on the kind of food we were allowed. But you warm to a manager who says one night, 'Sod it, let's slob out for a couple of hours.' It might not be in the textbook, and it won't be as nutritious as a bowl of pasta, but it works wonders for the mind, which is a major part of the package. Just escaping the hotel and the same four walls of your room has a beneficial effect.

Everything the manager did during that World Cup I thought was spot on. He treated us like responsible people, and for that I respected him enormously. Certainly the mood in the camp was dead right for our biggest challenge in Group F, a re-run of the France 98 game against our old friends Argentina. With those memories still fresh, you could feel the resolve in the squad stiffen. After David Beckham's sending-off and all the pain of the penalty shoot-out, the idea of losing again to them was appalling.

After we had been knocked out by them in 1998, there was a lot of bitter feeling on both sides. They weren't particularly gracious winners, whereas I feel we behaved decently in defeat. Four years on, half the cast from St Etienne weren't there any more, so the game wasn't strictly about individual revenge. We had no idea whether people back home were thinking of it as a grudge match because of the time difference, which made it difficult to have telephone conversations with friends and family. We weren't exposed to the usual hype on TV either, which probably helped, because it stopped us getting too hung up on old memories. Had we been at home, we'd have been glued to the television and might have become obsessed with 1998. When the media are repeating 'remember this, and remember that' it does get the blood going. In Japan, we were in our own fortress, detached but certainly with our own private memories of St Etienne.

In the conference room we ran through their team and the manager told us what he thought their strengths would be. He was mindful of the creative power of their midfield, Juan Sebastian Veron especially, though in the end he was not at his best. It helped that Eriksson had managed some of their players at club level, Veron and Simeone among them. He was full of insights about their team and went into great depth when describing their players individually. Ariel Ortega was one we felt we had to stop. We had to keep our lines between midfield and defence compact. If we got stretched in those areas, we knew Argentina had players who could operate off the main striker and cause damage in those parts of the pitch. I was already familiar with Walter Samuel, at the heart of their defence, because I'd played against him for Liverpool against Roma. I considered him to be world class.

Eriksson made one important change to our team which had a huge effect on the match: Darius Vassell gave way to Nicky Butt, who shored up the centre of midfield and offered greater protection to our back four. Emile Heskey and I were the two strikers. There was an extraordinary atmosphere in Sapporo's indoor stadium, and from the beginning we got right in among Manuel Bielsa's team. I hit the inside of the post early on, and was then brought down for a penalty. (I also managed to put Owen Hargreaves out of the game after colliding with him in the nineteenth minute, but that's not something I shout about.) I was one-on-one with the defender, running at the goal, after a good ball in from Scholes. Heaven. My favourite position. *Stick your leg out at your peril, because I'm going past you.* Out came the foot, and I felt the impact of boot and stud. If I'd stumbled it's possible I'd have been able to stay upright, but I was trying to beat him while also inviting the tackle. The mistake was his, not mine, and the foul was easily bad enough to bring me down.

I assumed people would be happy that I'd caused him to make such a costly defensive error, but when I got to the press room later people were asking me, 'Did you dive, did you dive?' I actually had a cut on the knee where he caught me, so I said to a few of the press men, 'I'll show you the cut where he kicked me if you want. I'll roll up my trouser leg.' I couldn't believe they were implying I'd dived without being touched. I'd never do that. But if somebody kicks you, sometimes you will go down. I could feel a trickle of blood from the impact of the tackle, and I thought, 'You cheeky sods, asking me that when I can prove I was kicked.'

David Beckham tended to be the first-choice penalty taker, but nothing was set in stone. So who would take the kick? Everyone thinks that because we're top professionals, playing for England, there should be no debate about who is entitled to take a penalty. But sometimes life's a bit more complicated than that. Unless the manager stands up and says, 'Listen, Michael, I want you to take the penalties,' I would never go up to David Beckham and demand to be given the ball. Nor would he do that to me. All we knew that day in Sapporo was that it was either going to be David, who was the England captain, or me, who takes the penalties for his club. The penalty was mine in the sense that I had made the run that caused the defender to commit the foul. I can remember David scooping up the ball, and asking him straight, 'Do you want the pen?' He wanted it, but you could see he was nervous. He wasn't jumping to take it, put it that way. Something was bothering him. Maybe lack of confidence, maybe just simple anxiety about how much was at stake. People watching at home on TV probably assumed that David had it in his mind from the moment I went down to take his revenge for what happened to him in St Etienne. It's a nice idea, but the situation was too stressful for him to be thinking in those terms. If I had said to him, 'Listen I'm going to take this pen, give me the ball now,' I'm not sure whether he would have handed it over or not. I've spoken to him about it since and we've had a good laugh about that little scene. Me, the guy who secured the penalty, and him, the England captain, with all those haunting memories from France 98. I don't think he was a regular penalty taker for Manchester United at that time. This was one of his first big ones, and we were able to share a joke afterwards about how nerve-racking it was. In the event, he smacked it hard and fairly straight – which in itself was probably a sign of nerves.

I was ecstatic when it went in because of what had happened to us all against Argentina four years before. I couldn't bear the idea of reading that David Beckham was a villain again (this time for missing a penalty). In David's celebration, a hatchet was certainly buried, and you could see the rush of relief on his face.

But we still had a whole half to get through. Most people remember the second period for our great defensive performance, but we did also manage to string together some sweet attacking moves. Teddy Sheringham, who came on for Emile, and Scholes both volleyed beautifully from outside the box. I managed to wriggle through a couple of times and drag one wide. In the game overall, we had more chances than them. But if you're 1–0 up against Argentina there's only one scenario for the last 10 minutes: they're going to bombard you. In the face of those attacks we defended brilliantly and deserved our win.

I came off 10 minutes from the end. I was knackered, as we all were, but the change was purely tactical. The manager brought on Wayne Bridge, who played on the left of midfield. We switched to a 4–5–1 formation and left Sheringham alone up front. Afterwards the manager attracted some gentle criticism for this. Winning provides great protection against your critics, but the argument against him, I recall, was that taking a striker off left us with no one to hit when we were in possession and trying to break out of our own half. Obviously Teddy isn't going to race into channels for you because he's not that type of player. So in the last 10 or 15 minutes we ended up hitting the ball into corners; Argentina were collecting it and coming back at us in waves. These weren't my own thoughts, because I would never criticize Sven-Goran Eriksson. But some experts outside the camp did highlight what they thought was a minor tactical error. Some felt that it would have been better to use, say, Darius Vassell, who would have pinned their defenders back by chasing balls down the forward channels.

There was definitely ill-feeling between the two sides again after the final whistle, and to my disappointment our opponents refused to swap shirts. For an Argentinian, normally an England shirt would be a nice keepsake, and vice versa. A few of our lads went up to ask their opposite numbers whether they wanted to swap but were brushed away. Frankly, in one sense we were relieved. Their attitude after the game confirmed our suspicion that we had messed up their heads. Those of us who had played against them in 1998 wore particularly broad smiles. Then, we'd shaken their hands and peeled off our shirts. In 2002 we were willing to do so again, but this time the feeling wasn't mutual.

People asked me later which shirt I would have wanted. Some of my colleagues are obsessive about collecting 'big shirts' from opponents. Some even make sure they're marking the player they want in the last five minutes so they can ask him for his top. I normally just swap with the centre-half, or whoever's been marking me. Any decent shirt I get, I give away, because they mean more to my friends than they would to me. After the quarter-final, for instance, I swapped with Rivaldo and gave that shirt to a mate, who was chuffed to bits. Wonderful though it is, Rivaldo's Brazil top would have just sat in my wardrobe doing nothing.

Having beaten a heavyweight ourselves, we settled down to watch two others try to knock each other out: Lennox Lewis and Mike Tyson, the day after our victory in Sapporo, thus opening a window on the world outside Japan and South Korea. Eager to see one of the biggest fights in recent boxing history, we asked the FA's video technician if there was any way he could pull the satellite coverage of the Lewis–Tyson fight in Memphis on to Awaji Island. He came up trumps.

I have enormous respect for Lennox Lewis, and I was pleased to see a British heavyweight achieving such a lasting victory, but strangely, as a boy with a modest two-fight boxing career, Tyson was one of my heroes. There comes a point in a fight where you go from supporting a boxer to just feeling sorry for him. I had admired Tyson's skills for so long, but it dawned on me after the first couple of rounds in Memphis that Lewis was in total control of the fight. It's not that I wanted Tyson to escape with one desperate punch; I just wanted it to be over before he got hurt. Some fighters will keep taking punishment almost to the point where they're in danger of being killed. Tyson seemed to be in the grip of that instinct and I started to pity him because he was outsized and outclassed. In his heyday it would have been a more balanced fight. If he hadn't been taught to do so from his earliest days, I don't think Tyson would have made it off his stool for the final round. He knew what was coming. And it came all right. As Tyson went down, we returned to our own, safer world.

With a draw against Sweden and a victory over Argentina under our belts, we suddenly felt we were in the driving seat in a really tough group.

17

Back to Hell: 2002 World Cup

The bitterness of the Argentina game faded swiftly, and we turned our thoughts to the maths. At World Cups it's dog eat dog, and we wanted Argentina out. If you've performed the hard task of beating a fellow heavyweight, you don't want to face them again a couple of bouts down the road. To have helped to eliminate the pre-tournament favourites was a tremendous coup. It cleared one of the major obstacles between us and a World Cup final.

More than anything, it gave us a huge injection of confidence at exactly the right moment. Beating the pre-tournament favourites gave us a measure of how good we could be, and the psychology shifted in our favour. The Nigeria game in Osaka on 12 June, though, was downright uncomfortable. It was 93 degrees. In that heat it seemed pointless to take risks, and it was probably one of the dullest games in recent World Cup memory. From a personal point of view, it was weighing on my mind that I hadn't scored. I didn't feel I was letting anyone down because I'd played really well against Argentina and OK against Sweden, but I was a bit disappointed with my performance against Nigeria and I grew desperate to get off the mark. I knew I could score in World Cups. That wasn't the issue. The point was this: as a striker, you're the main hope for the team. Normally I thrive on that kind of expectation, but by the time the group phase was over I was starting to think too much for my own good. *I mustn't let everyone down. The manager's sticking with me, he's invested his faith in me. I need to get a goal. Right now.*

The second-round match against Denmark was effectively over by half-time, so much so that England fans were doing the conga around the stadium before the break. I'd never seen them do that before. Not that dancing was uppermost in my thoughts. Five minutes into the game a Danish defender tackled me and caused my leg to crumple at an awkward angle. I felt something tighten. I'd never felt anything like it. It was part groin, part hamstring. I've had pulls, tears, tightness and just about everything else, but I didn't recognize this feeling. When it struck there were still 85 minutes to go so I played on for as long as I could. But it was niggling me. I couldn't sprint, and it was starting to really hurt. Still, I felt this pressing responsibility to help the team, to be the hero, to make sure we made it through. So on I slogged. Finally, 17 minutes after Rio Ferdinand had put us in front, I scored, which lifted the other weight off my back. At last I was in business. Emile grabbed another a minute or so before half-time. Then something clicked in my head. *Right. We've won the game, get off. We've got a massive quarter-final to play now.*

Selfish or not, when I'm playing for England I never come off voluntarily. It's my equivalent of the boxer who fights on to the end, whatever that end may be. If you spoke to Ruud Van Nistelrooy, Thierry Henry or Alan Shearer there's no doubt they would say the same. Try pulling me out of a game in the second round of the World Cup. But suddenly I saw sense. We were 3–0 up, and my motivation was to get it right for our quarter-final against Brazil.

I wasn't at all clear what the problem was. All I knew was that I had four days to prepare. For the first two I didn't train, concentrating instead on getting round-the-clock treatment. The pain was retreating, just a touch. In my room, I did all the things you would never want your team-mates to see for fear that you'll be ridiculed, such as little sprints from the window to the door. Over five yards of carpet – which is admittedly not the best distance for testing an injury – I couldn't detect any significant damage. The plan was to leave it as late as possible to resume training, so we decided I would rejoin the group for the session at the stadium the day before the game.

That session was upon us in no time. The game was just 24 hours away. As we were about to go to training at the stadium, our physio, Gary Lewin, and our specialist masseur, Richard Smith, suggested I go for a little jog before boarding the bus, just to make sure the injury had healed. It was sheeting down, the way I imagine a monsoon to be. Japanese rain can be torrential. We put our wet gear on, walked on to the golf course adjoining the hotel and started jogging up one side of the rough. As soon as I set off, my hamstring clamped. *Oh, dear God. I'm not going to be fit for a World Cup quarter-final against Brazil.*

We tried to go slow to ease it off, but I was at the point where I literally couldn't walk any more. I was lying on the fairway with the physio and Richard Smith working away to find out where the problem was. Richard was getting his fingers deep into muscle, massaging it to make it looser. I looked at my watch. There was an hour and a half before we were supposed to be leaving for full training. *I can barely walk.* We scrambled under a tree to shelter from the rain, and Richard continued to stick his thumbs into my leg.

I stood up, walked around a bit and said, 'It's getting a bit better.' Then it was back on the deck and more deep massaging. We were all sweating, desperate for it to come right.

After an hour of this I didn't know how much progress we'd made because I was so anxious for the problem to go away so I could line up for the biggest game of my life. Richard was really getting stuck in and the pain was so bad I could have cried. It turned out that he was deadening the sensations in the nerves around the injured area: it was evident that I had a fairly serious hamstring tear, up the muscle, and it's 99 per cent certain that I made the injury worse by playing on in the tournament. But at the time, the pain was retreating. After an hour I could go three-quarter pace without discomfort. So we jogged back to the hotel and I grabbed my kit.

On the bus to the ground I could feel it tightening again, so in the changing room we had another bout of intensive massage for half an hour. During practice it was reasonably loose while I was in motion. If I kept moving it was tolerable. I could run at three-quarter pace, and if I sprinted it wasn't painful, though I knew the potential for more serious trouble was still there. Somehow I managed to get through the training session without making it obvious to the manager that I was going through hell.

Back in the hotel, I saw the specialist. 'I don't know whether I can play in this game. It's really, really painful.'

'Don't worry,' he said. 'We'll get you through this.'

I never stopped to question that assessment. When you hear those words you keep your mouth shut. *OK, hit me with the good news and keep doing your stuff.* A bit naive, maybe, to assume that pain relief amounts to a cure.

I wasn't the only one fretting. Rio Ferdinand, who had a problem with his groin, was lying alongside me in the treatment room and struggling almost as much. But I was virtually begging him to get behind me in the queue.

'Rio, I need this fella. I need every bit of his attention.'

Rio smiled. 'I need him as well, you know.'

Richard Smith was a fantastic deep-muscle masseur, but the whole process by now was about getting me fit for one specific game – a policy which, of course, I wholeheartedly endorsed. I was soon coming towards the end of my hour slot and there was bound to be someone waiting his turn, so I had to plead again to Richard.

'I need every bit of your time. I'm struggling here.'

I had to kill the pain once and for all.

I was up until one o'clock on the morning of the Brazil game, frantically trying to make the problem disappear. When I woke up later, the stiffening was manageable but I knew I couldn't play in that state. So I was with Richard all morning as well, virtually all day. The only escape was for lunch and to pack my bag to go to the game. I got changed as quickly as possible, and by then Richard and I were inseparable. I couldn't spend a minute without him. The more I was able to lessen the pain, the faster I'd be able to go. We worked on it so much that by the time we got to kick-off at 4.30 I was hardly feeling the injury. I kept moving the whole time, even in the dressing room where I didn't dare stand still.

It was mentally draining getting on and off the treatment table so close to the biggest game of my life, I can tell you, and torture having to go through so much painful physio-therapy. Even if Richard had warned me that playing in that game might put me out for a couple of weeks at the start of the following season, I would have wanted to play against Brazil. A World Cup quarter-final? Of course I would. Put it this way: I would rather be the sort of player who tries to play through an injury than one who limps out of a game faking one.

On the pitch it was bearable, but I was doubting my ability to influence the outcome of the game. *Just stick around the box and see what you can pick up.* I'm not sure if Mr Eriksson knew I had gone to such lengths to be out there because I was using his office and the massage room to receive the treatment. Richard had so much confidence in what he was doing that if the manager had asked him about my condition he would have given the thumbs up. I was trying to act normally, to buzz around without injuring myself. Although the manager could see I was struggling, he didn't know how bad it was – and I didn't want to tell him.

In the game itself, on a stuffy afternoon in Shizuoka, I knew I could run three-quarter pace, almost full pace, and realized I would have to adapt my game by sticking around the box and hoping a chance would come my way. Thank God it did. Halfway through the first period, Emile Heskey played a ball through and I could see Lucio, the Brazilian defender, studying my movements. The flight of the ball was taking it about a metre in front of me, where he was standing. I could have kept running diagonally and tried to beat him to the ball, but defenders are pessimists and strikers are optimists. I just had this feeling that he was going to make a mistake.

My whole mindset is to look for defensive mistakes and then pounce. I fixed my eyes on the ball and realized that it was about to hit him. He wasn't concentrating on the ball; he was too preoccupied with me. *I'm going to take a chance here. If it hits him, it'll drop, and I've got first run on him.* Fortunately, that's exactly what happened, and I found myself bearing down on the keeper and then dinking the ball into a half-empty net. I was especially proud of the finish, because I had to wait so long to fire the gun. A flood of relief came over me. Even injured, I'd contributed something to the team.

I did very little in that game but score a goal. People will now be asking themselves whether I let my team-mates down. 'He shouldn't have played if he was injured,' they might say. Well, I just had to play in a World Cup quarter-final, and the Football Association's chief specialist had told me throughout that he would deliver me on to that pitch. So I don't feel guilty at all. If you told an international manager that his main striker was going to go out injured but before doing so would score one goal against Brazil, then I think he would sign the deal. As would most supporters. If I hadn't scored then I might look at it differently. In those circumstances guilt might be a factor. Even with hindsight I just feel fortunate that a chance came my way and that I was able to take it so well. I don't think anyone can accuse me of letting the country down. I did my job.

I've wondered since what it must have been like watching that game back home. I wonder whether the early-morning kick-off killed some of the tension. For me, nothing beats watching a night game, when it's pitch black outside. I can remember Italia 90 and Euro 96 so clearly, because those were the last tournaments I watched as a fan. After the Brazil game, I tried to put myself in the shoes of people back home, getting up at dawn. When I pictured those scenes, I got rosy images of Euro 2004 and the 2006 World Cup, both in Europe, with everyone packing the pubs after dark. Footballers love night games. There's so much more noise and atmosphere. Maybe watching us play Brazil in blazing heat during the day didn't have quite the same intensity.

Friends and family sometimes remind me that my goal

against the eventual champions touched tens of millions of lives, and for a while shaped the whole country's mood. That feeling is probably the best of all those that come with being a professional footballer. Scoring in the Premier League makes everyone connected with Liverpool happy, but in 60 years not many people will remember many of those moments – though I suppose every Liverpool fan will set aside a special place if you score two goals in an FA Cup final, as I did in 2001. But if you score against Argentina or Brazil at a World Cup, those memories are for ever, for every England fan. I know everyone will remember where they were when those goals were scored. To think I've made millions of people happy with a single act is a mind-blowing idea. I sometimes look at those World Cup moments and ask myself, 'Can I surpass them in my short time in the game?' David Beckham might feel the same way about his free-kick against Greece. In England we seem to have one of those outstanding moments every two or three years.

I've been fortunate to have two or three in my career so far. But they're useless if you end up losing the game. Though it pains me, I have to record that Rivaldo equalized moments before half-time. Ronaldinho did fantastically well in the build-up, and it was a great finish by Rivaldo, but there were also a few mistakes by us along the way. During the break the message in the dressing room was, 'Don't worry, lads, we're in the game. It's one-one, no problem.' You try to convince yourself that it's going to be all right, but in the back of your mind you get a dark sense that things have turned against you. I remember feeling, during that FA Cup final against Arsenal, that the game was ours, even though we were being outplayed. In the dressing room across the corridor in Shizuoka, Brazil must have had that same conviction. Rivaldo's goal was their lifeline, and I'm sure they felt they were back in charge. The manager and his coaching staff told us to forget about the goal, stressing that the timing of it was irrelevant. Mathematically, a goal scored in the first minute of a half is no more significant than one scored in the last. They pointed out that Brazil weren't outplaying us and urged us to get out there and grab another goal. At the time, a positive message is what we wanted to hear, but there must have been something troubling me in the back of my mind. I look back now and realize that their goal completely stole our momentum. And we never got it back.

If we looked deflated, it was more that Ronaldo, Rivaldo and Ronaldinho suddenly felt invincible. If they'd put a hundred men in front of me against Arsenal in Cardiff I was still going to score because I felt unbeatable. There's a zone you go into. It's like watching Tiger Woods, on the last hole of a tournament needing a good approach shot, knocking it to within six feet of the pin. Brazil were in that zone from the moment they cancelled out my goal.

When the knife was pushed in by Ronaldinho with his long-range lob, I stopped for a moment to work out whether he had meant to chip David Seaman from that far away. To this day I don't think it was deliberate. Don't get me wrong, I think Ronaldinho is some player. For their first goal he was brilliant. But even in training, if you tried to locate the top corner from where he was you might hit it once in a hundred attempts, so I can't accept his claim that it was planned. While I was watching the ball fly, I wasn't panicking about where it might end up. I just thought David would tip it over the bar. When it entered the net I told myself that it must have been the roof of the goal. But then I noticed the Brazilians celebrating, and it struck me. *Bloody hell. Uphill struggle. They've really got the wind behind them now.*

A lot was made of David Seaman's role in Ronaldinho's goal and his supposed miscalculation. All I know is that if I was the manager I would be encouraging my keeper to stand on the six-yard line for a shot that was being launched from so far out. Unfortunately for David, there was no one else for the public to blame. It wasn't as if we didn't have a wall, or gave away a stupid free-kick. He was the only available culprit. I wouldn't call it a howler. It was just classic bad luck, in the sense that 99 times out of a hundred it wouldn't have ended up where it did.

In the dressing-room later David was certainly blaming himself, though no one I spoke to thought it was his fault. The unfortunate aspect of these big championships is that there's always a certain fear stalking the squad. There's always, always going to be someone singled out. When I looked at him in such distress and in tears, I really felt for him. *This man doesn't deserve to be pilloried for that. He made some great saves in that tournament.* It was just his turn to carry the heavy can.

Until I'm in my late twenties I won't feel it's my duty to console a team-mate of David's seniority. And I was vice-captain against Brazil, which gives you a sense of how seriously I regard the dressing-room hierarchy. David Seaman had played twice as many games as me. If he wanted to talk to me I'd have responded, probably by saying, 'Don't worry, it wasn't your fault. It could have been any of us.' I would have consoled him in that way. If I'd missed a penalty, and we'd gone out of the competition, I'd have wanted to be left alone to speak to my own family, gather my own thoughts. It's the grieving player who has to make that decision. That's his right. You treat people the way you want to be treated yourself. I wouldn't want the full 22-man squad telling me not to worry because I'd just feel I was in a bigger hole. I'd leave it until a later date to say it wasn't his fault.

Personally, I haven't cried because of football since I was a kid. The nearest I came to tears was at the 1998 World Cup when we were knocked out on penalties by Argentina. But I went no further than watery eyes and a lump in my throat. No tears fell.

In the weeks that followed I began to realize how fortunate Germany were to find such a gentle route to the final. Good luck to them, because they didn't make their own draw. They played Paraguay, the USA and South Korea in the knockout phase. All the five teams we played were better than Germany's three. We had to face Sweden, Argentina and Nigeria, and qualified through the group of death to meet Denmark and Brazil. There are no easy quarter-finals, but for us to face Brazil while Germany were matched with the Americans only added to our frustration. I have huge respect for German football, but there's not a shred of doubt in my head that we were a better side than them in 2002. Team for team, I wouldn't put them in the top 10 at the last World Cup, yet they got to the final and we were knocked out in the last eight. Still, it's no fluke that they grind their way through every time, which brings us to the question of mental strength. There are plenty of people who are more naturally gifted than Alan Shearer, for example, but my God, you show me a more instinctive and committed player. Ninety-nine per cent of football is in the head, and German players are bred to be stubborn and clever. Take out Michael Ballack and Didi Hamann and Germany barely had a notable player in Japan and Korea. Their strikers were not a vintage bunch. So for them to get to the final was incredible.

Before Shizuoka, we definitely had the feeling that if we could beat Brazil we would win the competition. I can remember us saying it to one another. About 10 of us were watching a game together one night and were getting excited at seeing a major name go out. France and Argentina didn't get out of their groups, and Italy were beaten by South Korea in the second round. Rio Ferdinand remarked to me, 'All the best teams are going home.' I can remember testing the mood by saying, 'If we beat Brazil, we're going to win this.' There was a chorus of agreement. Nobody challenged me. I remember hearing a few 'definitelys' and a 'no problem'.

Brazil were a good team, but what sickens me is that they weren't a truly great Brazil side. We didn't play well in Shizuoka. That's the starting point in any post-match analysis. I wasn't fit and it was boiling hot. There are plenty of other elements in the mix. We could have played so much better. If we played Brazil again now, there wouldn't be a single trace of fear.

One of the first things I read when we returned home from the World Cup was that Sven-Goran Eriksson wasn't sufficiently emotional when the game was slipping away. He was accused of being too calm and not conveying a sense of urgency to the team. When I first heard that, it struck me that Arsène Wenger had won the Premiership with Arsenal without ranting or punching the air, and nobody ever criticized him for being too passive. In fact, a cool temperament had been picked out as one of his greatest assets. Suddenly, despite his excellent record, people were questioning Eriksson's character on the basis of one defeat. If you're going to find fault, don't manufacture one just because we lose one match.

The criticism didn't change him. He didn't start smashing tea cups or raving from the bench, and no one's complaining now. In every World Cup, the responsibility for a defeat is dumped on to one or two backs. Eriksson tried his heart out to win that game. He wanted it as much as any of us. Just because he didn't shout or bawl doesn't mean he was a less effective manager. Football has changed. Most successful coaches these days are even-tempered and analytical. It isn't about instilling fear any more. Football management isn't a job for bullies.

At the end of our time in the Far East he sat us down and thanked us for our efforts. We'd been together a long, long time. He walked round and expressed his gratitude to us individually. Right from the start, after his appointment, I felt he was an exceptional manager. The real test, of course, is when the pressure is on, at a World Cup or a European Championship. That's when you separate the good from the average. In the heat of competition, you see the difference between good Premier League players and real internationals, and the same is true with managers. In Japan, Sven-Goran Eriksson didn't need to go up in my estimation. But he did.

18

Gambling – the Truth

For the first time I'm able to set the record straight about me and betting, and the myths that began flying around after Euro 2000 and the 2002 World Cup. The England card schools have become the stuff of newspaper legend. I'm happy to share the real story.

The image of 'Michael Owen the wild gambler' arose after I took two hits in Sunday newspapers. In the first, reporters had gained illegal access to my betting accounts and painted a lurid picture of a two-year betting spree. In the second, a photocopy of a cheque I had written to my England team-mate Kieron Dyer for £30,000 appeared soon after we returned from Japan. However it happened, the cheque had fallen into the wrong hands and then resurfaced in the papers – another example of the goldfish bowl in which we live. This is my chance to tell my side of the tale.

I had a sleepless night the day before the story of my supposedly reckless two-year betting binge appeared in print. We had played Southampton away in the Premiership, and when I boarded the team bus and switched my mobile on there were about 20 voicemail messages from my agent saying that there would be a big story appearing the next day about me betting on horses. The warning was that the reporters had infiltrated my credit accounts and would be splashing the details all over the Sunday papers.

By the time the Liverpool plane touched down, there were dozens of journalists outside my house, so we re-routed to a hideout in Chester. Louise and my mum and dad joined me so that they could avoid being door-stepped by reporters. We sat up until the early hours of the morning discussing the storm that was about to break. My mum did ask whether it was really necessary for me to play cards and gamble, and I felt very low thinking about how the newspapers would twist things and how bad they would make me look. Maybe I shouldn't worry about what people think of me, but I do. I have pride, and I want them to think I do the right thing. In my defence, Dad said to Mum, 'Listen, Janette, it's not illegal to have a bet or play cards. It's not his fault that the papers have rung the company who run his betting account pretending to be him. We know him inside out, and whatever they accuse him of we know who he really is.'

The jounalist involved even tried to get into my bank accounts. I've heard the tape of a reporter from the newspaper saying to the official at the bank, 'Hi, I'm Michael Owen,' and supplying my date of birth and my address. My dad knew how much I was betting because he had seen my statements, and he reassured Mum that it wasn't beyond my means. I had a nice house and had bought houses for my brothers and sisters. By no means had I been throwing money away.

Yes, you can have a bad year on the horses, but I would never gamble to the extent of putting anyone else at risk – certainly not my parents, Louise or Gemma. I quite accept that it's easy to chase your losses by upping the stakes. That's a temptation all gamblers face. It's at that point that you have to take a look at yourself and impose some self-discipline. And that's precisely what I do.

The headlines for the World Cup cheque story were equally big: OWEN LOSES 30 GRAND, and so on. I took stick on two counts: firstly for losing that much money – which I didn't – and secondly for being rubbish at cards. I do accept that seeing a cheque for £30,000 with my name on it might have shocked some readers. They might have had the feeling that what we were doing was wrong. Even my mum was upset by it. But when you break it down, as I did, it's nowhere near as bad as it looks – quite apart from the fact that it's nobody else's business. I still don't feel ashamed of playing cards for money. I was quite naive to write a cheque that large, because it wasn't an accurate measure of my losses. To settle all the debts after a six-week trip to Dubai, South Korea and Japan for the World Cup tournament itself, the England players simplified the cheque-writing process so that some of us ended up paying each other's losses. It didn't mean I was £30,000 down, because I also had money coming in. In fact, I recouped more than half of that £30,000. So the most anyone lost on that long trip was £10,000.

It sounds like an unbelievable amount of money, but relative to the modern footballer's income it isn't. Nor is it necessarily bad value for five good weeks of companionship and entertainment. The money we staked bought us a good time, a good laugh and a lot of team spirit. The England team were performing as well as we could. It's not as if it was affecting anyone out on the pitch.

For some reason the card schools that are struck up on England trips are made to look like some sort of shameful activity. The issue first arose when there were pictures of us playing cards on the bus during Euro 2000. We are England footballers, not criminals. I'm sorry, but you will never stop grown men playing cards with a bit of money on the side, and that's fine – provided common sense is observed. We're talking about something completely legal which isn't harming anyone else and which, despite the hysteria, isn't even close to being out of control. We earn good money, and we're having a bet; it's not as if we're doing anything wrong.

In international football, some issue or other always rears up before and after tournaments. One month a couple of England players have had a few drinks on a night off; the next week there's a gambling culture in the squad. It seems there always has to be something negative for people to have a go about.

If anyone had asked me, 'Do you play cards in the England squad?' I would have admitted it. Why? Because it's not a crime. Nor were we irresponsible. The first thing to remember is that on a five- or six-week trip boredom can very easily set in. When friends come round to my house it never crosses my mind to play cards. For me, it's a feature of life on the road, and that's it. As a professional footballer, it's part of your regime to relax after training and games. You're not meant to be dancing, you're not meant to be running around, you're not meant to be doing anything stressful. You have to relax. You have to put your feet up.

I can't imagine anyone in any walk of life sitting in the same hotel room on their own for 12 hours every day for six weeks with only television in Arabic or Japanese to watch. Bear in mind that the time difference makes it hard to call home on your mobile phone. If you're not careful, even in a football squad, you can start to feel very isolated. So in the summer of 2002 of course the England players went into one another's rooms and talked about our clubs, exchanged gossip and discussed the World Cup. Some groups listened to music together; some sat around and talked. I know players who took a suitcase full of portable electronic equipment, and the DVDs to go with it. They must have spent thousands on high-tech gear. That was their chosen form of entertainment. What we did was spend £2.50 on a pack of cards, enhance our friendships and have great fun along the way. We were in Dubai for over a week, South Korea for a week and then Japan for three more. Take out matches and training and you have a fair amount of spare time on your hands. It just so happened that there were four or five of us in Japan who enjoyed playing cards. What's the problem?

This is how it worked. At the start of the Dubai trip, five of us began playing 13-card brag for £10 a point and kept a written ledger throughout our time there, in South Korea and at the tournament itself. There was me, Teddy Sheringham, David James, Kieron Dyer and Wayne Bridge. We never put money on the table. Not once. We had an exercise pad in which we kept track of all the points scored over the entire five weeks. There was no question of handing over money every day. At the end of the trip we added up the points to see who was in credit and who was in debt. It was very controlled and very confined. It never took place in the changing rooms and never on the night before or the morning of a game. We played on plane journeys or at the hotel in our spare time. It never got in the way of the football. And we weren't playing for amounts that we might lose sleep over, so nobody can argue that it might have affected our performance. If that had happened it would have been up to the player to act like a grown man and protect the team and himself. A World Cup is the pinnacle of my career, and I wouldn't have jeopardized that for the sake of a few games of cards.

If I thought locking myself in my room for five weeks would improve my performance in a game, I would gladly do it. However, it's beneficial to be taking your mind off the game, chatting to the lads, passing the trip away. If you're not enjoying your life, you can't play football well. Everyone has their own methods for relaxing themselves during high-pressure tournaments – each to their own. A 25-year-old England footballer will have got to that level by knowing what he needs to do to perform. He's a professional person. He doesn't need to be lectured like a child. On the day before or the day of a game I didn't turn a single card over until maybe the flight back to our base. Nothing was allowed to intrude on the football.

We certainly weren't being flash or arrogant, chucking £20 notes across the table. It was just a quiet hobby that we all enjoyed, with a running total recorded in a pad. On the last leg, on the way home from Japan, we came to the final reckoning. Naturally the losers wanted to get a bit back, and the winners wanted to hold on to their winnings. Louise was sitting behind me, studying my cards as I played, so nobody could accuse us of squandering money while our families were looking the other way. On the new British Airways plane we were able to arrange a table to lay the cards on, while our wives and girlfriends gathered with us in a circle. If the stakes had got out of hand I'm sure Louise would have given me a clip round the ear. Sven-Goran Eriksson knew we were playing and was relaxed about it. He knew we weren't staying up until three in the morning to play. There was no curfew because we didn't need one. As I said, we're all grown men.

Going back to my formative years, the bottom line is that when I was a kid I was ultra-competitive. It didn't matter what I was doing, I wanted to win. If I had the choice, I preferred to win a prize. My dad was much better at games than me when I was eight or nine. At that age, of course, he didn't let me fork out when I was on the losing side. Later, when I started winning regularly, I was devastated on the odd occasion I lost and had to hand over a quid. I was mortified. And it made me grab the bit between my teeth and want, even more, to play to win. When my dad wasn't with his mates, he would always be with us kids. A great treat for me was going down to the snooker hall. I don't know whether it was his idea or mine, but if we played snooker it was always for, say, 50p. You can't play sport for nothing when you're as competitive as me. Not that my dad is a big gambler. I was brought up to want to win, whether it was a prize or simply for pride.

If you see me now in training, in a five-a-side, you'll see my winning nature. I'll fight to the death. It all comes back to wanting to win that 50p. I see it as a big advantage in my make-up. I'm certainly not saying you have to gamble as a kid to acquire the competitive instinct to reach the top. The point is that my dad worked it to my advantage in the long term. Maybe he planned it that way. Maybe it was a useful by-product of the way he approached games of snooker or golf between him and his kids.

If someone I don't know challenges me to a game of golf, I can't stand on that first tee and say, 'Right, let's have a good game, chaps.' I'll say, 'Come on, what are we playing for?' Even if it's only a pound, or paying for dinner afterwards, it just adds that extra meaning to the contest. There's a winner and a loser. If we were just going out for a knock I wouldn't care about the game. I would be smashing the ball anywhere. But if there's something at stake I'll grit my teeth and concentrate. I can be as enthusiastic playing for a pound as I can for something bigger. My mum doesn't like gambling, but she's never had to have a go at my dad about it. For him it's just a normal hobby that could never take over his life.

I do understand the normal person's point of view if he or she says footballers are extravagant. Sometimes I feel embarrassed to earn so much for doing something I love. Yet nobody will criticize you for spending £50,000 on a race-horse. It's all relative to income and to personal taste. I'm unhappy about having to defend myself like this, because to put my losses at the 2002 World Cup into perspective I have to talk about how much I earn, which in turn makes it sound as if I'm showing off.

The going-over I received was another example of how judgemental our society can be. If you take all someone's passions away from them, what's left? If you can't have a game of cards when you're away with England, or have a bet from your own front room via a legal betting account, what sort of life is that? Would anyone take those pleasures away from me because someone's writing a newspaper story about me that's mostly false anyway?

Actually, after a week of it being in the papers I felt a sense of relief, because now everyone knew I owned a couple of racehorses and liked a bet. In the early days, Tony Stephens, my agent, wanted to play down the fact that I owned racehorses. It was because I was only 18, just a kid. The problem with us being slightly secretive about my love of racing was that when the story started to emerge it back-fired a bit on me. Because no one knew I owned racehorses, it came as a much bigger surprise when the news first broke, and suddenly it became a major talking point. In interviews, I talked about football, golf and snooker, but never men-tioned racing. So it was as if I had been harbouring some secret. In fact, I saw it referred to as 'Michael Owen's secret obsession with racing'. In retrospect, maybe we should have fed the news into the system gradually, been more open about it. But now I'm 26 it's obvious that I have nothing to hide because of my genuine love of horses. So when we issued our statement soon after the story of the £30,000 cheque broke, I pointed out that racing is the sport of kings. The Queen, I reminded people, owns and breeds racehorses. It makes me happy, and I'm fortunate enough to have the money to do it. I don't go stupid and I look after those around me. Discipline is the key. And I like to think I have plenty of that.

19

New Life: 2002/03

The biggest story of 2003 didn't involve me directly, but it shone a light on the high quality of English football. Five days after the 2002/03 season ended, the news broke across Europe: David Beckham was on his way to Real Madrid. David's success, alongside the likes of Zinedine Zidane, Raul, Ronaldo and Luis Figo, has encouraged other England players to believe that they, too, could thrive in any environment. I always felt I could, though I was not to know that I would be next on the magic carpet from England to Madrid.

An England player's perspective on a major transfer is different to that of the average fan. Inside the game, you become accustomed to hearing the rumours long before a deal is done. In David's case, the will-he-won't-he saga seemed to last all summer. There was so much smoke, so much gossip, about David possibly leaving Old Trafford that I assumed there must be a fire at the heart of it all. The Beckham–Ferguson scenario reminded me of the Fowler–Houllier situation: the relationship simply went downhill. In the end there was so much speculation that it was simply a question of where David might end up.

Though we took note of the incredible circus that

followed his eventual arrival in Madrid, a bigger question for his England team-mates was how he would get on where it really counted – out on the pitch. David was suspended for the Euro 2004 qualifier against Slovakia on 11 June, so I only saw him in South Africa for a few days and didn't discuss his plans with him. But I did get the gist of what was happening. We shared the same agent, and though Tony Stephens didn't tell me what was going on, I knew that United were willing to sell. Since David left England, I've spoken to him more about what life's like in Spain. Family life, especially.

Plainly David and I have taken different paths in life. He likes fame, I like privacy. That, I suppose, is the basic difference between us. Are we close? We're very friendly, but I don't talk to him regularly between England get-togethers. In fact, I don't have his mobile phone number. If I need to speak to him, I'll pick up the phone to my agent and ask him for David's number. People may find that surprising, but look at it this way. If I asked someone in a factory whether they had telephone numbers for each of their 30 colleagues, they would probably say no. They would have numbers for their three or four closest pals. Even though everyone's matey in football, the same principle applies.

In the England camp, David and I talk a lot. We're good mates. We might sit together for a meal and discuss issues to do with a game, or a fellow England player. He's the captain and I'm his deputy, so we need to have a good professional relationship. He consults me and I respect him for that. He doesn't talk to anyone as if he's the captain, or as if only his word counts. He asks for opinions. There are four or five of us the manager consults most: David Beckham, me, Rio Ferdinand, and Gary Neville – all the senior lads. There's more dialogue with David and Sven as captain and manager than I had been used to. Everyone wants to make the England camp an enjoyable environment to work in. With our team spirit and our growing maturity, everything is pointing in the right direction for the current generation of players.

When the job is done, though, footballers return to their lives outside the game. And we do have those other lives. Just because people don't know much about what I do away from football doesn't mean that I come home and do nothing. I get on with things that interest me, such as my family, my horses or my golf. At Liverpool, I tended to speak to Danny Murphy, Jamie Carragher and Didi Hamann. They were my closest mates. With England, if I need to get a number for a team-mate it's not hard. My number is equally accessible. I think you'll find that every professional footballer has two or three close friends who become daily reference points.

It's true that David and I are at opposite ends of the spectrum when it comes to our public profiles. Though I'm intrigued by his life in Spain, I wouldn't push him to tell me what it's like to be mobbed by photographers every day. A fan might wonder, but it wouldn't be of interest to me. I would simply ask him, 'How's life, and how are the children?' The normal questions. The Owens and the Beckhams have never been out socially as a foursome. We live totally different lives. I've never really asked for publicity because I don't want it. The paparazzi know I don't throw myself in front of them, and to an extent they accept that now. In contrast, David has been used to the limelight and the flashing lights. Now, if he turned round and said, 'I don't want this any more, get out of my hair,' he would have a heck of a job making all those people go away. I haven't earned the money he has because I haven't smiled for as many cameras or encouraged as much interest in my life. Victoria Beckham was a pop star in her own right, whereas Louise shares my desire to stay out of the public eye. It's all down to personal taste. Neither of us is right or wrong. We're just different people. And we get on fine that way.

Having David in the team has altered the whole experience of playing for England. But before anyone runs away with the idea that we resent the heavy security and the extra focus on him, I couldn't imagine what life would be like for me without David Beckham. I'm so grateful to him for taking all the media attention and the spotlight away from me. If he didn't exist I, and others, would have to put up with a lot more in the way of intrusion.

Look at it this way. Because of David, attendances for England matches have risen, and a lot more sponsors want to be associated with the team. The list of advantages goes on. Everything is bigger and brighter. The disadvantage is that everyone has to live under the tightest security when David's there. The bottom line, of course, is that he's a valuable player – a footballer at heart. When I retire, I won't give two monkeys about the fact that we had to have an extra policeman on the floor of our hotel, as long as I've got that World Cup winner's medal. He will have contributed to that, and I'll be thanking him for it.

Fame hasn't changed him as a person. I can still have the same conversations I would have had with him five years ago. It's the world around him that has changed. As a person, he doesn't think he's better or more important than anyone else. That's the key fact about David.

The start of David's new life came at the end of a long and mostly frustrating season at Liverpool. After our second-place finish the previous season, it was the club's intention to conduct a serious push for the Premiership title in 2002/03.

With that in mind, Gérard Houllier brought in Salif Diao, El-Hadji Diouf and Bruno Cheyrou at a combined cost of around £19m. All we felt we needed was an extra spark in one or two areas. We were down to two or three strikers, which is why Diouf was signed. After the World Cup we were especially excited to hear that he was coming because he had played so well for Senegal.

My own season started quietly with a run of seven League games without a goal. The sequence ended on 28 September with a hat-trick against Kevin Keegan's Manchester City at Maine Road. In my occasional barren spells, I do get grumpy. I admit that. I start to feel as if the world is against me. My suspicion is that some people are enjoying seeing me go through a bad patch. It's just my self-defence mode. But I could feel a rush of goals coming, and the hat-trick against City was my chance to ram a few words down a few throats. I'll always have that competitive streak in me. If I get criticism it becomes an obsession to prove the critics wrong. One goal, and a bit of confidence, and I'm off and running again.

Not long after our 3–0 win against City, I encountered hostility of a more threatening kind. In the second week of October England travelled to Bratislava to play Slovakia in our opening qualifier for Euro 2004. Our 2–1 victory is less memorable to me than the moment when we all rushed to our hotel windows to find out what the loud bangs were in the square outside. Gunfire was the answer. The first I'd heard of the trouble in Slovakia was through some TV pictures showing disturbances between English and local fans. I persuaded myself that the images were coming from some distant town and thought no more about it until the sound of guns going off prompted us to part the curtains. We congregated in the rooms of players who were staying at the front of the hotel, overlooking the square. Soon we were poking our heads through those windows to watch the fighting. The police were trying to restore order. If you hear a bang, normally you assume it's a car backfiring; only later did we discover that bullets were flying around outside a pub.

It was a grim trip in many respects. The pitch was in a terrible state and the game was in doubt until a couple of hours before kick-off. The last thing we wanted was a post-ponement. We wanted to get in there, get a result and fly back to Britain. But the pitch was atrocious. Back home, an under-10s game would have been called off in those con-ditions. If you stood still for more than two or three seconds you would sink up to your ankles. The game wasn't much better, but we did well to come back from 1–0 down. Slovakia were a decent side, too. They also gave us a scare in the home leg in Middlesbrough. At half-time we would have settled for a draw, but after the break David Beckham scored from a free-kick which the goalkeeper thought I was going to head, and then I got the winner with eight minutes to go. When our plane took off that October night, it was one of the nicer feelings we'd experienced when leaving a foreign city. When you hear gunfire a few yards from where you're sleeping, it does make you miss home.

Four days later we had another bad night, for different reasons, in Southampton, where the manager took a lot of flak for our performance in a 2–2 draw with Macedonia, which turned out to be David Seaman's last international appearance. We got carried away before the game, thinking we were going to rack up a big score, and in the match itself nobody seemed to be in their proper positions. Every time they had the ball they seemed to slice through us. We lost a bit of our discipline that night. It didn't help, of course, that they scored a freak goal from a corner. We weren't good that day, but we were surprised by how much hostility there was in the media. At the post-match press conference I had my shield up, defending Seaman, the manager and just about everyone else.

Seaman was jeered by some England supporters in his last match for his country. What a shame. People have such short memories. David was a very good England goalkeeper. Everybody grows old. To be a top-class keeper and then go out with the memory of your own fans booing you must be awful. Being chased out of the job is something I want to avoid. I don't want to give anyone the chance to say I'm in decline and have gone on too long. The example set by Alan Shearer sticks in my mind. I really respect Alan for retiring as an international player while carrying on with his club. He was able to leave the England squad with every-one remembering what a great striker he was. He wasn't booed or pushed out. He went out on his own timetable. Alan's experience of international retirement certainly looks preferable to that of David Seaman.

Back at Liverpool, we were flying in the Premiership and fancied our chances in the Champions League, having beaten Spartak Moscow 5–0 and 3–1, with a hat-trick by me in Moscow. That momentum was lost at the end of October when we were beaten 1–0 at home by Valencia, and then we drew 3–3 in Basle to finish a disappointing third in Group B. I have awkward memories of the away game in Valencia the previous month (they won 2–0) because it was the second major occasion on which I felt I was unjustly left out – the other one being, of course, the Worthington Cup final in 2001. I can accept being rested, but the low points of my career are when I've been dropped for games on the big stage.

The manager pulled me over before our Saturday,

14 September game against Bolton and said, 'I'm going to rest you for this one, because we've got a big Champions League game against Valencia coming up.' I didn't object, though I've always felt it's a bit dangerous to rest a striker a few days before a big game. If the two who play each score a hat-trick, what's the manager going to do? Houllier told me that day I was definitely going to play against Valencia on the Tuesday. We beat Bolton 3–2, and Milan Baros and Emile Heskey played really well. The Valencia game came along, and there was no knock on the door from the manager. Up to two hours before kick-off I was still assuming I was in the team. As it turned out, the manager dropped Milan, who had scored two against Bolton, and left me on the bench; Emile and El-Hadji Diouf were the two strikers. Hence it turned into one of my two major gripes. In fact, that game was one of the few times I went into the manager's office and confronted him. In those situations you have to stand up for yourself. I said, 'It's the most important game of the season, and I should play in that game.' Things heal over time, but if you scar me I do tend to keep looking at those scars.

Domestically, we won nine of our first 12 matches and drew the other three. Then, incredibly, as I said, our season went into freefall. When we travelled to Middlesbrough on 9 November, people were wondering whether we were on our way to a club-record number of games unbeaten at the start of a League campaign. We set ourselves up quite conservatively at the Riverside Stadium, with Danny Murphy playing just behind me as the lone striker. Jerzy Dudek famously dropped the ball for Middlesbrough's goal – the only one of the game – but we didn't play well, and that defeat started a really bad slump of 11 League games without a win.

By the end of that run you could see a total drain in the confidence of the squad. Even in training you could see the standard dip. We were looking at one another for someone to provide a spark of life. It didn't help that we went 3–0 down inside half an hour in the game against Basle that ended our participation in the Champions League. Bloody hell, did they sting us at the start of that match. Two or three times in your career you will say to yourself, 'This is just a nightmare. What's hit us here?' That was one of those games. It was embarrassing. Thankfully we salvaged a bit of pride by dragging it back to 3–3. In fact we might have won it because Basle had totally 'gone', but there wasn't quite time for us to score a fourth.

Jerzy was going through a bad patch. His mistakes against Manchester United at home on 1 December were highlighted across the land, but the truth is that we weren't playing well as a team. Jerzy's problems in goal opened the door to Chris Kirkland, who I think is going to become one of the best goalkeepers in the world. I have a very high opinion of Kirky. He'll be England's number-one goalkeeper for a long time to come. But he's been so unlucky with injuries. Soon after replacing Jerzy he damaged his knee ligaments against Crystal Palace at Selhurst Park and was out for five months.

I'm not sure whether there is a connection, but after our eleventh League game without a win the club reached into the past in search of help from one of Liverpool's greatest goalscorers. Five days before we finally broke our dismal sequence, on 18 January with a 1–0 win at Southampton, Ian Rush returned to Anfield as the forwards coach.

As a coach, Rushie understands the importance of doing things the players enjoy. If you don't relish going through a particular exercise, you end up looking at your watch and thinking you can't wait for it to end. Ian has been a top striker so he knows what goalscorers like doing on the practice ground. They enjoy slotting it past the keeper. So we do plenty of that from different angles, with different feet, and from a variety of starting positions. Just kicking the ball regularly into the back of the net is so fundamentally important. If I haven't scored in training for a while, you can bet your bottom dollar that when I bear down on the keeper one Saturday afternoon it doesn't feel quite as good as it would if I had smacked in 50 goals in training the previous week.

The other Liverpool coaches, who I respect enormously, are coaches for the whole team. The benefit of having Ian there is that he caters for my specific needs. And it's obvious that different players have different requirements. What I do in a game is maybe 50 sprints and walk; I hardly ever jog. My game is 'bang, go', whereas Didi Hamann would sprint maybe once in a game and jog around the rest of the time. People in football are beginning to realize that teams can be broken down into separate components, and I think you'll see a lot more specialist coaching in the Premiership. Football's a multi-billion-pound activity, the biggest in the world, yet in some respects we are light years behind some other sports. Mainly the individual ones, because in athletics, say, you have to be in perfect shape or you're only letting yourself down, whereas in football you have 10 other people to pull you out of it if you're not 100 per cent. We're trained to the maximum, but there's plenty we could learn from a rower or a cyclist. We're not at the forefront of sports science and technology, even though we're the world's biggest sport.

The win at Southampton stopped the rot, but it wasn't the turning point we had hoped for. Though our form was better, we still lost four of our remaining 14 games and found ourselves clinging on for a win over two legs in our

Worthington Cup semi-final with Sheffield United. It wasn't our biggest target, but at least it was a final, and our 2–0 defeat of Manchester United in Cardiff on 2 March enabled us to feel that we had salvaged something from an average season (bear in mind that expectations were at an all-time high following our second-place finish the season before). A goal for me four minutes from time put us 2–0 in front and gave me another happy personal memory from Cardiff.

Before that final, I was joined in England colours by Wayne Rooney, who made his international debut on 12 February at the age of 17 years and 111 days in the 3–1 defeat against Australia at West Ham, thus breaking my record from five years before. People on Merseyside talked about red corners and blue corners and a great new rivalry between the Liverpool and Everton strikers. I didn't consider Wayne a rival or a threat. The truth is that I was as intrigued as anyone to see what he was like.

By nature, I'm sceptical about glowing praise in newspapers or on TV. If I wrote a list of the players who were meant to be the next great thing there would be a lot of embarrassed people. The easy part is showing you've got talent; the hard part is keeping your place on the stage. I love seeing good young players coming through. Having seen Wayne only once or twice, I was full of anticipation, wondering what he was capable of. I must say I was impressed. He was tough and strong and had a nice touch. He also looked like a decent finisher. At the same time I was taken aback by how much praise he received in his first two or three Premiership games. Around that time a youngster called James Milner was breaking into the Leeds team, and people were making comparisons between Wayne and James, who is a totally different player. It took me back to when I was breaking through. I used to pick up the

Liverpool papers and see polls asking, 'Who's got the best striker – Liverpool or Everton? Is it Michael Owen or Danny Cadamarteri?' Then it was Michael Branch, then Frannie Jeffers, then Phil Jevons. I've got enormous respect for those guys – I was at Lilleshall with Michael and Frannie – but only when a player is in his early twenties can you really look at players side by side.

Some of the comparisons are laughable. At Liverpool, people outside the club were judging me in relation to Robbie Fowler when I was only 14 or 15. OK, that was a fair analysis because we both made it through. I must confess, though, that at the very start I was wondering how Wayne could have acquired such a reputation on the back of maybe 10 Premiership games. At the same time I was thinking back to my emergence as a Premiership player and trying to remember whether or not there had been this kind of reaction when I burst on the scene.

The answer is that it was my goal against Argentina at France 98 that brought me the kind of attention Wayne received in the wake of his promotion to the Everton first team. Maybe I helped people realize that you could call on kids and they would deliver. The likes of Wayne, Steven Gerrard and I have upped the stakes in terms of Premiership academies, which can't afford to miss a good player in their own ranks. So young kids coming through now will be put on incredibly generous deals, which wasn't the norm for us. To me, as a young player, £500 a week felt like a fortune.

When Wayne came on board with England, I felt like a senior England player for the first time. He was extremely nervous and seemed relieved when anyone spoke to him. For me, his arrival was the transitional stage between feeling like a kid myself and realizing I was the senior England striker. Steven Gerrard was quite pally with him. They came from a similar area and Stevie was the one to welcome him into the squad. After a dozen England get-togethers, Wayne was probably able to feel part of it. It's a good sign that he was so reserved in the earliest days. Too many kids nowadays come into the game ready to shout their opinions or show you their new watch. It's no bad thing to be humble at the start (or all the way through, for that matter).

People ask me endlessly what Wayne needs to do to thrive at the very top. I point to all the basics. It's all in your head. As long as you're prepared to develop as a player, to listen and to do the right things, then you've got a damn good chance of making it – assuming you've got the ability. And Wayne certainly has that. It all boils down to how you handle things on and off the pitch, and that's always determined between your ears. You need to trust your own judgement. If someone tells you you're the best player in the world, you know you're not; you know you're not the worst, either. You just keep a middle ground on everything. My main aim has been to be myself all the way through, and that seems to have been good enough. If he keeps on the straight and narrow, Wayne's ability will do the rest.

All the temptations are right there in front of you. Drinking and smoking are the obvious ones. You're earning good money and girls do fancy you. Some people can't handle those temptations. A career can be finished in one or two years. That's how violent it can be. Wayne's obviously got the footballing talent and the physique, so everything comes down to his ability to resist the things that will hamper his career. It comes down to his mind and how he copes with fame.

But back to Liverpool. Before the Worthington Cup final, I equalled Rushie's record of 20 European goals for Liverpool in a UEFA Cup match against Auxerre. At the time I just saw it as a headline, because I tend not to dwell on records that don't stand up to scrutiny (we play far more games per season in Europe now than Ian would have done). On the other hand, in 20 years' time I know how proud I will be if I can still say I'm Liverpool's leading goalscorer in Europe. Later, in April, I scored my hundredth goal for the club in 185 appearances.

Cardiff proved to be a false high, because the rest of the season was a slog to reach the Champions League for 2003/04. The last chance was our so-called '£20 million match' against Chelsea at Stamford Bridge on the last day of the season. I'd never played in a winning Liverpool side at Chelsea. It's a stinking ground for us. Despite that we made a great start, with Sami Hyypia scoring from a set-piece, but Marcel Desailly and Jesper Gronkjaer hit back for Chelsea.

The disappointment of not making the following season's Champions League creeps up on you. You don't feel it so much on the day; it only really hits home when you find yourself flying to Croatia for a UEFA Cup tie while another Premiership club is on its way to Madrid or Milan. We finished fifth in 2002/03, 19 points behind Manchester United. The Worthington Cup aside, we had two crushing disappointments in the knockout competitions, losing to Crystal Palace in the fourth round of the FA Cup and to Celtic in the quarter-finals of the UEFA Cup, which we joined after being knocked out of the Champions League. It was some small consolation that I scored 28 goals in all competitions.

Within days of the season ending I was on my way to South Africa with England. Our long trip south was an exercise in diplomacy that featured a famous meeting with Nelson Mandela. Everyone was knackered, me included. After our early start to fly to the other side of the country for the day, I could hardly keep my eyes open when I was shaking his hand. But now I can sit here and say I met Nelson Mandela. In my rocking chair I'll be able to tell my children and grandchildren. Some of our players got stick for not going, which was desperately unfair. Playing for your country means so much to some people that they want to prepare 100 per cent for the game. Gareth Southgate was particularly unhappy that people were questioning his motives for staying at the hotel.

Still, with England I finished an exceptionally long season on a real high. The date for our Euro 2004 qualifier against Slovakia was 11 June, a full month after the end of the Premiership season. In a non-tournament year, when you're exhausted, you don't take kindly to games that cut right through the holiday period. We had a week in South Africa, a week in La Manga, a friendly against Serbia and Montenegro and then another week preparing for an important qualifier against Slovakia. Yet in that match I felt an amazing sense of pride. This was my fiftieth cap, at 23 years and 181 days. I was England's youngest captain in a competitive match. At 1–0 down I was getting edgy, but two second-half goals from me saw us home, and I was so elated that the three-hour journey home felt like 10 minutes. Two goals, three points, and a holiday just around the corner. I had 10 days off and was then back at Liverpool for preseason training. I've been playing professional football since I was 17, and the most I've had off in a summer is 19 days.

And while David Beckham was on his way to Spain, I was making my own huge new start in life. In May 2003, I became a father for the first time.

20

Gemma

Gemma Rose Owen was born in the Countess of Chester Hospital on the first day of May 2003, at 6lb 8oz, in the maternity unit where Louise and I both entered the world. Our own happy childhoods had encouraged us to dream of creating our own large family. With Gemma we made our start. I was a dad at 23.

It was a normal day in training when the call that all expectant fathers wait for finally came through. I was down to play in an away game and Louise was panicking about me not being there for Gemma's birth. So we took the decision to have her induced. It was totally safe to do so. In hospital on the night we took that decision, Louise went through the normal tests and the doctor told her, 'I don't think you need to be induced. You're starting to dilate.' I left her that night and went into training the next day with my mobile on. Nobody called me in from the office during the session so I made my way to see the chiropodist. As I was doing so, a receptionist dashed over to inform me that my mum had just called to say Louise was going into labour.

In cars I'm not a speedster, but I have to admit that I put my foot down after flying through the gates of Melwood. I reached some silly speeds to get to the hospital in time.

Simon Bayliff had come up to handle the news of Gemma's birth. Simon started as Tony Stephens' assistant but now has his own FIFA agent's licence with SFX. He handles most of my commercial work and is on hand to make sure things in my life run smoothly. He had been through the process of babies being born before, with David Beckham. Still, I think he was a bit nervous in the passenger seat. The last thing Simon wanted was for Louise and the baby to be blinded by flash bulbs as they left the hospital through the front door, so he came up with a military-style plan in which my dad, as the accomplice, would bring the car to the front of the hospital and wait with all the doors open. The press and photographers would be poised for the big moment. Meanwhile, with all this commotion and excitement at the front of the hospital, Simon would slip us out the back unnoticed.

As every father knows, when you arrive at the hospital and realize that the labour is going to be a long process, you wonder why you risked your life to get there so fast. If you've never experienced the birth of a child, you don't know whether the labour is going to be 10 minutes or 10 hours. All I knew was that I didn't want to miss the moment. Having nearly killed myself on the roads, I stayed with Louise as she sailed through it in about two hours.

I helped her as much as I could. The midwives told us it would help if Louise got into different positions and didn't just lie on her back. When she stood up, I took most of her bodyweight. After Gemma was born, I felt as if I had done 20 training sessions, I was so knackered. The contractions were painful, obviously, but there weren't any complications. I was incredibly excited to see the baby, but when she came out I was more concerned with congratulating Louise, because I was so proud of her. I gave her a hug before I reached for the baby or started studying Gemma to make sure she had the right number of fingers and so on. Finally I composed myself to inspect my new daughter.

The name was my suggestion. I've always liked Gemma. Fortunately, Louise liked it as well. The significance of Rose, Gemma's middle name, is that it belonged to my last living grandparent, my dad's mum. It's not a double-barrelled name, it's just Gemma Owen, though people often refer to her as Gemma-Rose. When the photographers were hanging round the hospital, we announced that the baby was to be called Gemma Rose Owen, so the papers the next day were full of this little girl called Gemma-Rose.

The days and weeks after a baby is born present all sorts of new and strange challenges. Instinct tends to take over. Louise was an incredibly natural mother. For a long time she wasn't eager to carry Gemma out of the hospital, because she felt protected inside. Everything she needed was close at hand. If anything had gone wrong, there were experts everywhere she looked. I was the opposite. My male instinct was to bring her home.

When we finally left the Countess of Chester, there was a lot of press interest in the new arrival. We wanted Gemma to settle down for the first week so we kept her in the house to avoid being ambushed by the paparazzi. Louise felt safer at home. In the meantime we let all the papers know that we didn't want to be followed. In return, we promised to have a photo of the three of us taken professionally, and to put it on general release.

With Gemma, the scheme worked well. They left us alone until they received the 'official' portrait. It was a beautiful picture, not least because Gemma was born with a full head of hair. All the Owen children were born with a wispy top. As a baby, Louise came out with a full head of black hair, which is where Gemma must have got hers. Unlike Louise, she kept it for a long time. At nine months she'd already had two haircuts, but still had a fine mop.

For the first two or three months I was very excited about being a father. I loved everything about it. I didn't say this to Louise, but in my own mind I was expecting more. Gemma's reliance on Louise made me feel slightly redundant at times. If I'd gone away for six months it wouldn't have made any difference, it seemed, to Gemma's early development, which was all about the basics of eating and sleeping. Louise had done all the hard work in carrying Gemma around and giving birth, and I felt I just needed to play a bigger role. I'd psyched myself up into thinking I would be looking after her constantly, but in fact they didn't seem to need me all that much. My memory of the first two months is of Louise sitting upright at nights, breastfeeding and making sure Gemma was OK.

I now realize that for men such feelings are pretty much universal. It's only when a baby gets to four or five months and starts to smile and touch and grab that the father gets drawn in more. By the time she got to nine months, Gemma and I were like Siamese twins, joined at the hip. I hate leaving her and I don't like putting her down. If I leave the room, she screams. For a man – for me, at any rate – it just gets better and better. Now, if anything, Louise gets a bit uptight if it looks as if the baby wants me more than her.

Having a child, as all parents know, changes everything. If my football isn't going well, if I'm down because I've played badly or haven't scored, I can come back home on a Saturday and just look at her to restore a smile to my face. Nothing else could do that. Gemma's the only person who can bring me up from any depth. Louise still does all the nitty-gritty of getting up in the night if Gemma is unwell, because quite frankly we can't afford to send me on to the pitch exhausted after a sleepless night. I need rest, and I need to prepare perfectly. I'm fully aware that this places me in the privileged position of being able to come home and enjoy all the best things about having children. I will change Gemma's nappies and feed her, but all the stuff that would make me grumpy, like getting up four times in the night, is done by Louise. Right the way through she has been a fantastic mother.

Both our families are very close by for help and support. Gemma was my mum and dad's third grandchild. My eldest brother and my eldest sister have both had a child, so Mum and Dad have had a bit of practice. For Louise's parents, John and Sue, Gemma is a first grandchild. We're all fighting to have her. One of the advantages of having so many close family members nearby is that the baby gets plenty of interaction. At five or six months Gemma went through a phase of just feeding and lying on her back when she might have at least wriggled, but I'm happy to say she came out of that and began developing fast.

Before you become a parent, you're quite naive about what it entails. In my teens I was constantly aware of what a great childhood I'd had, so it was easy to tell myself I would have a massive family myself at the first opportunity. But as soon as you have your first child, reality sets in, and you realize what hard work it is. If I had to put a number on it now, three children would be my ideal. I wouldn't rule out the possibility of having five, as my parents did, but it's easy for the man to say that. I suppose Louise would have the final say. She is drawn to the idea of having a large family, partly because she has seen mine in action and can appreciate how much fun you have when there are lots of brothers and sisters around. When we first started going out together, Louise used to have a whale of a time at my mum and dad's house.

Having Gemma has increased my sense of responsibility and my awareness of the future. As a parent you don't just live for today any more. I have a family now and it's my job to look after them. In theory, money shouldn't be an issue, but it does make the signing of contracts and so on a much bigger business. You want to set up everything perfectly for your children. By the time Gemma is seven, my career will be nearly over, so I have to do everything I can to be successful on the pitch to help my children through life. For that short period, there are bound to be sacrifices, because the family is partly shaped around my need to go on being a top footballer. The closer to match day I get, the more I have to conserve energy, and rest. But I'd like to think we'll all feel the benefit. My ambition is to give my children an upbringing that is as happy and fulfilling as my own.

21

Life and Death

It was a cold day in early January 2004 and I was strolling through a gate back into our home when I heard the scream. As I turned, I couldn't see the horse and I couldn't see Louise. Suddenly I saw a familiar creature haul itself off the ground, distressed, and without its rider. Without Louise. My career as a footballer has been built on pace, but I've never needed to run as fast as I did that winter's day.

I was closest to the scene of the accident and came sprinting from the house, leaping over the fence to where Louise was lying. Her mum and dad, Sue and John, had also heard the scream and were rushing along behind. Louise knew straight away that it was serious. As I arrived, I heard her say, 'It's bad. My pelvis has gone. Definitely. It's bad.'

Every afternoon at the same time, Louise went up to the stables attached to our house to exercise the horses. That day I had followed her, along with Sue and John and our baby daughter Gemma. With my sister Lesley's boyfriend and John, I had been messing about on the quad bikes in the adjoining field, and was coming back in to see how long Louise was going to be. I watched for a couple of minutes, but Louise then happened to mention that her mount, Isabelle, wasn't performing the dressage exercises especially

274

well; she said she wanted to stick with it until there was some improvement. Being the headstrong person she is, she didn't want to come in until Isabelle was doing everything perfectly. It was growing cold, and I didn't want to stay out much longer. If Louise had expected to be five minutes I would have held on, but it looked as if it was going to be more like 20, so I started making my way in. My presence wouldn't have prevented what happened next anyway. I'd walked about 50 yards when I heard Louise's wail. I felt my insides collapse and set off at a sprint, not daring to imagine what I would find.

Isabelle was a young horse who tended to be stubborn. It was quite common for Louise to engage her in a battle of wills, though the horse had never done anything malicious to a rider. All through the routine that day she had been 'arguing' with the reins. While cantering round, Louise had asked her to slow down in a particular corner of the ménage, but as she pulled on the reins Isabelle had reared up on her hind legs so violently that she ended up vertical. Louise stayed on at first, but Isabelle lost her balance and fell backwards, dumping her full weight on Louise. It was when the horse crashed on top of her that she let out that terrible scream.

It was the worst of all scenarios. Horse and rider were jammed up against the fence and Isabelle began thrashing in an effort to get back up. She managed to get a foot into the surface, but then lost her balance again and fell back on Louise a second time. In her final attempt to scramble off the ground, she kicked her feet out and began trampling all over Louise. As she was stamping and flailing, she flipped Louise over on to her side.

My first job, obviously, was to run to Louise, and after that I lurched instinctively towards the horse, who was running around, shaken and maybe even upset at what she had done. I grabbed her and led her out of the manège. I passed Isabelle to Sue and then went back to help Louise.

Describing it now, she says it was an instant, intense pain which then faded for a while. During that phase she felt completely numb. Imagine her fear as she lay in the dirt, at the mercy of her own imagination. But by the time the ambulance came the pain was building up again. She had the shakes – real, heavy shaking, which made the pain even worse. The more she shook, the more it hurt. She just couldn't control the spasms in her body. I tried to make sure she stayed warm.

Though she was in a bad way, strangely I wasn't panicking. I reasoned that she wasn't going to die there so I never lost my self-control. Somehow, logic took over, and I was soon thinking very methodically about what we needed to do. To me, it was a problem that needed to be solved. Though it hurt me to see her in such agony, she needed me to think, not to break down sobbing. She needed me to cope. The one great fear that did take hold of me was that she was going to be paralysed for life, because for a while she couldn't feel anything from the waist down. She could wiggle her toes, which gave us some comfort, but she couldn't feel any sensation below the hips.

This was Louise's second bad riding accident. At the age of 16 she'd broken her femur and was stuck in hospital on traction for 13 weeks. So her dad's immediate response was, 'Oh, not again!' He admits that he wanted to get rid of the horse for good.

While John phoned the ambulance, I called the Liverpool club doctor, Mark Waller. That week we were playing Yeovil Town away in the FA Cup. I had been due to travel down to Somerset to return to the first team after another spell on the sidelines with an injury. Luckily, I hadn't felt

I was fully ready, so I hadn't made the trip. Mark was on the road back from Yeovil when he took my call. He did what he could to offer comfort and advice, talking me through the initial stages of caring for Louise while the ambulance was on its way. When it arrived, I got in and travelled with her in the back. Once we were at the Countess of Chester Hospital, where Louise had given birth to Gemma only a few months earlier, I called Mark regularly for more information on what the hospital doctors were telling me. He helped me interpret the bulletins that were being fired my way.

They started by gently checking the places Louise was pointing to. Then they set about X-raying the area where all the damage had been done. The pelvis, which is like a circle, was shattered: Louise had suffered seven breaks of the bone. Although that number was alarmingly high, there wasn't a great deal of displacement; the bones had largely stayed together. She'd also fractured a vertebrae in her back in two places and broken a finger. The grand total was eight or nine breaks, including a hip, which was the real killer. Mark Waller's initial hope was that Louise had 'only' broken her pelvis, so when the hospital doctor told me about the pelvic damage I was quite relieved. *Oh, she'll be out in three or four days.* What made it much worse was the fact that one of those breaks had spread down into her hip. For weeks, she couldn't put any weight on that area.

Louise's only concern was for Gemma. Straight away she was gripped by the fear that our daughter would become increasingly anxious if she was separated from her mum. Until then, Louise hadn't spent a single day away from Gemma. She kept saying to her mum, 'Please don't leave her. Even if you have to give up work, just please don't leave her.' She wasn't worried about herself. It was all about Gemma and minimizing the trauma for her.

277

By that stage I was quite calm about the problems confronting us. Being a footballer probably helped, because I was familiar with serious injuries and having to deal with their consequences. Liverpool were fantastic. Gérard Houllier, who was still the manager then, was straight on the phone saying, 'Take as much time off as you need. Make sure you stay close to her.' Liverpool have always been a club of decent people who understand what really matters in life. But I didn't think for a moment that I would have to stop playing and take a month or so off.

I knew we could cope. I knew that, with the help of our families, we could adjust and create some stability for Gemma. By then, John was thinking straight too, though he was still angry that a horse had done that to his daughter. Like me, he can think clearly under pressure. Louise's mum, in a nice way, was the highly emotional one.

Even during the rehabilitation stage – and there was still a lot of uncertainty for three or four weeks afterwards – I had this conviction that she would be all right. Louise is young, fit and healthy. I never think of the worst-case scenario. My career has taught me that injuries can be overcome. My own most frightening accident was the blow to the head I took at Derby County. For a while after that I was adamant I wasn't going to kick a football again. That day I thought I was going to die, and I was convinced I was going to pack in the game. I said to my mum, 'I don't want to play any more.' For the first week I thought, 'I don't want to do that any more. It literally does my head in!' Concussion was largely to blame.

I worked my hospital visits around training and matches and took every chance I could to be with Louise. If we were training in the afternoon, I would go in on the way to Melwood and then see her again on the way home. The hard part was travelling to away games, which might prevent me from going in for a couple of days. Overall, though, the average was more than one visit per day.

The minute I said goodbye to her and shut that hospital door behind me, I felt so guilty that I was able to return to Gemma while she was in that bed. Often I just wanted to stay with her throughout and go to sleep alongside her in the same hospital room. But Louise was eager for me to be at home with Gemma as much as possible to maintain some semblance of normality. We brought Gemma in to see her in hospital, but she's only a tot and after an hour she started to get fed up. For Louise, the most painful part was missing her baby. It was awful for her having to wave Gemma goodbye. Even in their precious hours together she wasn't able to pick Gemma up and give her a proper cuddle on the bed. She wasn't allowed to put any weight on her body. Gemma was at the age where she was wanting to be mobile, to grab and pull herself into new positions. She couldn't understand why Louise wasn't getting up and moving around with her. Louise often said it was breaking her heart to have their time together so affected by her injuries. She was away from home for a month.

We didn't have any difficulty protecting Louise's privacy in the private hospital she went to after the initial treatment. It was in the Countess of Cheshire, where she was first taken, that we had to deal with the paparazzi. Every time I turned up there were half a dozen photographers outside the front door. I figured out a couple of back routes, but they knew the number plates for every one of our cars and always spotted us coming through the gates.

The very first time I visited her, I was intending to park in the main car park and go in through the front door like any other visiting relative. But as I drove through the gates I saw the photographers leaping into position and a bizarre idea came into my head. My mum, Janette, was following a couple of miles behind, so to avoid the lenses I came back out, went round the roundabout again and phoned my mum to head her off. I said, 'They've recognized the car, so meet me in the such-and-such hotel car park a couple of miles down the road and I'll get into your car, which they won't spot.' I jumped into my mum's vehicle and lay down on the back seat so no one could see me. Ten minutes later we were gliding through the gates again. But guess what: they recognized my mum straight away. From the back seat I called, 'Stop the car here,' crawled out of the passenger door and made a run for the front door. Looking back, I wonder why the hell I went to such lengths to avoid being photographed. Under scrutiny, you don't always think straight. I felt it was a private family matter and wasn't comfortable with the idea of having it all recorded in the press. When you're distressed, you don't want to be pictured walking into a hospital with a bunch of flowers and a concerned expression on your face, you just want to be left alone. But now I do wonder what I was so worried about. Running across busy traffic just to avoid being in a newspaper wasn't the smartest plan.

At the Countess, people inside the hospital had cottoned on to who Louise was and there were a couple of minor intrusions on her privacy, but at the Nuffield, the private hospital where she went subsequently, she was left in peace. She was deluged with cards and flowers, some from complete strangers. A lot came through my fan mail. My team-mates and the staff at the club all sent supportive messages. The wives of the club physios came to visit. It was a classic Liverpool response to something bad happening to one of the family. By eight o'clock, Louise was usually exhausted from all the attention and quite happy to go to sleep.

Her rehab started in bed, with knee-lifting exercises. Even

they were difficult. Muscles waste with amazing speed. Then it was non-weight-bearing exercises in a chair. She came home on crutches, still not able to bear any kind of load. A month after she returned they said she could start putting weight on her left leg, which was the one with the broken hip. That meant she could start picking Gemma up again without pain. A lot of hard work in the gym restored her strength, though six months later she was still banned from running.

Needless to say, she was back on a horse at the first opportunity. We bore no grudge against Isabelle. For the first week in hospital, mind you, Louise was saying to me, 'I can't ride again. I'm so lucky to come away from this with no long-term damage. Imagine if I'd been paralysed and left in a wheel-chair. I've got to think of Gemma. I feel guilty about being away from Gemma. All I can think about is what she must be thinking, with her mum not there. I'm not riding any more. It's over.' I don't know what changed her mind. Time, I suppose. By May, she was back in the saddle – on Isabelle.

What her favourite horse did that cold winter's day was a one-off. We honestly didn't think it came from anything spiteful in her nature. We also think she scared herself doing it and has been calmer and wiser ever since. We think she'll always have a stubborn streak in her nature, but as she grows older and has more schooling she'll understand completely what Louise is asking her to do. They had an argument that day, and Louise lost. She didn't do anything wrong in terms of her handling of the horse. She had been told in lessons to stop an uncooperative horse in its tracks and then start again. That's what she did with Isabelle. It's not as if she gave her a smack with the whip to cause her to rear so violently.

Our family crisis didn't affect me on the pitch at all. Not even one per cent. I've never been one to carry anxiety from my private life into a game. In fact, as the days passed I was becoming happier because Louise was gradually returning to her old self. I was calm about it throughout. One of my philosophies in life is that everything will always turn out fine. I have such a positive outlook. What gets me through bad patches on the pitch is the knowledge that they always pass and that I will start playing well and scoring again soon. I knew Louise had been broken up, but my mind was fixed not on her injuries so much as on the moment when she would return to being 100 per cent sound. I'm not capable of thinking, 'I can't play well because Louise is lying in hospital.' As a starting point in life that's just too negative.

If there's been a change, it's that Louise isn't taking riding quite as seriously as she did before. She's not thinking of riding in competitions or being out there every single day. When I bought Isabelle as a present, the idea was that riding her would be an occasional pleasure. But my fiancée has a bit of a stubborn streak. She can't do anything by halves; she has to be the best at it and see it through to the end. She thinks it's a waste to spend £10,000 on a horse and then not do much with it. I disagreed. People buy a Ferrari or an Aston Martin and enjoy driving it once a week; they don't have to throw it round Silverstone to get their money's worth. Louise couldn't see that at first, but now she's coming round to the idea of riding as a gentle hobby. She had been aiming to compete in regional dressage and showjumping tournaments. Isabelle was bred for showjumping. She moved so sweetly, though, that we thought she could be a decent dressage horse as well. Local shows were the starting point, and Louise had also affiliated her at regional level just in case.

The accident caused us to re-evaluate many aspects of our lives, right down to the question of how we were bringing Gemma up. Until that day Louise hadn't had a single day away from her baby so our daughter wasn't used to being with anyone else for more than a few hours. We felt we had to change that. With our second child, we resolve to organize the early months differently. We'll encourage him to have strong attachments to other family members. As she was lying in hospital, Louise wished she'd let Gemma out of her sight a little more. She wished she had allowed herself a day away from motherhood every now and then.

But it made us appreciate just how close our families are. Louise's mum, Sue, dropped everything and lived at our house for a month. My mum was in every day, along with my sisters, Lesley and Karen. We've all been brought up in the same small area of North Wales, and you tend to take family closeness for granted until something happens to show you the benefits of being so tightly bound. To have a strong family bond has always been second nature to us. In a crisis we all pull together. If my dad's hurt himself, for instance, what are his sons supposed to do? They're meant to rally round. Throughout my life it's been that way. So much so that I feel shocked when anyone makes a remark about how close we all are.

'Your family rallied round. That's really incredible, isn't it?' they say.

No. It's just par for the course.

The news was broken to me by Ian Cotton, the Liverpool press officer, in the changing room after I had come off the pitch in a UEFA Cup match against Marseille, in France on 25 March. I felt myself go numb. *That wasn't meant to happen. This was never meant to be about life and death.*

Mike Flynn, an interior designer who had worked on our new house, Lower Soughton Hall, had been found dead by his wife, Sue, at their home in Shropshire that morning. He had taken an overdose, taken his own life some time after we discovered he had apparently been using money I put into a building account for his own ends. We were trying to recover that money at the time, but nobody could have foreseen that events would take such a terrible turn.

The following day, still in shock, I sent my condolences to Mike's family. I never wanted anyone to lose their life over a legal dispute about money. It was just that it looks like he saw a chance to use my money for his own personal gain. I had met his children and posed with them for pictures. I've thought a lot about why Mike did what he did. Maybe he felt he would never be able to show his face again when what he had done came to light.

His involvement at the Grade II Listed house we'd bought in the autumn of 2001 began when he started to come round to measure up for curtains and work on the minor details. As the refurbishment gathered pace, Mike began to take a closer interest in the wider issues we were addressing in the process of modernizing the house. Soon Mike began to question some of the decisions we had made. 'Why are you putting that wall there?' he'd say, or, to my mum, who was the link between me and all the tradesmen, 'If you did this or that, Michael could have a bigger bathroom.' That kind of thing. There was always the major obstacle of planning permission, which we had to apply for through CADW, the Welsh equivalent of English Heritage, but some of Mike's ideas were good, and gradually he eased his way into doing more.

Soon Mike was taking on more responsibility, and we were paying his company, Décor by Design, not just for furnishings but also for structural work on the house. He had turned himself into a kind of site manager. Money was passing through his hands. The trouble started when we discovered that we had paid way in excess for security – some £276,000, when the firm that carried out the work had received only £164,000. When we started looking further, we uncovered more financial discrepancies. We then had to stop using Mike on site and employ solicitors to find out where the money had gone. His assets were frozen by the civil court which ordered him to disclose what had happened to the money that had been paid. Mike had been due to attend a court hearing on the day he took his life.

All I ever wanted was my money back. I just didn't want to be taken for a ride. My brothers and sisters have to work nine-to-five to earn a few hundred pounds a week, so money is precious. If he had stayed alive and had spoken to me after it all came out, I would have talked to him. When I need to be hard, I can be, but I don't think Mike was a nasty person deep down. It was just that it appears we caught him in the middle of taking my money and he took all his own decisions from then on.

Looking around our home now, it's hard to comprehend that something so dark can have been associated with such a beautiful place. It remains a painful memory.

At the time Lower Soughton Hall came on the market, I wasn't looking to move. I'd built my own house a mile away from the street where most of my family were housed, and I was perfectly happy where I was. A lot of estate agents and property developers send brochures to the players at the training ground, many of them aimed at recently arrived foreign players who might be looking to buy. I picked one up one morning at Melwood and saw the word Northop, which was only five miles from where I lived. I thought, 'No overseas player is going to want to live that far from the training ground,' so I took a closer look.

I couldn't believe that anything so nice could come on the market so close to my family base. When I first went to have a look, I fell in love with the grounds and the gardens. The house was lovely too, but inside there were too many small rooms. I went away thinking that the overall property was let down by the house. But a couple of weeks later we came to view it again. *What the hell was going on in your head? How can you have hesitated for one second?*

The next stage was to bring in our own architect, who gave us all sorts of ideas about altering the living space. It dawned on me that this was the house of my dreams – the house of anyone's dreams – so then and there we decided to get serious. I'd just scored my hat-trick for England against Germany in Munich, and a couple of days after that match we put in a bid of £2.3 million. The previous owner wanted to stay for a few more months while he sorted out his new home, which gave us time to file our planning applications for the many alterations we hoped to make. Louise and I walked up to the house with our dogs from time to time, wandering across the adjacent golf course, just so we could look forward to the day when we would stride through the door.

Once we got the keys, the builders flooded in and started knocking things about. We couldn't wait for the dust to clear so we could move in. It felt like an eternity, but we finally moved our stuff across from the old house in September 2003. Initially I'd told myself that I would oversee every fine detail, making decisions on every aspect of the scheme. Then, after a few weeks, I found myself saying, 'Oh, just do it,' or passing it on to my mum. Gradually I stepped back from the project, while maintaining my say in the major issues.

The house has got everything I ever wanted from a home.

The main intention was to find a nice house with enough land for us to have horses and a few stables in a small yard. There were boxes there already but they needed renovating. We also put in a planning application for a swimming pool, a gym and a mini cinema. Everything we wanted seemed to fit into the plan we had. The house is surrounded by a golf course, which is just heaven for me, and we have 30 acres in which to ride our horses or bomb around on our quad bikes. We had to buy that land separately – from Steve Morgan of Redrow homes, who, ironically, later tried to assemble a takeover package for Liverpool.

We've tried to keep the house's original features, to preserve its character. We didn't want to march in and turn it into some modern creation. The idea was to inject a contemporary side through the swimming pool and the gym area but to keep the main house traditional. It had fireplaces in every room, which we managed to retain. Everyone who visits tells us that we've got the balance right. That pleases us no end.

The one problem was our application for a new garage by the side of the house. There are two cottages in the grounds, but the parking areas around them aren't suitable for us, safety wise. The council turned it down on the grounds that it might be an eyesore. We didn't contest it, because the local authority have been really helpful to us over the last couple of years. We understood their point.

Obviously security is a prime concern these days. It became a major issue again in the 2003/04 season when Gérard Houllier received death threats when the team started going through a really bad patch. A day or two later, I was walking out of the stadium when Chris Bascombe of the *Liverpool Echo* asked me for my thoughts on the vile threats directed at the manager. I said it was happening more and more in football (my dad tells me there was nothing like that in his day). I sympathized with Gérard and said it was terrible that abusive messages had been scrawled on the training-ground walls. I also mentioned that David Beckham and I had had the same problem. My words, accurately reported, were then picked up by the national press and became major news.

Halfway through the 2003/04 season, on 20 January, my family were involved in a so-called security scare, which, I'm happy to point out, was actually nothing of the sort. Under the headline 'Owen's pregnant sister in kidnap terror' it was reported that Karen had been grabbed by masked men outside the health club she uses at the St David's Park Hotel near her home. The truth was that two guys tried to wrestle the keys of her BMW X5 out of her hand when she came out after having a swim. It was a carjacking, not a kidnapping. There was a gang in the area at the time who were going round stealing high-performance cars. We were astonished when we read the Sunday papers and saw it blown up into a major scare story. The article was full of unnamed 'insiders' and 'family friends' who had talked about new 'fears' over security, but it was all down to two fellas trying to steal Karen's motor. She's a tough little cookie and she fought back. She's five foot three inches and ready to take on the world. So much so, in fact, that she managed to keep the car; the two assailants ran off. If she loses her head, you don't mess with my sister. We all thought of it as one of those things that might happen to you once in a lifetime. I didn't even question her about it for long. It was a minor incident. She did report it to the police, but nothing else was said about our security or any implications for the future.

Another drama that season was the Sunday newspaper investigation into Kieren Fallon, the champion flat-race jockey, who was quoted from a hidden tape recorder saying,

'Michael Owen is a good friend of mine. Loves racing. Every day he will ring. Every single day. I will say, "I've no horse today." He says, "Give me one anyway. Just pick one . . . because I have to have a bet."'

Now, I'm friendly with one or two jockeys. They've ridden for me and we share a love of horses and racing. For example, Frankie Dettori has stayed with us when he's been riding at the Chester meeting, and I've been on *Question of Sport* with him and substituting for him. Frankie is interested in my football career and might occasionally ask for tickets. If we're playing down at Highbury, he might ask for my help to get in because he's a big Arsenal fan. Kieren has been to a couple of Liverpool games. I speak to them from time to time. If I have a free Saturday, I might be flicking through my address book and I might call them to see whether they fancy a horse that day. Kieren rang me after the *News of the World*'s 'exposé' to apologize for what he had said, but I hadn't taken offence. I thought a lot more would be made of it in the media generally, but it seemed to blow over quite fast. My reading of it was that Kieren was trying to impress some new contacts and exaggerated the number of times we speak. Certainly it's total rubbish to suggest I call him every day for tips.

Going back to Mike Flynn's sad death, I'm sometimes asked whether it made me more mistrustful. The answer is no, for the simple reason that all my closest friends are ones I acquired long ago, at school, or good mates at Liverpool. There are a select few in my inner circle. I can share a phone number with someone and talk to them every now and then, but that's as far as it goes. I've got my own circle and nobody can really break into that. The reason I've adopted that approach is that there are people who will try to creep into your world for the wrong reasons.

You can never trust anyone as much as you can your family. They are the ones I can turn to and confide in, whatever the circumstances. That's the meaning of family, to me. Obviously there are friends I trust, but it's on a different level with fathers and mothers and brothers and sisters. You never lose your family. They're always there. Despite the terrible tragedy of Mike's death, I'm proud to have created such a wonderful home for my immediate family, Louise and Gemma. Proud that we turned a lovely house into something even better than it was before. No family could want for more than we have now.

22
Farewell to Houllier: 2003/04

The second half of the 2003/04 season, then, seemed to be dominated by news, and it wasn't over yet, because in May Gérard Houllier was sacked as the Liverpool manager. The message I left on his mobile when I heard was, 'Thanks for everything you've done over the last six years. I've certainly developed as a player with you as my manager. We've had some great times together and I hope we'll stay in touch.' Stevie Gerrard and Jamie Carragher, who were with me in England's Euro 2004 squad when the announcement was made, also called Gérard to express their gratitude for all he had done for the club. Three days later, when the fuss had started to die down, I spoke to him too.

It was the end of an era, the end of a major phase in the history of Liverpool Football Club, and we all felt it. It was 24 May when Gérard appeared alongside Rick Parry at a press conference at Anfield to confirm that there had been a parting of the ways. My thoughts had already turned away from club football to Euro 2004, but when I heard that Gérard had been dismissed, during our first day away with England at our pre-tournament training camp in Sardinia, I felt sickened, even though the possibility of a sacking had been building up in the press. It's not that I made a judgement either way on the board's decision; it just wasn't nice seeing that happen to someone I knew and cared about. I knew how much Gérard had put into Liverpool, and how much the club meant to him.

The following day, the media flew down to Sardinia for a press open day and I made a point of saying that I hadn't done anything that might have contributed to Gérard's fall. Steven Gerrard and I were highly sensitive to the suggestion that we had walked into the chairman's office threatening to leave unless the club made big-money signings. I would never do that. I didn't want to be blamed falsely for a man losing his job and I told the football correspondents as much.

Gérard going left me with such an odd feeling. I've never really been in the situation where you walk into training for the first day of a new season and have to impress a new coach or a manager. As I tried to think ahead to the new Premier League campaign, I realized that there would be an edge, a buzz, to going into work that was going to be new to me.

Probably the majority of fans felt there was a need for a change, and it's obvious that the board felt that way too. Managers are unlucky in one respect: if they're in a job for too long, everyone can grow tired of hearing the same voice. The exceptions, obviously, are Alex Ferguson and Arsène Wenger. You can grow stale working in the same factory or office, just as you can at a football club. Towards the end of the 2003/04 season, in which we finished fourth in the Premiership, there was a touch of that staleness among the supporters, the players and the board.

We grew enormously under Gérard Houllier, but then we arrived at the point where we really needed to win the League to reach the next stage of our development. When we fell back from the verge of winning the title, finishing fifth and then fourth, there was a feeling that we had been trying for six years and were now slipping further away from achieving our aim. That shift in momentum counted against Gérard. We went backwards in his last two seasons, and it was perhaps inevitable that he would be held responsible when the board sat down to assess the team's position. The Treble-winning season of 2000/01 and the second-place finish in the Premiership the following season were our two peak years. Though we amassed a great tally of points in 2001/02, I preferred the previous campaign, when we won so many trophies.

Looking back now, I feel that Gérard's great strengths were as an organizer and manager in the wider sense. He could have walked into any business, spotted what was wrong and put it right. I don't think he was the world's greatest tactician. He wouldn't respond to a problem on the field by coming onto the touchline and changing the shape of the team. He didn't see the game the way a Ronnie Moran would. Gérard would get everyone organized and understanding their job. He was a very, very good manager of the whole team. Individually, every player knew what he was supposed to be doing. Gérard knew a tremendous amount about football and a very great deal about individual players. If you talked to the other lads in training about a game you had seen the night before, Gérard had watched them all – home and abroad. He had countless channels beamed into his house. He's a real student of the game. Problem-solving on the pitch might not have been his speciality, but managing the team was.

Deep down he was a cautious manager, and he took quite a lot of stick for being conservative in his tactical approach. Towards the end of his time at Anfield he came under a lot of pressure to adopt a more extravagant style of play, and maybe he tried to appease the press and the fans by deciding to be more adventurous. He hated people saying we were a boring team and tried really hard to change that perception. His starting point, though, was always the clean sheet. Above all he wanted us to avoid conceding goals. And there's nothing wrong with that. We had a lot of success from being defensively sound. We had developed a method that we all understood. We all defended like mad and had a couple of quick strikers who could hit teams on the break.

We weren't dazzling going forward, but we became good at nicking goals. So we won a lot of games 1–0. We used to sit deep and suck teams in before hitting them on the counter-attack. I wouldn't say we were a long-ball team, but we certainly liked to get the ball forward fast. Counter-attacking is sometimes frowned upon, yet Arsenal are often stunning when they break out of a defensive position and sweep the ball upfield. Manchester United, too, have used the likes of Andrei Kanchelskis and Ryan Giggs to suddenly turn defence into attack. Gérard grew frustrated with people saying that Liverpool were only a counter-attacking team because he felt that lots of other sides played that way. The difference was that those other teams had a longer build-up phase before scoring their goals. We rarely strung together nice passing moves; our goals tended to come from quick counter-attacks or maybe a ricochet in the penalty area. I'll admit that we rarely created great chances. I'll also admit that it sometimes became frustrating.

People may say that to win the Premiership you have to play an exciting brand of football. But at the same time you can't suddenly change the players you have into something they are not. A team will develop in tune with the individuals who make up that side. If Gérard had bought different players, the side might have developed in a different way.

For example, he always favoured a defensive midfielder. In that system you have five defensive outfield players straight away. We had some defenders who lacked natural pace. They were excellent at what they did, but they didn't want to be involved in sprinting competitions with quick centre-forwards. So it was no good us advancing to the halfway line and then squeezing teams in their own half. That would have made us vulnerable to the lightning counter-attack. Breaking down other teams wasn't our forte.

I felt there was a downward slope in those last two disappointing campaigns, and when things aren't going well people tend to form their own little groups and talk constantly about what's going wrong. The whole chemistry at the club was deteriorating, I felt. In Gérard's final season, the process accelerated to the point where many fans and experts were questioning the quality of the team.

Emile Heskey had dips in form, and he attracted some of the negative attention as a result. At the end of 2003/04 he left Liverpool to go to Birmingham City. I certainly liked playing alongside Emile. When he's firing, he's special; and when we fired together it was a really powerful partnership. But Emile's form tended to be in peaks and troughs, and I had the odd injury during our time in the squad together, so I wouldn't call ours a massively successful or consistent combination. But we won a few trophies together and helped each other along the way, and I enjoyed playing with a fellow striker up front, because two versus two defenders is a lot more appealing than one versus two. If you're up there on your own and you get past one centre-half, you've got another one to contend with. The trend now is to have a withdrawn striker playing behind the front man. Generally, though, strikers like to play with a partner, and I'm no exception.

But Emile wasn't the only one to take the slings and arrows. Obviously the homegrown players are more protective of the club's traditions. We feel part of the fabric of the club. Ironically, at a club like Liverpool it's the English lads who take the heat when things aren't going well because there is a closer relationship between them and the fans. The supporters feel they can express themselves more easily to the traditional Liverpool lads. Other players seemed to be exempt from criticism, and that irritated some of the homegrown boys. It's hard to take stick when you're trying your absolute best. We've got the club in our blood.

From a personal point of view, I started the 2003/04 season at the top of the charts. I was flying, playing really well, and there were plenty of goals. On 24 September, against Olimpija Ljubljana in the UEFA Cup, I overtook the club's European goalscoring record, held by Ian Rush, with my twenty-first in continental competition. For part of Rushie's time as Liverpool's main striker the ban on English clubs in Europe was in place, of course; had that not been the case I'm sure he would have reached an unbeatable total. Still, to be the all-time leading scorer in Europe for Liverpool is quite something, but you have to sit back to appreciate it and I know I won't do that until I've retired. It's on the back burner until I'm 60!

So far so good, but then a freak accident wrecked the last few months of 2003 for me. Against Arsenal at Anfield on Saturday, 4 October, I went to challenge for a loose ball down at The Kop end, managed to block Ashley Cole's clearance, but then felt my standing leg slip and turn in a single movement. I felt something go, something pop. Being stupid, I convinced myself it was nothing and tried to run it off. I hobbled around for another 10 minutes, but it wasn't getting any better. I knew I had to come off. On the X-rays, thankfully, there was no crack. In fact there was no damage bone-wise, but the following day the injury blew up. There was terrible swelling and lots of funny colours. We knew there was something wrong, but it didn't seem to make medical sense that I was pointing to those particular areas.

The Turkey–England game was coming up fast. I had seven days to recover. As there was no obvious structural damage, I joined up with the squad hoping that in a few days it might settle down. But it was quite evident after two or three days – the key stage after an injury – that I couldn't even walk without still feeling pain. So the England medical staff sent me back to Liverpool where I had a variety of tests and saw several specialists. Nobody had seen anything quite like it.

When I'd first walked in to the treatment room on the day of the Arsenal game, they'd assumed I'd broken my leg or damaged my cruciate knee ligament. It looked awful on TV and felt atrocious, too. It wasn't an ankle injury, I was feeling it in my shin, but there must have been bleeding that affected parts of my ankle. It was hard to pin down. We had seen, on the scans, that a lining along my shin bone had split apart. When we did some research we discovered that there were only a handful of cases of that ever happening. The research suggested that with this kind of injury the bone always breaks after the lining has split; mine must have split open, ready for the bone to break, but then not taken the final step. On the replay, you can see me jump and lift my leg at the last moment – maybe just before the bone gave way. In a way, I suppose, I was fortunate.

Missing the Turkey game in Istanbul hurt me a lot. It was one of those games you just have to play in. Everyone was talking about the atmosphere and the rivalry between the two countries. Those are the international games I love:

big stakes, hostile environment, huge adrenalin. But I had no chance of taking part. Still, maybe that was a good thing. If I'd been half fit, I would have been so desperate to play that I'd have been knocking on the manager's door telling him I was OK. If you're injured, you might as well be injured properly so there's no temptation to talk your way into the team. As it turned out, we drew 0–0 to finish top of our Euro 2004 qualifying group.

We didn't know what treatment I should be having and we weren't sure about the timescale. I was just starting to come back to feeling sound again, with the swelling gone, when the manager asked me whether I could battle through and play against Leeds on 25 October – just 21 days after the accident. Everyone knew I wasn't match fit because I hadn't trained properly for weeks, but results hadn't been going well so the manager wanted to throw me in. I played and I scored, but I wasn't really on the pitch in the true sense. I was there in body but not contributing much. I played in the following game against Fulham, too, and it flared up again. So we gave it more time, and eventually it healed.

The international get-together prior to Turkey–England will be remembered for the so-called mutiny over Rio Ferdinand's suspension by the Football Association for missing a drugs test, at Carrington, the club's training ground. We first heard about Rio's problem from the Manchester United players when we met them at Manchester airport to fly down. The Liverpool, Everton and United players were all there – about ten of us – and it was then that we were filled in on the story. *This could be a problem.* That was my initial response, but I never imagined it was about to start such a major row.

It soon became evident that a huge political issue had erupted. Rio was looking at a long international ban and would not be lining up against Turkey. At Sopwell House, the England team hotel, we began debating what we should do. At no time did we say 'We will not play'; we just wanted Rio in the team. I wasn't going to fly to Istanbul anyway, but I felt strongly enough to take part in the discussions organized by the players' committee, who had sounded out the rest of the squad. The whole group was unanimous: if we were going to fight Rio's ban, we had to fight it together. We issued a statement, which read: 'It is our opinion that the organization we represent has not only let down one of our team-mates but the whole of the England squad and its manager. We feel they have failed us very badly.' We argued that the FA's actions had 'made the team weaker' for a vital match.

Yes, we took up a strong position to help a mate, but that's all it was. It wasn't about money or anything else. Our intentions were honourable. We saw a friend, a family member, in distress and wanted to help. We didn't feel disloyal and we didn't mean to offend England fans. We wanted him to play, and we didn't accept that at that point he'd been proved guilty of anything. Yes, he had been foolish to miss a drugs test, but we didn't accept that he should be punished before he had been given a chance to defend himself at a formal hearing. Rules are there to be obeyed, clearly. If Rio was shown to be guilty, we all knew he was going to be punished. But there hadn't been a trial and there hadn't been a verdict. In athletics, and in other sports, he would have faced a hearing before starting his suspension. There is a tradition in this country that a person is innocent until proved guilty, but in this case that didn't seem to apply.

So the players felt aggrieved. Not for one second, though, did they consider pulling out of the game. I hope people won't blame us for standing by a friend. It's one of my beliefs in life that you always stick by your mates. I can understand people saying, 'You cheeky buggers, you're privileged to play for your country,' but I would stress that we were never going to turn our backs on England. In fact, the events before the Turkey game brought us closer together. As ever, the manager was spot on in every respect. He couldn't do anything to help Rio because the issue had been taken out of his hands. He let us know that. Given the choice, he would have wanted Rio to play. Eriksson was great with us all the way through.

With that drama out of the way, and England through to Portugal the following summer, I worked to get fit. In the League, Liverpool were already in trouble. It was a gradual slide. You lose a game and you think, *It's slipping away.* You lose another and you think, *This is getting hard, now.* There isn't the sudden smack in the mouth you get when you go out of a cup competition. Arsenal, Chelsea and Manchester United were playing well and we weren't picking up points. The Premiership was turning into a three-horse race.

As the winter months passed our focus began to change: the priorities became to finish in the top four, qualify for the Champions League and maybe win a cup. But by the end of February 2004 we'd bombed out in the domestic competitions, at the hands of Bolton in the League Cup and Portsmouth in the FA Cup, and for the last couple of months of the season after yet another exit from a cup competition, the UEFA Cup, our only target was next season's Champions League. While we felt relieved to finish fourth, we didn't just forget the previous seven months. We knew we had failed.

As the mood darkened, I did look with envy at the leading teams. *If I was in this or that team, I'd fancy my chances of getting X number of goals.* But that's true of all professional footballers. They make comparisons. I dread to think what it must be like for a striker who plays in the lower half of the Premiership. He must think, 'Well, if I played for Manchester United, they're all tap-ins!' When we weren't playing well and not creating anything, and people were accusing me of not performing, I wasn't getting much of a kick half the time. Not that I would look at Thierry Henry and think I would be doing exactly the same as him if I was playing for Arsenal. Thierry's on a different planet.

As my confidence dipped, I ran into problems with my penalty taking. Around the time of our FA Cup defeat at Portsmouth on 22 February, everyone seemed to be talking about my run of misses. As a striker I've always wanted to take the pens. In theory it's an ideal opportunity to add five or six to your total for the year. We're all selfish gits that way. But I should make an important distinction here: there's a difference between being confident and being mentally strong. While I'm always confident, deep down, on the edge of that, there's a margin where my day-to-day self-belief can be affected by events. When I'm not getting chances and scoring goals, I admit I'm capable of getting frustrated with myself, the team, the fans, with everything.

Nothing's perfect when things aren't going well, and I was going through a patch when I wasn't scoring regularly and chances were at a premium. At that point, I suppose, you would have diagnosed low confidence. I would step up for a penalty not feeling it would go in. I just wasn't in that mode of believing it would end up in the net. In practice, the manager would say, 'Stay behind and take ten penalties.' Every one would go in. Even with the keeper trying his hardest, I could put every one on a postage stamp. But when it came to a game it felt totally different. Again, it was down to a lack of confidence because I wasn't getting chances and I wasn't scoring goals. I could no longer sense what it was like to hit the back of the net. Consequently I missed a couple of penalties on the bounce, though I had scored the first four of the season. People forget that when you miss two on the spin. It was open season on me. But that's OK, it happens to everyone over a career. Steven Gerrard took the next one and missed. Emile Heskey took one and missed. El-Hadji Diouf took one and missed. I remember Ruud Van Nistelrooy missing two in a row. Then, the best penalty taker of them all, Alan Shearer, missed one from the spot. Nowadays you'll see more penalties being saved than ever before, because the rules favour the keeper.

I admit that I felt low, fed up. I'm a normal person. If I'm going to work and it's not stimulating me as much as usual, I can get into moods. Or, rather, I can have mood swings: happy some days, sad on others. I went through patches during the 2003/04 season I hadn't been through before. I was frustrated, I wasn't getting chances. I was taking all the blame in every newspaper column or on every TV show, despite the fact that I had missed half the season with an injury. That's how it felt.

I was getting about three kicks per game. In some games I was letting my shoulders sag a little – but that's only because I'm human and because I want to do so well for the team. I know I have to rise above it, and I do. Even Tony, my agent, said, 'You don't look happy. Try to play with more of a smile on your face.' Some players might be able to kid the fans, but if I'm not happy you'll be able to see it a mile away. Equally, when I'm firing on all cylinders you'll see that too. I can't kid people.

After my run of penalty misses, Houllier still wanted me to take them. But if I'm honest, I just spat my dummy out. I couldn't be bothered with the hassle I was getting. If I had

missed another one it would have led to more critical comment about the club and the team, which wouldn't have
helped the manager or the players. I hadn't scored for three
or four games, and maybe I was having a bit of a sulk inside.
Though I would have taken a pen in the next match without
hesitating, I just thought, 'I'll leave it to Stevie Gerrard to
take the next one.' Then, once Stevie had missed, Danny
Murphy took over.

Stevie's emergence as Liverpool captain took some of the
weight of expectation off me. He is the biggest hero on The
Kop these days. If I played five good games in a row they
would have probably sung my name first, but Stevie played
really well last season and was the player of the year by
an absolute mile. His game has really improved. It wasn't
so long ago that he was getting dragged off at half-time,
and everyone was saying, 'What's happened to our young
English star?' What a difference a few months have made.
A season ago he was getting grunts from the crowd every
time he gave the ball away; now he's playing so well nobody
says a bad word about him.

Having been handed the captaincy by the manager, Stevie
also became the spokesman, if you like, for Gérard Houllier.
He was the one who had to defend the manager when share-
holders and fans were having a go at him, as they were for
much of the season. The truth was that we had players who
weren't performing well enough, and the manager shielded
a lot of us when we didn't deserve to be protected. Gérard
bore the brunt of all the frustration building up around
Anfield. He was laughed at for some of the things he said in
defence of the team. But he said those things to protect the
players and we should be thankful to him for that.

Towards the end of the season, in the second week of
April, there was a big showdown meeting between the

manager and the players at which Gérard said we needed to do an awful lot better in the final few games. We'd just surrendered a 2–1 lead at Arsenal with some amateur defending – amateur play, all round. After our 4–2 defeat that day, suddenly fourth place was no longer in our hands. The turnaround was going to Old Trafford on 24 April and beating Manchester United in their own back yard. That had a huge effect on our confidence. Having beaten United away, you're bound to feel good about facing Middlesbrough at home the following week. We won that one 2–0 and then beat Birmingham 3–0 away on 8 May. After the United game, there was just a new air about us – and it helped, of course, that Newcastle, who were also contesting fourth place, hit a run of bad results.

When things are going wrong with a club, you see endless newspaper columns examining the reasons. There is no success to write about so the whole focus falls on individuals – whether they're fit, whether they're performing properly, whether they're staying or going. I entered the 2003/04 season with two years left on my Liverpool deal. By the summer I would be 12 months away from being out of contract, so inevitably there was constant chatter about whether I would be staying at Anfield after the summer of 2005. The rumour mill starts like this: a report appears saying 'Michael Owen still hasn't signed a new contract'; then everybody gets it into their heads that there's some kind of delay and the issue gets analysed endlessly, even if the negotiations haven't even started. Partly because the team was performing so badly, the speculation started incredibly early in the campaign. Liverpool came to me around Christmas and said, 'We'd like to talk to you about your new contract,' but we didn't have our first meeting until April. So I had five months of people having a go at me, calling me disloyal or saying I was waiting to see if we made it into the Champions League. Lots of silly things like that.

By the end of the season it seemed as if I had been 'holding out' for an eternity, but it was only because the speculation started way before we actually sat down for our first set of talks. Prior to our last game of the season, against Newcastle on 15 May, we had just the one get-together, and our second was straight after the season ended. I didn't point out any of this at the time because it's advisable not to stoke the fires. If I had said, 'I've only had one meeting,' it might have looked bad on Liverpool's part for not dealing with it earlier, or bad on my part for not getting it sorted out. I was having to take it all on the chin and not respond. We had already decided among ourselves that we were going to deal with the issue properly in the summer. I had to bite my lip and take an awful lot of abuse. We were never in any rush, and Liverpool always knew I wouldn't walk out on them on a Bosman free transfer in 2005. I shook the manager's hand and assured him that we wouldn't drag it out, that we would get something resolved in the summer, and everyone was happy with that.

The other point is that Tony Stephens, my agent, had taken a sabbatical and wasn't around until April anyway. After many years of rushing around the world with SFX, he wanted to spend more time with his wife and catch up with his baby grand-daughter. Without Tony I was in no position to enter detailed negotiations. So both sides were happy with the agreement to wait until May or June.

Never once did I walk into Anfield and say, 'Either we reach the Champions League or I'm off,' or demand that they buy such and such a player, or else. Ridiculous. The manager makes the personnel decisions and the chairman gives him the money to spend. That's nothing to do with me.

I just play. Obviously I felt we needed to strengthen, because finishing 30 points behind the champions Arsenal was an enormous gap. But I would never make threats or put pressure on the people responsible for those decisions. It's not my style.

Naturally I don't appreciate being accused of disloyalty. It didn't sit too well when I picked up the tone in the local papers or heard fans questioning my commitment on radio phone-ins. *If that's what everybody thinks, then sod it. What more do I have to do to show my loyalty to Liverpool Football Club?* But then you come to your senses. *Well, it's only one moron out of how many millions of people who support the team?*

It's an amazing feature of modern football that people have so many platforms on which to express their opinions about you or the club: phone-ins, fanzines, letters columns and so on. They can give you a distorted view of what the fans are thinking. If you see one critical letter about you, you start questioning yourself. *Is everyone saying this about me?* It can damage the bond you have with them. I don't mind if someone calls me a rubbish player or says I haven't done this or I haven't done that. But the word 'loyalty' really sets me off. I am as loyal as they come. For example, at the end of the season I renewed my deal with Umbro, who I've been with all along, signing for another 15 years (well into my retirement). The money didn't come into it. I just like the people. And if I like the people, I want to work with them. I'm straightforward like that. I'm a loyal lad who wants to be successful. When people do question me as a human being or doubt my loyalty, it hits below the belt.

When the season finally ended, of course, a takeover battle began. On one side was Steve Morgan – who, by coincidence, built the houses in the street so many of my family members occupy – and on the other was Thaksin Shinawatra, the Prime Minister of Thailand. I don't suppose any club is going to be as lucky as Chelsea, who found themselves being bought by Roman Abramovich, a Russian billionaire with many millions to invest. Every major club is probably on the look-out for that now; they all want a bit of that kind of investment. Liverpool are fortunate to have a massive fan base around the world, which makes them an attractive club to put money into. And that's what was needed. I can't believe that any club would turn that down. Whatever money they get, they need to spend it on things that improve the team, because they've already got great facilities, a wonderful youth system and a new stadium on the way. Liverpool need a top-class team to front it all. They already have some world-class players, so the basis is there; they just need a few more to lift them from fourth to second or first.

On the international front, as Euro 2004 approached, Sven-Goran Eriksson's well-publicized April meeting with Peter Kenyon, the Chelsea chief executive, didn't bother me in the least. From where I was standing it certainly didn't have any effect on the morale of the squad either. Ten years ago, when there weren't so many photographers and journalists, those meetings were probably going on all the time, it's just that we didn't know they were taking place. Now everyone's scared to talk on a mobile phone in case someone takes a picture of them and reads something into it. I don't think anyone in football is naive enough to be shocked by the discovery that the England manager may have had a chat with Chelsea about a job.

As players, we never thought for a second that he wasn't going to lead us to Portugal. Besides, after international tournaments there's always a question about whether the manager is going to be around for the next one, which is two years away. I know myself that if I was an international manager, knowing that it would be two years before I saw really serious action again, I'd be twiddling my thumbs, wondering whether I should go back into club management. Everyone has a right to protect his own interests and position. In football, people are quick enough to have a go at you if results turn against you. Eriksson spoke to Chelsea knowing that a couple of bad results at Euro 2004 would have some people calling for him to be sacked. We're always quick to chop an England manager's head off, so he has to look after himself. When you're a fantastic manager – as he is – why not be in the frame for the best jobs going? If a journalist is offered a job on the best paper in the world then he's going to go – for money, or prestige, or whatever it is. Just because it's football, this big word 'loyalty' comes into play. Eriksson had already shown loyalty to the England job. He had been doing it for more than three years when he listened to whatever Peter Kenyon had to say. If he had accepted another job, starting after Euro 2004, I would have said, 'Good luck to you, you've earned it.'

Because of all the problems at Liverpool, as well as Mike Flynn's suicide and Louise's accident, a lot of people automatically assumed that 2003/04 was the worst season of my life. But I didn't remotely think of it as a hellish year. Mike Flynn's death was a tragedy, plainly, and Louise's fall was deeply upsetting for us all, but otherwise I've developed the capacity to work through problems. I was injured a lot, yet I still scored 18 goals, which amounts to one every other game. Even if I'd had a nightmare season I would never, ever look for excuses. The basic facts are that I had a freak accident, against Arsenal, and the team was not performing at its best. Anything that happens off the pitch has no relevance. When the ball is knocked six inches off the centre circle for that kick-off, I wouldn't register the world's worst disaster.

You hear so many excuses. 'We've had a new baby and I haven't been getting any sleep' is one that springs to mind. But there were no excuses for what happened to us at Liverpool in 2003/04. Sadly, it was Gérard Houllier who ended up paying the price.

23

Euro 2004

I can't pretend that the 351 minutes I played at Euro 2004 were the most fulfilling of my international career, but I will defend myself against the suggestion that there was something bothering me during our four matches in Portugal, or that my relatively quiet start to the tournament was down to a lack of form.

The way our team was set up, I had to perform an unselfish role, providing the forward point of our attack, but I grew more comfortable in that position as the competition wore on and had the minor consolation of a goal against Portugal to set against the agony of another penalty shoot-out defeat. There is something else I ought to say at the outset. If we defended too much against France and Portugal in the two big games we lost, it wasn't the manager's fault. Sven-Goran Eriksson had urged us to stay on the front foot and keep chasing goals. But we, the players, fell back into a defensive state of mind. If people need to blame someone, they should blame us.

It seems incredible that I've played in four international tournaments and scored in them all. Incredible, also, that England have been knocked out of two World Cups and two European Championships since 1990 by way of penalty

Still my greatest moment in football. Jamie Carragher, Gary McAllister and I celebrate Liverpool's 2001 FA Cup final victory over Arsenal.

The Liverpool team bus parts an ocean of happy fans. I'm desperate to see more trophies at Anfield.

Steven Gerrard and I have come up through the ranks and share a special bond. Here we are celebrating the 2003 Worthington Cup win.

Almost as big as me, the UEFA Cup was our last piece of silverware in the epic Treble-winning season of 2000/01.

Germany 1, England 5. It was only a qualifier, but who will ever forget it? Here I beat the German defender Christian Worns for the first of my three.

My second, and a touch of Alan Shearer in the goal celebration.

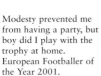

Modesty prevented me from having a party, but boy did I play with the trophy at home. European Footballer of the Year 2001.

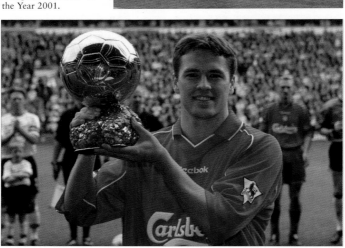

A goal against Denmark at the 2002 World Cup, followed by an injury crisis. Would I be fit to face Brazil? Only after going through hell.

One-on-One. I love a sprinting competition. Here, I'm in a duel with Argentina's Diego Placente.

Sven-Goran Eriksson and Tord Grip, his assistant, encourage senior England players to express their views.

An opportunistic goal against Brazil in the 2002 World Cup quarter-finals. A moment of promise, followed by crushing disappointment.

Signing off for summer. Two goals for me, as England captain, in a 2–1 win over Slovakia on 11 June 2003.

Roy Keane must love this picture. The Manchester United captain is flat out while I race through to score in the 2003 Worthington Cup final.

A headed goal in World Cup qualifying against Liechtenstein in March 2003. I've worked hard on my heading over the past six years.

Young and younger. I thought I had a meteoric start – until Wayne Rooney came on the scene! Here we celebrate an England goal.

A goal at last. Euro 2004, and my first of the tournament, in the quarter-final against Portugal. Look how high I jump.

It was a complicated swivel manoeuvre, but I found the net after a mistake by Costinha.

With blisters and cramp, I hobble back to the half-way line, where my England team-mates look less than ecstatic! The hell of another penalty shoot-out defeat was about to swallow us up.

Baby Gemma with one of our beloved dogs. They make good pillows.

A father at 23 (*main*). A night out with brothers Terry and Andy (*top inset*), and a family of horse lovers. The Owens queue up for a pat, with Louise holding the reins (*bottom inset*).

Louise and I settled well into our new Madrid environment.

Real Madrid were the only club I would have left Liverpool to join. Sixteen goals in 45 appearances, 26 of them starts. Not bad for a supposedly 'bit-part player', then.

Joining Newcastle meant pairing up with
Alan Shearer, one of the legends in the game.
I even saw the inside of his house for ten days!

A pain in the metatarsal. I spent
plenty of time in the gym doing rehab
as the World Cup clock ticked down.

I missed this one during England's thrilling
win against Argentina leading up to the
2006 World Cup Finals – but I bagged the
crucial winner, from a header of all things.

shoot-outs. They just won't go our way. But I won't entertain the idea that we are carrying some kind of curse. I have faith in our team and our players, and I know we'll be one of the leading contenders at the 2006 World Cup.

When the 2003/04 Premiership season ended, we had a week away together in Sardinia, and then it was off to Manchester for the Summer Tournament, a triangular competition involving us, Iceland and Japan. This was the formula the manager had adopted two years earlier, before the Japan–South Korea World Cup. Both times we worked really hard in those two weeks. Sardinia and Manchester were Dubai revisited. The fitness work calmed down only on the Wednesday before the match against France. So we arrived in Portugal toughened by a fortnight of hard labour.

The Sardinia trip was the first overseas adventure Gemma has any chance of remembering. She came to La Manga on a short England trip once but was only a couple of weeks old at the time; she'd also been on a couple of flights to London, but Sardinia was her first major expedition. We stayed in a lovely hotel but the weather was awful for the first five days. Everyone was locked up in their rooms, which was much tougher on the wives and girlfriends. At least the players had the distraction of training. Gemma was great. You'd think a child would get bored being stuck in a hotel room all day but she always found things to do. For the last couple of days the sun finally broke through and the mood lifted as everyone converged on the pool.

Our first prep game, at the City of Manchester Stadium on 1 June, was against Japan, and I carried my good late-season form into a match we drew 1–1. For my goal, in the twenty-fifth minute, Stevie Gerrard made a terrific run and let rip with a powerful shot that bounced off their goalkeeper. If you really strike the modern football it just flies everywhere, and as soon as I saw the pace of Stevie's shot I knew it was going to run loose. It was just a case of working out where it would land. It was my dad's type of goal. In his own playing days he would always follow the ball in for the rebound. Funnily enough I hadn't had one of those tap-ins all season, and was starting to wonder whether it was sensible to keep burning energy following up shots. But if you keep doing it you get your reward. I stayed on for 77 minutes before giving way to Darius Vassell. In the players' lounge afterwards my dad gave me a knowing look, as if to say, 'That was a striker's goal – the sort I taught you.'

We played particularly well in the Iceland game four days later, when Wayne Rooney captured the public imagination with two goals in a 6–1 win. By now Wayne was really bubbling, but few inside the camp could have predicted the things he would do in Portugal. I scored a good goal too, but it was ruled offside (linesmen – the scourge of my life). We had already done our hard physical work against Japan, so everyone bar Jamie Carragher stayed on for just one half. When you change virtually the whole team at half-time the performance usually drops off a bit, but this time it picked up.

By this stage Frank Lampard had established his place in midfield at the expense of Nicky Butt. Our problem was that we had lots of talented midfielders, none of whom was naturally left-sided, so the manager was trying to fit four top-class midfielders into three positions and work out which one was going to have to play on the left. Against Japan we used a midfield diamond, with David Beckham on the right, Paul Scholes at the front, Frank Lampard in the holding position and Stevie Gerrard to the left. But the flat midfield four we switched back to against Iceland worked particularly well, so we stuck with that formation from then on.

Our team hotel for the tournament, near Lisbon, was first-class, with a games room and TV lounge where we sat and watched the other games. But there was a downside. At previous tournaments we'd all been on one floor, which helped to create a team atmosphere; in Lisbon we were spread across two levels, with two long corridors per floor, so people were less inclined to wander between rooms. You couldn't feel much of an atmosphere when you were in yours. Still, once we went downstairs the camaraderie was really good.

The new element for me, of course, was being away from Gemma on a tour for the first time. Our daughter had just started speaking on the phone, which was a real lifeline. Obviously she didn't understand a lot of what I said, but by then she knew a dozen or so things to say to me. She would shout 'dada' or 'bye-bye' down the phone without getting upset when the conversation had to end. Missing your child certainly makes it harder to be away from home, especially in those moments when the phone goes dead and her voice is still there in your head. The child doesn't think of it that way, of course. She runs off and plays. As I said, Gemma never cried when our conversations came to a halt. As soon as I sensed her getting bored listening to me I would say 'Go and stroke Poppy' or 'Go and stroke Tank' – our two dogs. Louise told me that Gemma would put the phone down and wander straight off to stroke the dogs.

The France game on 13 June felt like an epic showdown, though it was only our opening game in Group B. There was no screaming or wall-punching in the dressing room, but you could tell everyone fancied playing against the French. The only change to our settled line-up was Ledley King coming in for John Terry, who had a hamstring injury. Of course, Frank Lampard headed us into the lead, and we defended that advantage for the next 52 minutes before Zinedine Zidane twice kicked us in the teeth.

This was the game for which I attracted the most hefty criticism, after being replaced, in the sixty-ninth minute, by Darius Vassell. The way the game panned out just didn't suit me. I just didn't get to show what I can do. France were the former world and current European champions, so our starting point was that they had a lot of dangerous forward players we were going to have to stop. We felt we would probably need to keep a clean sheet to win the game. We certainly weren't expecting to score three or four goals against them, so the hope was that we might nick one – perhaps from a set-piece, which is how it turned out. Tactically, we set out to smother their best players. It was just a pity that we made a few mistakes at the end of the game to give Zidane his chances.

I was playing more of an unselfish role for the team. Sometimes you have to do that. My job was to keep the length of the team – that is, provide a forward point. That way I would keep the French defenders wary and pinned back in their own half. People will always notice you having a quiet game, but they might not be so quick to analyse the reasons why.

I was standing right next to Frank when he scored from David Beckham's free-kick. As we were running off to celebrate, Wayne Rooney said to me, 'Blimey, I thought you'd scored that.' Frank had made contact with his head a yard in front of me, and the next thing I saw was the ball nestling in the top corner. God, that was exciting.

There was no great rethink by the manager at half-time because everything was going so well. We were leading 1–0 and defending efficiently. I couldn't remember Jame-o having to make a single save. Wayne and I were continually dropping back on to their central midfielders, which consumes a lot of energy and makes it harder to launch your own attacks. But against a team like France you have to help out defensively or they'll overrun you. You can't leave your own midfielders to cope with theirs on their own. But a couple of mistakes and two French goals in injury time undid all the good work.

When I saw that Darius was coming on, I knew it had to be me coming off, because Wayne was having a lot of joy. People tend to forget that I had a hand in him playing really well. I was stretching France as far as I could, which meant that their defenders couldn't advance to the halfway line and start pressing us from there. Yes, I was disappointed to come off, but only really because I hate being substituted. Hate it.

Strikers have a different view on these things. As a group, we would point out that Thierry Henry did very little against us but still made the run that won them the penalty. Equally, Ruud Van Nistelrooy struggled against Germany two nights later but was left on the pitch to score the equalizer. In the 2001 FA Cup final, of course, I scored two goals in the last seven minutes. I suppose, though, you could argue that it's different when you're 1–0 down. I totally understand why Eriksson took me off. He was trying to protect a lead, but on the personal level it didn't stop me being disappointed.

Our defeat came about in an astonishing sequence of events. We're 1–0 up, Wayne gets brought down by Mikael Silvestre in the penalty area and the ref reaches into his pocket – maybe for a red card? *They're about to go down to 10 men and we're about to go 2–0 up*. But Silvestre stays on and David Beckham has his penalty saved. We continue to defend really well, but then comes a free-kick, following a tackle by Emile Heskey on Claude Makelele, and Zidane advances to curl the ball into our net. *Shit. One-one, with 91 minutes on the clock*. Almost immediately after that Stevie plays a short back-pass, Jame-o rushes out, takes Thierry Henry at the knees and it's a penalty. Zidane again. And it wasn't as if they'd been bombarding us. We were heading for quite a cosy win and everyone was buzzing on the bench. Then, all of a sudden, we'd lost the game 2–1. Astonishment. *Hell, we might be out of this tournament now*. But the message from the coaching staff was, 'Get it out of your system.' After 24 hours I was once again certain we were going to qualify from the group.

A word about Zidane and his two cracking goals. Standing close to him, you never know which way he's going to go, you're scared to commit yourself, his feet are just lightning quick and he's as strong as an ox. Your inclination is to just stand a yard away from him in case he makes a mug of you. It's as if he's got the ball on a string. I spoke to Carra on the coach on the way home, and he was saying, 'Zidane had a quiet game until he scored the two goals.' In response, I was explaining what it's like being that close to him and feeling his potential to produce something incredible. Sometimes you come off the pitch and everyone says, 'That guy who's supposed to be brilliant was really crap today,' but you just know he's got it in him to be special. This was one of those cases. Zidane might not have shone for the first 90 minutes, but if you're standing close to him it's a different kettle of fish. He looks like he's got ice in his veins. Look in his eyes, and that will tell you everything about him as a player.

The England players were and are full of respect for him, and not just for his skills because he's not one of those who starts shouting his mouth off or running to the crowd to celebrate. As we walked in after the final whistle, I looked up and saw Zidane striding straight to the dressing room while the rest of the French players were dancing around on the pitch. Fair play to them, they had won the game in the most dramatic circumstances, but I couldn't help noticing the contrast with Zidane, who just headed straight for the tunnel. He's an unbelievable player, but what we respected most about him was that he wasn't rubbing our faces in it, unlike some. There's no messing with Zidane. He doesn't need to tell anyone he's brilliant. He just is.

The loud singing in the French dressing room didn't bother me. I suspect that we would have been singing too had we won the game. As we sat down, someone said, 'Shut the door!' but then several others insisted, 'No, let's leave it open and hear them singing, just in case we play them again in the final. We'll all remember it.' We weren't saying they should have stopped singing, we just wanted to use it to our benefit further down the line. We would have been silly not to. So the door stayed open.

The squad was soon confident again and totally relaxed. For 20 minutes after the France game we were shell-shocked, struck by the thought that we'd have to win two games to survive. But our self-assurance soon returned. We just fancied our chances. Big time. We watched the other games and began to feel that France and England were the best two teams in the competition. Didi Hamann, my Liverpool team-mate who was in Portugal playing for Germany, left a message saying, 'Bloody hell, I didn't know England were that good. I've watched you in friendlies but I didn't realize you were so well organized. The German players watched it together and everyone in our team was impressed with you.' Didi's a close mate so he could have got away with taking the mickey, but he went the other way. He was just very complimentary.

Eriksson didn't say anything specific to reassure me after the France game. He didn't take me to one side to tell me my place was safe. The current manager picks the team early before games, which is reassuring for those who aren't sure they're going to make the cut. It settles your mind to see the team for the next game being played together in training. Not that I thought I was about to be dropped.

Though there was no special discussion with the England coach after the France match, I did take part in an important conversation with another senior manager who paid a special visit to our hotel. Rafael Benitez, the new Liverpool boss, arranged a pass from the FA to see the three Anfield men – me, Stevie Gerrard and Jamie Carragher – as well as Sammy Lee, who doubled up as a Liverpool and England coach. He told us his plans for next season, how he operated and what he expected out of training. He wasn't sure who would be in his coaching staff, but he did say that Sammy would be staying while also promising to bring in his own people. Phil Thompson, Gérard Houllier's assistant, had already left the club.

Benitez also said that he wanted Stevie and me to stay and be part of the rebuilding process. At the time every single newspaper was speculating about Stevie moving to Chelsea, so that was the new manager's main focus. Though he also addressed my situation, I got the impression he felt Stevie's possible move to Chelsea was a more urgent issue. He made it clear that he felt he could move Liverpool up the table to a position where we would be challenging for the title.

Benitez stayed for around an hour and a half. Sammy was involved at the start of the discussion but then the manager asked him to leave so we could carry on the conversation for the last hour. I imagine Benitez was worried about us feeling uncomfortable talking about the club's training methods and so on in front of Sammy. He didn't keep telling us how good we were, as some new managers might, and he was obviously confident in his ability to turn things round. We'd already studied his track record in Spain and noticed that he had won a lot of trophies while spending hardly any money. That guaranteed him instant respect from the whole football world. The Spanish league, after all, is a hard one to win. Yes, he wanted us to stay, but the emphasis was on the team and how he would develop it. He said he believed in thorough training methods and a good team ethic; he certainly didn't say 'You're the best players in the world and if you stay we can win the League.' His point was that we could all improve as players and that he would help us achieve that aim.

Talking of preparation, there were a few innovations from the England medical and back-up staff. One was ice baths after training sessions and matches. The idea was to jump in one for five minutes (alternating with ordinary baths) to bring the body temperature right down. Some of the players were suffering with blisters and obviously the ice cooled those. I didn't use them religiously after training, but on the warm-down days after games I did my five minutes.

I managed a couple of trips out of the camp to clear my head. Even though the security is tight round England these days, the manager was very relaxed about our families coming in to see us, or us leaving the hotel to see them. As long as you let the security people know where you're going, he's fine. In that sense Portugal was different to every other championship I've known. Getting out of the camp is especially beneficial if you're in a bad mood. To see Gemma and Louise gave me a great boost. My mum and dad, and brothers and sisters at different times, were staying in Cascais Marina, just west of Lisbon, on a boat that belonged to Steve Smith, a family friend. One Saturday I made it down there for a barbecue with Louise and Gemma and some friends. We had an excellent time.

The build-up to the Switzerland game – our second – on 17 June featured a tactical debate that was described in some quarters as a 'player revolt', which it wasn't. The manager, of course, had used the midfield diamond formation for the friendly against Japan, but not against Iceland or France. Switzerland played with Hakan Yakin, their number 10, just in front of their midfield, behind the strikers, so we trained for the Swiss game with the diamond in place to see how it might keep Yakin under control.

When we finished the final training session and walked back into the hotel, Steve McClaren, the manager's assistant, was sitting waiting for us, looking slightly concerned. Steve called five or six of the senior players over and said, 'Everyone looked a bit flat in training today. Was it the long trip up in the coach, or is it because we've just lost to France?' We were at a loss for an explanation. Yes, we were disappointed with the result against France, but nobody had a burning issue they wanted to air. Our mood was pretty good. 'What about training. Is everybody happy with training?' Steve persisted. 'Yes,' we all said. Gradually we got round to discussing the formation. We had used a flat four-man midfield against France, and one of the lads remarked on how pleased we were with the way the formation worked. Then someone asked whether the diamond we had used in training that day was the system we were going to be using against the Swiss. The midfielders were only enquiring because they wanted to go to bed knowing what to expect in the game. Steve simply said that the manager wanted to keep both options open. That evening we came down to dinner and learned that the manager had held a meeting with the four midfield players. They'd discussed the two options and Eriksson had made his decision. The following day we played a flat midfield four. The manager has always been open-minded about that sort of thing. It certainly wasn't a mutiny by those players, as some assumed.

In the game itself, in Coimbra, a two-and-a-half-hour drive north of Lisbon, I set up the first goal by chipping a pass from David on to Wayne Rooney's head, but was later substituted again, this time after 71 minutes. With 65 minutes gone I looked up and saw Darius Vassell stripped and ready for action on the touchline. That's always a strange feeling, because you go from concentrating intensely on the game to wondering whether you're about to come off. You think, *Is it me or is it my strike partner?* For a moment, your concentration is broken. If you've been replaced once already in a tournament, there's a little memory of it lodged in the brain. I wouldn't compare it to Euro 2000, where I ended up a nervous wreck, but if you're not performing 100 per cent and you're not playing the full 90 minutes it will start to affect you in the end. Against Switzerland, whom we beat 3–0, I was a bit more involved than against France, but I still wasn't playing the way I knew I could.

Our first was an important goal, and I was pleased to have crossed the ball for Wayne to head in. Setting up a goal is the second best feeling, though it's not a patch on getting one yourself. My main job is to score, and I came off the pitch without a goal again, frustrated. But I was happy for Wayne, who I got to know properly for the first time as the trip wore on. There are no cliques with Eriksson's England. Although there are groups of players from clubs with bitter rivalries, everyone mixes really well. Wayne felt especially comfortable with the Liverpool players. He turned out to be a really good lad – very funny, without always realizing he was being amusing. He's hilarious without even trying to be.

With three points on the board, we moved on a few days later to the Croatia game, with people and pundits asking out loud whether there was something 'troubling me'. The search was on for an explanation as to why I hadn't scored.

Let's get it right. Strikers depend on service. If people didn't see what the problem was in the France game then they certainly could have done against Portugal where I was lively and felt as if I would score every time I got the ball. When England score and then just defend, you see how ineffective I can be. Against Portugal I was firing on all cylinders in the first half, but then we lost our impetus and the Portuguese started retaining the ball and attacking non-stop. As a striker, there's not much you can do in those situations except maybe 'drop off' the most forward position to hunt for the ball and help the team. Against France I did have a quiet game, there's no hiding that. But you can only work with the balls you get. People will say, 'Well, Wayne managed fine,' and he did, but his job was different to mine. Part of my brief was to help 'stretch' the team by providing a forward point to the attack. That helped to create space for Wayne to do his work in behind me. It was up to me to be selfless and give Wayne a little room.

My first real chance in the tournament was the chip I dinked on to the roof of the Croatian net. The ball fell a couple of inches away from the ideal spot so I couldn't quite take it in my stride. I had to take it with my knee in the end, and the break in my step gave the defender half a second to come across and apply pressure. If I'd taken another couple of touches he might have had time to put in a tackle, so I decided to take it early. Close, but not quite there.

Our performance against Croatia was encouraging. We attacked right the way through the game and were dominant throughout, winning 4–2, with two more goals for Wayne. I desperately wanted to break my duck in that game. I've gone two games without a goal plenty of times, but when the stakes are so high people are quicker to ask questions. Three games is even worse. Yet I felt an awful lot better coming off the pitch at the Stadium of Light. I knew I'd played well. I knew I'd had a hand in three of the goals. We were through to the quarter-finals, with six points. I was in a really buoyant mood going back to the hotel.

By now, Roo-mania, as some called it, was in full flow. Wayne was receiving a huge amount of praise and attention both in Portugal and back home. Naturally I was in a good position to assess what was going on around him, because something similar had happened to me after my goal against Argentina at the 1998 World Cup. The difference was that I only started in the last two games in France whereas Wayne had come to Portugal as a member of the first eleven. Right from the start he looked comfortable at that level. When you're in the England team there's nothing more frustrating than seeing a clamour for a player who's not quite good enough to play for his country. You just know when a player isn't going to measure up. You also know that people are usually calling for him to be promoted just because they're bored with the players we've already got. Bored, maybe, with David Beckham, because he's been playing for many years. Bored, perhaps, with Alan Shearer, because he's scored so many goals. 'Let's get the new young blood in!' people cry. It's frustrating when you're an older player. But Wayne was an exception to that. You could see he was a proper footballer. He wasn't being built up out of proportion because he had the talent to support what people were saying about him. Obviously it got a bit out of hand at the end of Euro 2004, when people seized on the point Eriksson had made about his impact being comparable to that of Pele. The fact is, though, that Wayne was there on merit and performing well in every one of our games.

As a kid, there's a natural urge in the blood to just play. It was the same with me at France 98: you don't think of missing, you're not scared, and often you don't even know who you're up against. You watch football live and on TV, but you don't analyse it in the same way. At France 98, I didn't know much about the Argentina players I was taking on; it's only later that I realized I was being marked by Roberto Ayala, one of the best defenders in the world. At 18, you're really not bothered; now I would know who I was up against. It's not that I would be scared, just more aware. You have no fear as a kid. You could see that in Wayne's body language, not just on the pitch but around the hotel, where he would walk around laughing and joking. He is a top, top lad. He mainly hung around with me, Stevie and Carra. He had a great tournament, and he deserved it for being such a good player and a nice lad to boot.

People have asked me since whether I worried about the edge of aggression in Wayne's play, and whether it might get him sent off in an important game. I confess I was a bit concerned before the tournament. Concerned for him, really. I know what it's like to come up against very experienced foreign defenders in huge matches. Some of the tackles he put in during the two warm-up games, particularly the arm he threw during the Japan game, might have got him a red card in the actual tournament, because it's possible that his opponent would have rolled around and exaggerated the force of the blow. But in Portugal everything went to plan. In the France game he had a five-minute red-mist period, but we laughed about it afterwards. You need that bit of aggression in your game.

There's no doubt Wayne has the ability to become a world-class player. To get to that highest level you need consistency – the capacity to keep showing how good you are. As long as he keeps on the straight and narrow his ability will see him through. And his physical abilities are beyond doubt. From now on it's all about the decisions he makes.

The quarter-final against the hosts, Portugal, on 24 June will be remembered as one of those classic English dramas, with the obligatory penalty shoot-out at the end. And it all started so well – not least for me, still chasing my first goal. Jame-o let loose with a long clearance and I could see their defensive midfielder, Costinha, back-pedalling. I couldn't get in front of him to challenge for the header so instead I kept floating just behind, in case he failed to get his head cleanly on the ball. As he retreated I thought, *He's not going to get that. The best he'll do is flick the ball back to the keeper.* It was similar to my goal against Brazil at the World Cup: I took a chance on the flight of the ball. When I noticed that the two defenders beside me weren't advancing, I gambled on Costinha not making proper contact and waited for the ball to bounce in behind. As I ran to meet it, I could have volleyed it with my left foot, but instead I turned full circle and took it with the outside of my right. It just felt natural at the time. In it went. You don't practise things like that. It was just a natural movement. Maybe another striker could have volleyed it coolly with his left foot, but it felt natural to me to pivot round and stroke it with the outside of my boot.

It was a big relief, and an important moment in the game.

To go 1–0 up so early was a cracking start. Having said that, somebody wrote that England need to be drawing or losing early in a game to get the best out of the players. Certainly on each occasion we scored in the tournament I felt we developed a negative mindset, as if we just wanted to keep hold of what we already had. It's like having a baby: you just don't feel safe letting it go. Once you've scored a goal and are defending for your lives, it's hard to knock that caution out of yourselves and open up. Hard to take risks.

Don't forget, we hung on against Argentina at the last World Cup in similar circumstances and everyone said what a great defensive performance it was. Gritty and stubborn. If Argentina had scored, people would have said, 'Why did they defend so much when they were in front?' This time the boot was on the other foot.

After a few days thinking about it, I felt we definitely would have beaten Portugal had we remained positive. If we'd kept going forward I'd have fancied us to score a few. Their defence was really rocked and our midfield players were passing the ball well. It's not that the manager ran on to the touchline and screamed, 'Right, you've got to defend now!' At half-time Eriksson was telling us to get forward in search of another goal. He wanted the defence to squeeze up as far as possible and the midfield to close the opposition down. He was right, but it's evidently harder than it sounds to act on those instructions. When the opposition is pouring forward, it's hard to turn a game around. Maybe if we had kept going from the start Portugal wouldn't have been in such a dominant position. We might have stayed in front.

After Helder Postiga's equalizer, eight minutes from time, I felt the momentum shift and I saw in them the same rush of confidence I'd felt after scoring the equalizer for Liverpool in the 2001 FA Cup final against Arsenal. We'd put so much effort into keeping our lead, so the switch in momentum really hit us hard. A huge frustration from the match, which turned into a national talking point, was Sol Campbell's disallowed goal. I was close to the incident – or non-incident – and have absolutely no doubt that his challenge was legal. Quite simply, it was a goal. As we all rose for the header, John Terry was underneath Sol and I was underneath John Terry. Sol touched John as he climbed for the ball but he didn't touch anyone else – certainly not their goalkeeper, Ricardo. I'd never heard of a foul on your own player before.

As soon as Urs Meier, the Swiss referee, blew the whistle, he was pointing towards the goal to indicate a foul. He didn't look at his linesman and he didn't seem to be in any doubt. I do feel that goalkeepers get too much protection these days. When you jump with a keeper you have to have your arms down by your side, and as soon as there is the slightest contact the referee looks to blow. It's as if the goalkeeper has become separate to the other 10 players in his team – with a kind of special status. I felt especially sorry for Sol. That was the second time he'd scored with his head in a major tournament only to have the referee stop play for a non-existent foul.

At the end of full-time, while we swallowed as much fluid as we could to keep our muscles from seizing up, the manager again stressed the importance of squeezing out as a group and not getting trapped in our own half. His message was to stay positive. We stood in small huddles, urging each other to remain confident. After 90 minutes of hard graft, we would have to begin again.

New drama was packed into those extra 30 minutes: first the shot Rui Costa smashed into the roof of our net and then Frank Lampard's late equaliser. In the last five minutes of extra time I started getting terrible cramp in my calves. When the whistle blew and we found ourselves staring down the barrel of the gun again, I swallowed as much fluid as I could and stretched to loosen the muscle. By now, I had a blister that was turning red raw, so I sat on the pitch and had my foot strapped up. In truth I was a bit of a mess. Had we beaten Portugal that night, I wouldn't have been able to train for a few days. I would have played in the semi-final, but I'd have needed time to let the blisters calm down before throwing myself around in practice.

Penalties. Again. As I lifted my right leg to take my penalty, I felt a spasm of cramp – which is why I scuffed it down the middle. You can see that as I walked back to the halfway line I had to keep stopping to stretch my hamstrings. I had two options: stand there and stretch quickly or lie down and wait for somebody to carry me back, which would have been a bit embarrassing. Until you've had it, you don't know how painful cramp can be.

Everyone who is English knows by now that David and Darius were the two who missed for us. David's standing foot slipped in the loose turf and his spot-kick ballooned over the bar. In training the previous day he had done exactly the same thing: his standing foot had given way in identical circumstances, leaving a massive divot. As I've said before, there's always an inquest into why we've been eliminated from a tournament, and David and the manager took most of the stick this time. Eriksson was criticized for being too negative after we scored. Again I say, in his defence, he was telling us to squeeze out and push up, to get the ball and pass it more – in short, to attack. If the players don't do that, he can't be held responsible. In David's defence, a few of the lads had the same problem with the turf around the penalty spot when we were practising penalties the day before. David must have a heavy impact with his standing foot, because he left a massive divot. Several of us tried to fill the hole before we took our turns. The pitch was quite a mess. The manager had even mentioned it to UEFA the day before. But you won't hear me blaming our defeat on a patch of loose soil.

I can only imagine what the country must be going through when the England players gather round to swig drinks and discuss who's going to take the penalties. People probably think the order is decided beforehand and pinned on the dressing room wall. But the manager has no way of knowing who will be on the pitch by the end of the 120 minutes, so there are always last-minute adjustments.

In a penalty shoot-out, every man looks inside himself to see what he can find. Some won't want to take one. Their great fear is of letting down the team. It's a tough business. No-one really wants to go out there, alone, with the whole country's fate on his shoulders.

I wasn't asked whether I wanted to be one of the initial five. It was just assumed I would take my turn. There was no question of David not going first – despite his miss against France. When the manager came past, as I was having my blisters strapped, I called out: 'What number am I?' I felt confident and calm. Why? Because I'd scored in the game itself. Believe me, that makes a huge difference to a striker. If you have a goal under your belt, it's *Give me that ball and I know I'm going to score*.

But we lost the penalty shoot-out 6–5. I was down. Really down. *It's all over. Another chance gone*. Those were the words inside my head. You could hear the Portuguese players and their crowd singing. Among us: silence and sorrow. After the France game, lots of positive things had been said inside that changing room, but this time there was no escape from the reality that we were out of the competition. Adrian

Bevington, one of the FA's press officers, came in and asked me whether I'd speak to the press. By the time I got back from the interview zone, the manager was telling the other players that we needed a bit of luck in big competitive games. He mentioned the narrow defeats against Brazil, France and now Portugal on penalties. Just that ounce of luck. At the same time, we all accept that's up to us to make sure we win those matches.

Since the tournament ended, a lot of experts have looked at the question of fatigue, and asked whether the top players were exhausted from having played in so many high-intensity club games – especially in the Champions League. When you're running around like mad in the heat, as part of a good team with a chance of winning the tournament, the issue of tiredness doesn't enter your head, and I would certainly never use it as an excuse if I had a quiet game. It's only when you lower yourself on to the sofa at home that you ask: 'How did Greece win Euro 2004?'

A pattern is beginning to develop. France have nose-dived in two consecutive tournaments. A lot of their players play in England. The Spanish and Italian players are Champions League regulars. It's not the number of games that matters so much as the standard – the intensity. With respect to the Greeks, you won't find too many of their players in the later stages of a Champions League campaign. At both the 2002 World Cup and Euro 2004, a lot of the so-called big powers did seem to run out of gas.

As for the England team, it was yet more grief and another early flight home. A few days after I put the key in the door, I was watching Sky Sports News when I saw a bulletin: 'Big announcement at three o'clock at Liverpool'. *What can that be about? We've got a new manager, we've got everything else in place.* I dialled Jamie Carragher's number but couldn't reach him. I called Stevie Gerrard but his phone rang out. So I texted Stevie and asked, 'What's this big announcement at three o'clock? Is it anything to do with you?' His answer was, 'Yeah, we've just had a meeting and I've decided to stay at Liverpool.'

Liverpool fans were thrilled. And as I digested that welcome news, I had no reason to suspect I would soon be boarding a flight to Madrid to become a team-mate of Zidane, who I had admired so much at Euro 2004. To America, yes – for Liverpool's pre-season tour – but to Spain? But then it came: first the serious interest from the world's biggest club, while I was in New York for the Liverpool vs Roma game on 3 August, and then a whirlwind of talks, goodbyes, packed bags and hellos that finished with me joining David Beckham (and later Jonathan Woodgate) at Real Madrid. I felt so proud, and so grateful for my thirteen years at Liverpool. It was time to test myself again. Time to start afresh.

24

Magic of Madrid

Look at the score sheet for the Real Madrid–Barcelona match on 10 April 2005, and you'll see goals from Ronaldo, Ronaldinho, Samuel Eto'o, Zinedine Zidane, Raul . . . and Michael Owen from Chester. With one swing of the boot in a pulsating 4–2 victory over our great rivals, I knew the decision to leave Liverpool for a new challenge in Spain had been justified.

There was lots of other proof, of course, but there was something about that magical night at the Bernabeu that made all the hard work worthwhile. A huge contingent of family and friends had flown over to watch the game and I ended up having to buy 35 tickets to get them all in. I was so happy they weren't coming out to see me sit on the bench. And I was buzzing like crazy after the game; not so much because I scored in an important win, but more because of the nature of the game. It was a stunning contest, with endless attacking and some wonderful goals.

Someone told me later there were over a billion people worldwide watching the two heavyweights clash. It was a great advertisement for the game – and I was part of it, in a three-man strike force, together with Ronaldo and Raul.

To be in the company of all those great goalscorers was

deeply satisfying. The two Real–Barcelona games last season generated the best atmospheres I've played in – though Celtic–Liverpool in the UEFA Cup was right up there with the most intense. For the first 10 minutes of the Real–Barca derby I was just anxious to make some contribution, to be involved. Sure enough, I received the ball in a good position and beat a defender down the line. That got me into my rhythm. My goal came from a superb pass by David Beckham, who had sent the ball into a strong headwind. With a defender breathing down my neck and the goalkeeper rushing out, I needed a good first touch. I got that, and drove it hard and low past the keeper's feet. I played well in that game and came off just before the end to a standing ovation. That feels pretty good, when there are 85,000 people on their feet, together with 35 friends and family members.

I say all this to emphasise how much I enjoyed testing myself against the very best, and how satisfied I was with my year's work by the time summer arrived. Sure, there were peaks and troughs in a year when I had to fight my way into the team under three different coaches. But when I returned home to North Wales in early June, I was pleased with my statistics in Spain. I scored 16 goals in 45 appearances – 26 of them starts. I played the last 10 games of the season in the Real starting XI – in the club's best spell of the season, in terms of results. That year, by some stroke of luck, none of the club's strikers suffered any serious injuries, so for me to play so many matches – and for two successive coaches to alter the formation to get me into the team – was a big feather in my cap.

I said on England's mini-tour of America that I've become a more rounded person from having to live abroad, learn a language, adapt to new challenges. I've certainly become a better father. My ideal day is trying to make Gemma happy.

The same goes for Louise. I considered it a big responsibility to make sure they weren't too homesick. We made great efforts to be part of normal life in Spain and to settle in our nice rented home in La Moraleja – a tranquil suburb of Madrid.

When Liverpool won the Champions League in May, people inevitably asked: 'Don't you wish you'd stayed at Anfield?' I don't deny that I'd have liked to win the European Cup, but equally most people had recognised my transfer to Spain as the chance of a lifetime: 'What a wonderful move. One in a million footballers get to play for Real Madrid,' many of my Liverpool team-mates had said. When I look back at my career I'll be proud that I was brave enough to grasp that opportunity.

If you said to the man on the street, 'You can win the Champions League or you can play at Real Madrid with all those fantastic players', I think opinion would be divided. I have no regrets. It's been highly eventful and a great experience for me as a footballer and a person.

But I ought to start at the beginning. As soon as I found out Real Madrid were interested in me back in the summer of 2004, they were the only club I would have left Liverpool to join. The possibility first arose when I was in America for Liverpool's pre-season tour, and events gathered pace from there. When Liverpool were informed, I spoke on numerous occasions with the new manager, Rafa Benitez, who asked me how I intended to respond. We had some good, frank conversations. But when it came to answering the big question, I could hardly get the words out.

I knew I wanted to have a crack at playing for Real Madrid, to chance my arm in a foreign league and sample life overseas, but when Benitez was asking me to clarify my position I just couldn't seem to say: 'I want to leave.' The way

I saw it was that one in a million footballers are invited to play for Real and one in ten million decline the invitation. I didn't want to be one of those people. It wasn't that I actively wanted to get away from Liverpool. I'd simply received an offer I felt I couldn't refuse. I did tell the manager, though, that if it didn't come off for any reason I would be 100 per cent committed to Liverpool for the coming campaign.

As a Spaniard, and a former manager of Valencia, Benitez understood the lure of the Bernabeu. He knew full well that Real were the big glamour club in world football. 'Even if I go, and we never speak again, I want you to know that it's not because I want to leave Liverpool,' I told him.

He didn't urge me to stay – and I don't hold that against him. Not one bit. Football's a business. I had one year left on my contract. We'd progressed a long way down the line on contract talks with Liverpool but clearly they felt exposed, even though I'd promised them I would never leave on a 'Bosman' free transfer. I wouldn't have put the club in that position. If I was to leave, I wanted Liverpool to receive a decent fee. Being picky, you could say they might have expected to collect more than the £10 million package they received. Then again Real Madrid might not have been willing to pay any more than they did. None of that was anything to do with me.

It all happened in a rush, with only a week or so of real uncertainty. The first time I was sure I was on my way was when I sat on the bench for Liverpool's Champions League qualifier against Grazer AK in Switzerland on 10 August. If I had played in that game, I would have been Cup-tied for Real's European campaign, so by then, clearly, a deal was close.

I flew over to take my medical one afternoon and was due to fly back the following day. But then I was told the Real president, Florentino Perez, was intending to interrupt his holiday to present me to the media on the pitch. So I did my medical and signed in public within a day and a night.

If I was nervous on my first day at the training ground, it was only because I couldn't be sure what people would think of me, not as a player, but as a colleague. That part was quite nerve-wracking. By nature I'm shy. When the training began, I pushed myself hard to make a good impression. 'Average to quite decent' is the mark I gave myself after that first fortnight. That's how I imagined my team-mates would be assessing me. Then I went through a patch of being really quite good, enjoying every second of it, really flying. It's then that you earn the respect of your colleagues on the training ground.

Socially, I tried to remember what I'd been like at Liverpool when a new player turned up. At Anfield I wasn't inclined to impose myself on a new arrival. My experience at Real made me realise I should have made more of an effort. In the early days I clung to any conversation any team-mate was willing to include me in. Now I know how it feels to arrive at a club in a foreign country.

What a cast of characters I came across. With David Beckham, Jonathan Woodgate and later Thomas Gravesen, there was a core of English speakers to turn to. But my job was to make new friends. Cesar Sanchez and Ronaldo are probably the two I got on with best. The three of us would go out most weeks for a game of golf. Ronaldo was a sod to play against at first. He was a 16-handicapper, so I would have to give him six or seven shots. And he would beat me. Then it was 14 and 12 and finally down to eight, the handicap mark we now share. In the meantime, he took plenty of money off me. Get him on an open course where there's no out of bounds and he can really hit the ball. On a tight course where there are trees and so on he finds it harder. Mind you, I can be pretty wild myself.

As a Real Madrid player you go out together more than I remember us doing at Liverpool. The team spirit is fantastic. You have meals together and the odd night out. The famous Ronaldo house parties are less frequent, though, since he got married.

Zidane doesn't speak much English so it was hard for us to communicate much at first. Like me, he's quite shy and doesn't force his personality on you. He likes a laugh, but doesn't make a noise for the sake of it. What I have discovered is that he's an extremely nice fellah. And he still has that aura. I don't get star struck by other footballers, because I'm around them all the time, but I'll never forget how impressive he was in the England–France match at Euro 2004, when he dragged his team back into the game.

It wasn't so much the free-kick and penalty he scored in quick succession so much as the way he behaved in victory. He clapped the French fans briefly and then walked down the tunnel with his mouth closed. There wasn't the slightest urge on his part to rub our noses in the defeat.

Real Madrid have so many attacking players that it's hard to identify a single nucleus to the team. However, Zidane is probably the most gifted individual. With him it's real ball-on-a-string stuff. When it's on the end of his toe it just doesn't leave him. You never see a touch out of place and he's just a joy to watch. I wasn't born to manipulate a ball the way he can, but players can be effective in different ways. If I was a manager picking one player on the basis of overall impact on the team, I'd probably go for Thierry Henry, because he's going to score you 25 goals a season and cause havoc in the opposition's half.

As the No 10 and No 11, Luis Figo and I sat next to each

other in the dressing room and at the training ground. He speaks perfect English and is another really great guy. If there was ever a problem, Luis would always help, especially with translation. With the Spanish-speaking Raul and Guti the other side of me in the changing room, Luis's language skills were a bonus. He's another one with great touch and skill: an impressive player.

Some of the players I didn't speak to much at the start because of the language barrier later developed into friends. Raul is a good example. The more I got to know him the more helpful and friendly he seemed. Roberto Carlos and Ronaldo, though, are the two biggest characters in the dressing room. Roberto Carlos wears a permanent smile and has a nice attitude to life. Brazilian players, I've found, have a positive outlook and value a good social life. Santiago Solari, a near neighbour, is also a great lad. His English is top class. Helguera is another fun living guy, with his own unique sense of humour. Iker Casillas, our goalkeeper, tried his best to speak to me in English. He's probably the player who impressed me most. I already knew about the top outfield players, but I hadn't realised just how good Casillas is. He's even better than he looks on television. He's phenomenal.

Having the Beckhams so close obviously helped. When we were living in a hotel in the early part of the season we went round for Sunday lunch one afternoon and the children all played together. Louise talked to Victoria and would go round to visit. They helped us choose a nursery school for Gemma. We didn't have a weekly schedule of getting together but it was quite frequent and we would all see each other at the school. Obviously I was with David every day at the club.

David's incredibly high public profile must make it hard for him to trust people. As a friend, I trust him and I'm sure he trusts me, yet sometimes I'm careful not to ask him intimate questions about his life in general in case he thinks I'm fishing for information, which I never would. So we tend to talk mostly about football and each other's ups and downs on the field. We've definitely become closer since I moved to Madrid.

The first time I put on the famous Real Madrid No 11 shirt was for a match at Mallorca. Raul picked up an injury after 15 or 20 minutes, and, given the choice between me and Fernando Morientes, Jose Antonio Camacho – the first of my three managers – gestured to me to go on. I'd been expecting 15 or 20 minutes at the end to bed me in. In that white jersey, I felt something I hadn't for an awful long time. Enthusiasm can make you almost hyper-active. If I'd tried to carry on the way I did in the first few games I'd have been on my back with exhaustion by Christmas. You simply can't keep it up.

The language barrier was another challenge. On day one, hello and goodbye was about the full extent of my Spanish. The longer you're at a club like Real Madrid the more you're expected to understand. The Madrid press are constantly asking foreign players whether they've acquired any new Spanish phrases. After my third press conference, I told my teacher: 'You're going to have to give me a sentence to say,' and so I hit them with: 'I'm improving my Spanish bit by bit.' The room erupted.

Abroad, you go through phases of missing things. Being in a hotel room for so long was murder. For three and half months, Louise, Gemma and I were in a businessmen's hotel in a quiet area where there were no parks for our daughter to run around. I felt awful leaving for work at 10am every morning. Coming back at 1pm, I'd often find them bored to tears. So we went out and about in Madrid, locating the parks and all the landmarks. Even then, it would be lights out for Gemma by 7.30pm, and Louise and I would tip-toe round in the pitch-black. In that situation, anyone coming over to visit had to book their own hotel room, which raised the cost, with flights, to around £500. Moving into the house was an absolute must – and we couldn't get through the door quickly enough.

With that move we had a base where friends and family could stay. The Easyjet service from Liverpool was a real bonus. We found a small nursery school for Gemma nearby. The weather was great. We settled into the Madrid life – though relying on phone calls to discover what's going on back home is always hard. In the darker moments, I missed my family, my house, my old team-mates, the golfing, my dogs, the whole English package – even the rain.

For seven or eight years I'd followed the same ritual of getting in my car and driving into Melwood. Suddenly that was gone. Carra, Didi, Stevie G and Danny Murphy were no longer by my side. By the end of my time at Liverpool I was one of the senior players, one of the jokers, an organizer, a key member of the card school. In Madrid I was a new kid on the block again and it took time to adjust.

My new team-mates had advised me to expect the un-expected at Real Madrid, and within 48 hours of him giving me my first start, Camacho had gone and a new head coach was taking over. I wasn't too dismayed because football clubs are run differently in Spain. The board often chose which players to buy and the coach works with whatever he's been given. Some people wondered out loud whether I was one of those purchases, and whether Camacho, who spoke no English, wanted me in his squad in the first place. All I can say is that actions speak louder than words. When Raul got injured, Camacho turned straight to me and put me on ahead of Morientes, a long-established goalscorer for the club.

Mariano Garcia Remon, the new man at the helm, was another non-English speaker, but we eventually developed a good rapport. I made my competitive debut at the Bernabeu against Deportivo, thinking: 'Right, this is my big chance. It's a home game and all the stars are playing.' I'd broken the cycle of making brief appearances and turning out in the Copa Del Rey with many of our reserves. But after about seven minutes, David Beckham chipped a ball over and I felt my hamstring go tight. I could have cried on the pitch. I was so distraught. Foolishly, perhaps, I struggled on to half-time, trying to run it loose. I'd waited two months for this chance, and I would have taken it on one leg .

I mentioned it to the manager at half-time and he sent me back out to give it another try. I lasted about five minutes. I'd played that game at half-capacity. The press decided that I'd blown my big chance and proved once and for all I wasn't a *galactico*. On top of that, I was now injured, with two England games coming up, against Wales at Old Trafford and Azerbaijan in Baku. That was when despair really bit. I'd been pushed to the back of the queue with Real Madrid and couldn't even look forward to a few days with England to relieve my frustration.

Off the pitch, I had Gemma and Louise to take care of as well, so it's fair to say that I hadn't appeared entirely happy with my new life. Inside, I was determined to make a go of it, but the Madrid public might have found me a bit subdued. It was a vicious circle.

I flew to Manchester thinking I had a chance of playing the second of our two World Cup qualifiers, but not holding out much hope of facing Wales, my country of residence. I spent much of my first 24 hours back in England on the phone to Gary Lewin, the England physio. My head was spinning with this latest injury setback. I was pretty depressed.

But the hamstring seemed to loosen as the week wore on. A couple of days before the Wales match I was able to join in a full session and really push myself. I was out of that claustrophobic hotel room. Louise and Gemma were home with me. I had one full day back at the house. And I was back in the old routine, with no language barrier. It was a relief to feel like a major figure again. For a few days, at least, I was escaping the bit-part role I'd acquired in Madrid.

Thank god I made it. I played well against Wales and then went to Azerbaijan as captain and scored out there.

I came back a different man.

A Real Madrid coach had watched me play at Old Trafford and our manager back in Madrid had received good reports of my performance in Baku, where we'd registered a fine victory in a cold, hostile environment. Away games in Eastern Europe are invariably tough. They're seldom pretty, and you grab a 1–0 win with both hands. It was some turn-around. I boarded a plane back to Madrid full of excitement, with a new belief about me again.

Whatever the reasons, I kept my starting place for the next game and scored my first goal for Real Madrid, against Dynamo Kiev in the Champions League. The rest is history. When I scored the only goal, again, in a 1–0 win over Valencia that weekend, I thought: 'This is me. I belong.' The same writer who'd written, 'Let's face it, Michael Owen isn't a *galactico*,' was now calling me an authentic killer. The papers were full of it. They called me 'Mr Goals' and 'El Killer.' Those headlines must have filtered back to England, because whenever I rang my mates they would say: 'All right, El Killer?' Didi Hamann was one who enjoyed the joke.

Back home, people pointed out that I'd come to England's rescue several times. Now England had come to mine. Those World Cup games were the absolute turning point. I'd still have backed myself to become an established Real Madrid striker, but boy did I need the boost to stop my hopes being buried for another few weeks. To go into work with that new feeling about myself was wonderful. Soon I was so well established that the manager was playing Raul in midfield just to accommodate me. I felt a million dollars.

In Baku I took over the captaincy from David, who had been booked after his infamous clash with Ben Thatcher. At the time, I assumed David had gone in hard on Ben to settle a score. I put it down to the fact that Thatcher must have kicked David a few minutes earlier and a bit of needle had crept in. Later, David confessed that he'd got himself booked deliberately to use up a suspension while he was injured and therefore unavailable for the trip to Baku. All I'll say is that David was fairly brave to choose Ben as his victim. Thatcher's no pushover.

While I worked to hold down a first-team place, it became fashionable to say that I'd adapted my game to suit a new style of play and accommodate Ronaldo, the club's most senior striker. I don't think that's true. For the first few games I kept it simple. At every opportunity I showed for my team-mates to give them an option, even when I wasn't strictly 'on' for the pass. It was an eagerness to please. But really, Michael Owen only knows one way to play. I don't have much of a choice. My game is about getting behind defenders, trying to beat people, scoring goals. I've improved my linking play, but that hasn't changed me as a player.

With Raul, I played the way I've always played, at Liverpool and England, because Raul tended to drop off the centre-forward's position and link the play. Ronaldo was a bit different, because his eyes were locked on the goal. Like me, he lights up when he sees a chance. He doesn't peel wide the way I sometimes do. If you study his runs, they mostly come through the middle, over the width of the penalty area. There was a much bigger difference between me and the club's other strikers than there was at Liverpool, where Cisse, Baros and Sinama-Pongolle were quite similar to me in style. There was a much clearer distinction between me and Ronaldo, Raul and Morientes, who later joined Liverpool in the winter transfer window.

The new found stability I enjoyed in the run up to Christmas was short-lived. In January the club relieved Remon of his first-team duties and appointed Vandlerlei Luxemburgo. The sheet was blank again. I was making my third fresh start with a Real Madrid coach. When a new man takes over a top team, the temptation is always to stick with the players he knows have been successful for the club. Equally I was in the team and playing well.

His first game in charge was an oddity: a seven-minute match that was arranged to complete a fixture that had been abandoned in the 83rd minute. I was hopeful of starting. There had been lots of talk about Morientes leaving the club and I felt I'd moved up a peg. So it was a massive blow when he played three strikers and I wasn't one of them. I was back to fourth in the batting order. He explained to me later that he'd wanted a very direct seven minutes, with loads of long balls up to the strikers. He felt Morientes was the obvious choice to complement Raul and Ronaldo in that kind of game. But still I had the sense of tumbling down the list. I thought it was going to be a long couple of months before I got another sniff.

I actually enjoyed watching those seven minutes, because they were so crazy, and in the dressing room afterwards it was as if we'd won a major trophy. In the ensuing few days I fought hard to keep my spirits up. I felt I was back to square one. With the transfer window now open, newspapers began gossiping about which club might be interested in which players, and inevitably my name was thrown into that swirl simply because I was spending so much time on the bench. Maybe people detected a touch of frustration from my body language.

I should say, though, that I didn't say anything disloyal or detrimental to the team. Not long after the new manager had taken over I attended a press conference at which I was asked about Newcastle and Birmingham and whether I was aware of their interest. Some real nonsense appeared in some Sunday papers back home, suggesting I'd issued an ultimatum to Real Madrid. Can you imagine me doing that? It reminded me of a story that appeared during Gerard Houllier's last weeks in charge of Liverpool. The allegation then was that I'd marched into Gerard's office and told him to buy new players and do this and that. That's really not my style. Even if I ever wanted to do it I'm too shy. I get paid a wage to play football and, beyond that, keep my mouth shut. Often the headlines are the problem, not the articles themselves. The trouble is that the headlines find their way back to Spain, and then you end up defending yourself against a nothing story.

In one sense it didn't do any harm for the club to be reminded that I'm ambitious and don't enjoy sitting on the bench. If I didn't feel eager to get out there on the pitch there would be something wrong. I can't imagine being a professional footballer and preferring not to play. I could also console myself with the knowledge that I was good enough to play for Real Madrid. My ability wasn't the issue. There were simply lots of other factors involved, and sometimes rightly so. As a senior, home-grown striker at Liverpool I had the same expectation that Raul and Ronaldo had: they wanted and expected to be in the starting team. Besides, when you take the season as a whole I took part in as many games as any other Real Madrid player. Those who assumed I'd disappear into the wilderness were too full of doom and gloom.

When we invited *Hello* magazine into the house for a special feature, with plenty of photographs of us at home, there had been a lot of negative publicity about me struggling to get into the team, and I started to worry that people might get the wrong impression of our life in Spain. As soon as we moved into the house I was a new man again, so I did lots of things to show I was enjoying myself in Madrid. I went to the basketball, for instance, and the Madrid Open golf. I wanted people to see me with a smile on my face.

There was never the remotest possibility that I would give up or bail out in the January transfer market. The idea of coming to Real Madrid and waving the white flag after five months was absurd.

The warmth of the crowd had a comforting effect. The Bernabeu is not an easy stadium to please. In Madrid you really earn your praise. I do feel I won the fans over. The last thing you want is to be whistled or booed in your work-place. I've seen some of the biggest stars in the game jeered and 'white-hankied' for giving away three passes in a row. In England it's quite common to have your name sung by the crowd. In Spain it's more rare. But I heard mine echoing round the stands. *'Michael, Michael Owen . . . Owen'* they sang. It didn't half send a shiver down my spin.

Despite my anxiety, this time I didn't have to wait so long to be given my chance. The games came more regularly. And the crowning moment was definitely that 4–2 win over Barcelona, for which the manager changed the formation. I knew something was up when the he took us to the

Bernabeu to train to escape the eyes of the press. I was to play on the right of a three-man attack.

In that match we cut Barcelona's lead to six points, and there was a real buzz about the dressing room. We had a squeak of winning the league again. We won eight on the spin after that, but unfortunately Barcelona didn't stop in front. The result that finally killed our hope of winning La Liga was a 2–2 draw at Seville, when they equalised in the final minute, but the damage was done much earlier in the season.

Though Real finished the season empty handed, England's World Cup qualifying campaign was swinging along nicely. For me, though, there was a touch of turbulence after the Azerbaijan match at St James' Park, Newcastle, on 30 March. At the press conference the day before, Poland's 8–0 victory over Azerbaijan had been the centre of attention. The press were convincing themselves that we would also beat Carlos Alberto's team by a cricket score. So I was bombarded with questions like: 'How many are we going to win by?' and 'How many are you going to score?' No matter how much I tried to dampen those expectations, the next day's coverage implied I thought I was going to blitz our visitors and score four or five.

Carlos Alberto clearly thought I'd made all sorts of brash promises about what I was going to do his defenders. I didn't, of course, but by the time he attended the post-match press conference, that was no longer the point. I was at a low ebb anyway after that game. Although we'd won, I picked up my second yellow card of the campaign and would be suspended for the most eagerly-anticipated game in the group: against Wales in Cardiff on 3 September.

As we were pulling out of St James', Matt Dickinson, who ghosted my column in *The Times*, alerted me to the fact that

Carlos Alberto had laid into me in front of the press, calling me a 'midget' and suggesting I'd been disrespectful and was badly brought up. So I was braced for the back pages the next morning. The hardest part was trying to say the right thing by way of an official response. I pointed out as calmly as I could that I hadn't actually said the things that had upset him so much, and urged him to check the quotes attributed to me. I was trying to maintain my dignity. The last thing I wanted was for the story to be dragged out for another four or five days.

What I really wanted to say was: 'I think I've been brought up as well as anyone in this world, I'd never be disrespectful and I never predicted I would score five goals.'

The yellow card was a real disappointment. I mean, I get booked once every three months. For the first booking, in Poland, I'm not sure whether the caution was for pulling a defender's shirt or kicking the ball away. If it was for the latter, I didn't hear the whistle go before taking my shot. In the Azerbaijan game, when I was booked for handball, it was just a natural reaction for me to raise my arm. The ball grazed my hand. It's not as if I punched the ball into the net.

When the yellow card was raised I was sick with anguish. It gave me an insight into how Roy Keane must have felt to miss the 1999 European Cup final through suspension. Mine doesn't compare with that, but I was inconsolable to be missing the gritty, partisan atmosphere of the Millennium Stadium. Playing at home for England is wonderful, but, for me, you can't beat walking into the Lion's Den of a hostile environment. Those are the games I really get a tingle for.

Apart from Chelsea winning the Premiership, the year's other big story domestically was that incredible night in Istanbul. Liverpool had an amazing season in 2004/05. They were knocked out of the FA Cup by Burnley, finished fifth in the league behind their arch rivals Everton, and were beaten in the final of the Carling Cup. If Stevie Gerrard hadn't scored that brilliant last-gasp goal against Olympiakos at the end of the Group Stage they would have been out of the Champions League. Yet that goal led to them winning the European Cup. In football, as in life, everything can change in one moment.

I didn't leave Liverpool on bad terms, so I can only be pleased for the club and all my friends who are still there. Besides, there's no guarantee Liverpool would have won the Cup had I not left for Spain. Maybe I'd have missed a chance that someone else scored from. You can't assume that history would have turned out the same had I rejected Real Madrid's approach.

I watched the Liverpool–AC Milan game from the sofa of our house in Madrid. Louise put Gemma to bed and then rejoined me in front of the TV. At half-time, when Milan were leading 3–0, I was texting my mum and dad back in England, saying: 'I hope for the lads' sake it's not embarrassing for them.' I was also surprised to see Didi Hamann not starting the game. The drama was incredible. There were six minutes of mayhem when Liverpool scored their three goals, a quieter phase in which everyone had time to compose themselves, and then that astonishing double save by Dudek from Shevchenko, who really impressed me throughout.

'Carve Liverpool's name on the trophy now,' said Andy Gray when Dudek somehow kept Milan at bay. 'Don't tempt fate now, Andy!' I shouted at the telly. But he had the courage to say it and he was right. A tense penalty shoot-out was the final instalment.

John Terry and Frank Lampard were the driving force for Chelsea as they won the Premiership, and Carra and Steven Gerrard were the key figures for Liverpool in the Champions

League. And all four are English, which pleases me no end. I'd like to think anyone who gave Carra stick when he came into the team as a midfielder or a full-back will be looking at themselves in the mirror. Carra's fiercely, fiercely competitive, and if someone else isn't doing it for the team he'll scream down their ear until they do.

I watched him get cramp in Istanbul and get rid of it to keep on running and tackling. When they won the Cup, he was the fastest to run to Jerzy and celebrate. If anyone deserved to win it, Carra did. He's in the city full time, being reminded constantly of what it means to play for Liverpool, and the pressure it brings. He wants success so badly. He deserves a special medal he can wear for the rest of his life.

Straight after the end of our domestic season I jumped on a plane to New York to play for England against Colombia in a 3–2 win in New Jersey. Seeing so many young players making their debuts in a winning team was great, and there was also my hat-trick to send me into the summer content. Those three goals took me above Sir Tom Finney, Nat Lofthouse and Alan Shearer, and left me fourth on the all-time England list with 32, just 12 behind the next one up, who is Jimmy Greaves. Bobby Charlton leads the way, of course, with 49 followed by Gary Lineker, who got 48.

To reach the 30s by the age of 25 gives me a real chance of breaking Sir Bobby's record. Sometimes I have to stop myself confusing club football with the international game. 'It's only 18 goals – I should do that in a year,' I think. In fact five or six years would be a more realistic time scale. I definitely think it's possible provided I stay fit and keep my place in the team. Form and fitness are the two biggest obstacles. There are a lot of young whippersnappers coming through, as well, but it's realistic to hope I'll be in the England team to the age of 29 or 30.

The text message banter with Alan Shearer remains lively. 'Still not done it!' he would tease when I was still chasing his total of 30. I gave as good as I got. 'I've never been ten England games without scoring', I would retaliate. And, 'In your day you always played 90 minutes. Nowadays we get taken off at half-time in friendlies.' The texts flowed back and forward. All in good humour. Alan was the first one to congratulate me when I moved past him and on to 32 goals. Then it was time to indulge my other sporting passion with a private box at Epsom for The Derby. Heaven.

25

Black and White

In nine hectic months after my last kick for Real Madrid, I got married, signed for Newcastle after a deadline day drama, joined forces with my old friend Alan Shearer, went back to Anfield in a black and white shirt, broke my foot in a collision with the England goalkeeper and became a father again – this time to a son, James Michael Owen.

There are no quiet years in my life. Except maybe the season in Madrid, which I chalked up as a valuable experience but not one I wanted to extend by another year. Lately I've come to admit it to myself: right from the start of the 2004/05 campaign, when I arrived at the world's most famous club, I knew inside that I wanted to come home after one season. That feeling only intensified the longer I was in Spain. That said, we weren't negotiating with or speaking to any possible employers back in England while I was wearing the white No 11 jersey, so it wasn't possible to know I would be coming back until the day before the transfer deadline, in August 2005, after an exhausting series of discussions with Newcastle and Liverpool. Long before that process got underway, I had joined up with Real as normal for the start of a second season at the Bernabeu, played in all the warm-up games and even travelled to the first match of the Spanish calendar, by which time there had already been five Premiership games.

During my last appearance for Real Madrid at the end of the previous season I did gaze round the stadium a bit and walk off hoping I would be returning to the Premiership. It sounds all wrong to say that when you've been playing for a club like Real Madrid. At the same time, I've always been a bit of a home boy, always liked the security of being around my family and friends. I don't mind admitting that. I lived away from home at Lilleshall for two years when I was a kid and that was probably easier than the year I had in Spain.

Had I been the first-choice striker, starting every game, I suppose I would have felt more wanted and needed. But even when times were great – when I started at the Bernabeu and scored against Barcelona in a 4–2 victory in El Derby (the highest of the highs in football) – I would still go home to see my family feeling that if anyone asked me whether I wanted to return to Britain at the end of the season I would still say yes.

People assume I hardly played for Real that season, but the statistics tell a different story. Somebody told me I actually played in more games than anyone else that year, either starting or as a substitute. I would also point out that in the season before I arrived, several of the major stars were constantly injured. As soon as I appeared, they all seemed to be fit. And yet I still managed to appear in all those games. Who knows: Ronaldo and Raul were injured a lot as I made a fresh start at Newcastle, so had I stayed I would have played in a fair number of games in my second year. My goalscoring record was good. I scored 16 times in 29 starts.

There were those who thought, 'Well, when he played he did well, but he didn't play much – so that's a negative.' I see it in a rosier light. People underestimated my contribution.

Also, because I was fresh, I played well for England and had one of my best international years. So I certainly look on 12 months with Real Madrid as a positive time in my career. Short but sweet.

That summer, Madrid assumed I might want to return to the Premiership and made it clear to Tony, my agent, that he could start speaking to other clubs. My time in Spain drew to a close when the president Florentino Perez took me aside before a game.

'If you want to go home, that's OK.'

'It's important to be enjoying your life and doing what you want to do. We don't want to keep you if you want to go. We'll listen out for bids.'

The next direct conversation with him came when he informed us that Newcastle had bid £16 million. He told me that Real Madrid wanted to accept that offer. My response was that I wanted to hear from all the interested parties before I committed myself to any move. Tony had been given free reign by Real to speak to other clubs and obviously there had been interest from Liverpool. As the process unfolded, I met Rick Parry, the Liverpool chief executive, and Rafa Benitez, the manager, for some very constructive discussions. We talked football a lot. I thought it would be a question of the two clubs then agreeing a fee, but I also knew that Newcastle had made a huge bid, so I went up there to speak to them.

There was a constant dialogue still with Rick Parry and Rafa Benitez as I weighed up Newcastle's terms. I was impressed with what they had to say, but I still wanted to rejoin Liverpool. I said as much in the press at the time. One newspaper claimed I had been wined and dined by Newcastle while Liverpool had taken me to an empty terraced house. It was hardly that but both sides understood the need for secrecy. It was very private. Up at Newcastle, I visited the chairman's lovely house, but the full extent of 'wined and dined' was a glass of Coke and a couple of sandwiches.

Graeme Souness, the Newcastle manager, kept offering encouragement by phone and text and I knew all about the passion of the fans. I was left in no doubt that I had the opportunity to be a hero to the Geordie people. For Alan Shearer, joining Newcastle had been a homecoming, and he had turned down Manchester United to go back to his roots. That wasn't a factor for me, and I was quite honest with the Newcastle fans in saying that my first preference was to return to Liverpool. From my earliest years I saw myself as a Liverpool player with my own roots in the area and the club.

I spoke to Alan a lot in those crucial days and hours. He's a good friend anyway. Alan really wasn't giving me the hard sell. He wasn't telling me that Newcastle were 'desperate' to sign me. He was very frank. He listed to all the good points and he outlined some of the bad. He stressed that it was a nice area with friendly people who would appreciate me as a player.

He wasn't pulling any wool. The message wasn't 'you've got to come here', though he did keep stressing the positives. He said it would be fantastic for the city and promised that the fans would love me. There was no begging on his part.

D-Day was approaching, and Real Madrid were still saying, 'Liverpool don't have to match or top Newcastle – but they do need to make a fair offer.' The overriding sense, if anyone ever wants to experience it, is of being in a complex game of cards. I knew I wanted to leave Real Madrid. And I knew that Newcastle were offering around a third more than Liverpool. A difference of a million pounds or two might have prompted Real Madrid to take my wishes into account and send me back to Anfield. But for them the difference was simply too big. I had a decision to make.

I could have held out and said to Real: 'I want to go to Liverpool or nowhere'. To which they might have responded: 'Right, you're going nowhere. We'll see you at the Bernabeu for the next game.' I could have taken that route, hoping they would give in at the last moment. But if they had held their ground, I would have been at Madrid for another six months, minimum, and in a World Cup year I couldn't allow that to happen.

The other option was being a damn sight happier and taking Newcastle up on their wonderful offer. My wife Louise, my mum, my dad and my financial adviser all contributed to the debate. It all happened so quickly in the end. All the while I was trying to gauge how much Liverpool were offering.

If I had known they were bidding, say, £8 million, I would have signed for Newcastle there and then. But if the figure had been £12 or £13 million I might have called Real's bluff and hoped they might be persuaded to accept the lower fee.

Real tried to persuade me that they had my interests at heart, but it was also true that they were bowled over by the size of Newcastle's offer, which eclipsed anything else on the table. Just 12 months ago, they had bought me in deal worth £10 million: £8.5 million in cash, plus Antonio Nunez who was valued at £1.5 million.

There were several other teams offering me a new start. Dave Whelan, the Wigan chairman, is a real patriot and made a very generous offer via Tony. The gist of it was that Wigan would help me to come home and give me a very open contract that would enable me to leave at a suitable point if a big club came in for me, provided Wigan were reimbursed the sum they had paid to Real Madrid. That was very decent of him. We also spoke to David Moyes at Everton and there was interest from Italy.

But Newcastle were a strong second option, way above another year in Madrid. I had spoken to Sven-Goran Eriksson and asked him: 'What's my situation if I'm still in Madrid and don't play regularly for my club during a World Cup year? Where do I stand?' That was an important element in my decision. I knew that Real were buying Robinho and Julio Baptista. Ronaldo and Raul would be staying on. So I really did need to act.

I would never complain about the anxiety of those dying moments when I had to reach a verdict. Putting it into perspective, I was guaranteed a terrific job whichever club I ended up at. I was either going to be welcomed back to my old home with open arms – as Ian Rush had been – or become part of a rival tradition where there was huge passion for the team and the game. It was a win-win dilemma, and I would never ask for sympathy about having to be in that position.

My mind was to-ing and fro-ing. Should I accept Newcastle's offer? Should I hold out at Real Madrid? What would be the hidden consequences of staying or going? I repeat: either way, I was guaranteed a top job with a great club. It was simply the process of having to make the decision that caused me so much angst. The only time I had felt such extremes was when I was pulling out of my house to leave Liverpool and join Real Madrid.

My parting with Liverpool had been totally amicable. 'Do you want to go?' the Liverpool manager had asked me back in the summer of 2004. 'No I don't,' I replied, 'but I do want to sample something that will stay with me for the rest of my life.' I just knew that if I had turned down Real Madrid I would have been left wondering what it's like to play abroad, never mind for a club who have won nine European Cups.

Finally, I said yes in my own head to Newcastle sometime after midnight.

The following day was deadline day. I had spoken to Rick Parry to check whether there had been any last-ditch upping of the ante. I needed to have all the information at hand before I made such an important move. I asked Rick to give me one figure – the sum that Liverpool had offered Real Madrid. That was the last conversation we had.

It wasn't me putting pressure on him to increase Liverpool's bid. Certainly not. I wouldn't dream of doing that. I just needed to know what the gap was between the two offers. Rick's message was: 'It's come at the wrong time for us. We can't bid any more than we have.' He was fairly sure that Madrid wouldn't accept the lower bid. As soon as he said those words to me, I resolved to go to Newcastle and throw myself into that new challenge.

The minute I signed a four-year contract for Newcastle on 30 August 2005 I was excited once again. The stress of decision day passed quickly. I snapped straight out of it. It was as if somebody had smacked me in the face. I was home. I was a Premiership player again. Newcastle really wanted me. And soon I was on my way to an unveiling in front of 20,000 Newcastle fans at St James' Park, which was mind blowing.

When you think of an unveiling you imagine ten or so photographers in front of you and you holding up a shirt and smiling with a ball under your arm. You don't see 20,000 faces, 20,000 replica shirts. Alan had said to me: 'If you do sign, you wouldn't believe the reception you'll get. The place will go crazy.'

He was right.

Freddy Shepherd told the crowd I would be a 'Geordio Galactico.' I liked that. And I liked his honesty. He says what he thinks. When we first him, Tony told Freddy that we had spoken to Liverpool and others and the chairman's reply was: 'I don't care who've you spoken to, Newcastle's the place!' Straight away he was on the front foot. That was impressive. Football is a big business, but it's nice to deal with someone who's also a passionate supporter of his club.

Louise and Gemma accompanied me to the stadium for the big day. I collected my new Newcastle kit in the chairman's office and then walked out on to the pitch to do some interviews. They had a massive goody bag for Gemma full of footballs and kit. 'I want to look like Daddy,' she piped up.

So we put a mini-Newcastle kit on her above her smart pink shoes. As I looked to the side of the pitch halfway through the ceremony, Gemma was running on to join me. It was totally spontaneous. It wasn't for effect. In fact, I did worry that people might think badly of me for parading my daughter as a Newcastle fan when we had only been in town for a day. But it was all just off the cuff.

Louise shed a tear as the warmth of the crowd washed over us. I was also highly emotional. Just imagine: there are 20,000 people in a stadium – and they're all there for you, chanting your name. I felt a lump in my throat.

I was filling up. I'm not surprised Louise cried.

Alan had stressed that Geordie people love their goalscorers. The Newcastle No 9 shirt is one of the most famous in all of football. Alan had nine and I took No 10 – my England number. I knew all about Jackie Milburn, Malcolm MacDonald, Kevin Keegan, Andy Cole and my good mate Shearer. If I was the sort who insists on being star of the show, I wouldn't have joined Real Madrid. But if someone tells you you're going to be a hero to the fans it does give you a special feeling when you step out to meet the crowd.

I stayed at Alan's house for about ten days. It took a while to sort the logistics out, car, house and so on. We were in Alan's guest house next to his main home. The Shearers were extremely kind, but after a while you start to feel you're treading on toes, so the next stop was a hotel, where we stayed for a month or so before finding a house to rent.

I was so excited to be playing for Newcastle that Saturday. Staying at Alan's house, I had the buzz of waking up thinking: 'Three o'clock kick-off. Today, the Premiership.' Every footballer loves evening games, for the drama, the lights. At Madrid sometimes we would kick off at 10pm. Waiting was dull. It's a full day of just laying on your back trying to understand Spanish TV. I did that twice a week for nine months. It drove me mad, especially as I had a wife who wasn't happy and a young child who was starting to talk and was saying she wanted to go home. I would dwell on that in my hotel room.

I had played a full pre-season and was in pretty decent shape. I had scored a lot of goals as well. I was scoring so freely that it crossed my mind Real Madrid might try to keep me after all! Some of my pre-season appearances had been cameos or 45-minute run-outs. So for my Newcastle debut against Fulham I probably wasn't fully match-fit. But adrenalin got me through. By the time I joined, the team were struggling. We had lost three games and drawn one. On the first day at training I could detect a lack of confidence. At Real Madrid, we had been wiping the floor with everybody in pre-season, so it was obvious to me that Newcastle's early results had affected morale.

We drew that game 1–1 and were probably fortunate to get a point. I hardly got a kick. I was brought down for the free-kick from which we scored the equaliser but there wasn't much happening overall. It was in the next game, against Blackburn away, where I struck my first Newcastle goal and felt the full buzz of being back in the Premiership. We won 3–0. You can't beat the sensation of team-mates jumping all over you and the whole side jogging back to the dressing room saying, 'Get in there lads!' There's nothing like scoring a winning goal to put you on another planet. Once I broke that barrier I began to score pretty regularly.

The first half of the Blackburn game had been quiet. I got a free-kick on the edge of the box from which Alan scored. Then Charles N'Zogbia took a wide position, cut back on his right foot and crossed the ball for me to make a run in behind the defender. I leapt and nodded the ball into the corner. Great feeling. Really, really great feeling. It was our first win of the season. From then on the victories came thick and fast. It was great, in the dressing room at Ewood Park, to feel I'd made a contribution.

I knew everybody expected me to give the place a lift. That's what they had paid all that money for. I felt I was doing my bit.

'Right, let's ride the crest of this wave,' I thought. And in the next game at St James' I scored again in a 1–0 win against Manchester City. By then I was flying. My victim that day in a chase for the ball was my old rival Richard Dunne, the City centre-half, who I've been grappling with ever since my schoolboy days. He was a big lad even at 15 and he hasn't shrunk.

I had another good chance to make it two mid-way through the second half but a good save from David James kept it out.

The Newcastle crowd make a proper racket when a goal goes in. In Madrid, the audience turned up to be entertained and didn't start roaring just because the ball reached the edge of the box. A lot of businessmen treat the Bernabeu as a night at the theatre. They don't think it's their job to spur the team on. In England, there's a sense of everyone being in it together. The crowd are there to cheer the team on. I went to the Liverpool-Chelsea Champions' League semi-final as a spectator and I'll never forget that atmosphere.

At St James' when you score, all you see is a mass of black and white striped shirts celebrating. There aren't many teams who are better supported than Newcastle. When things are going well it's a great place to play. It's just a question of recapturing the mood of a few years ago when Kevin Keegan's team were on the rampage.

Graeme Souness was someone I had always admired. Watching *Match of the Day*, after playing for Liverpool, I would always make mental notes about the managers coming on to be interviewed. Carra and I both thought Souness would have been great to play with. Really tough, no messing about. And that's the way he was as a manager. An old school type, who gave us a glimpse of how things were when he was winning everything as a player.

After Gerard Houllier, it was interesting to see a more traditional manager in action. Souness was incredibly positive about me coming to Newcastle. He was constantly on the phone to stress how good it would be for me. Persistence was certainly a feature of his recruitment policy. Come to think of it, he was fairly persistent as a player as well.

One aspect I didn't enjoy was that people were constantly talking about Graeme's chances of keeping his job. When we started winning a few games it quietened down but as soon as we lost one it was back to 'Souness's job, Souness's job'. One defeat seemed to set the speculation off again. I asked myself: 'Is it going to be like this for the whole season, or until he goes?' I began to feel that Graeme was never entirely secure in the post.

And I didn't like the fact the everybody was constantly

raking over his future. Instead of blaming the players, most observers would talk about Souness hanging on to his job – and that became the sole focus, which I thought was unhealthy. Graeme's departure started to seem inevitable one way or another, and that's not the way it should be.

My best performance in a Newcastle shirt was probably West Ham away. The second half against West Brom was also a great team effort. We beat Bryan Robson's team 3–0. The West Ham game was just a very entertaining contest.

We were one of those inconsistent teams capable of real flashes of brilliance. On our day we had a cracking starting XI, low on numbers but high on quality. When we played well in 2005/06 it was an exciting team to be part of. We had Emre and Nobby Solano – both creative players – and me and Alan up front. Stephen Carr is a fantastic right-back when he's fit. Charles N'Zogbia is excellent when he's confident. Alberto Luque, who joined for £11 million, could be exciting. Lee Bowyer is a good player, too. So is Scott Parker. There were plenty of them. We were just short on numbers. Injuries affected us more than they did other big clubs.

Of course, no review of the season would be complete without a few words on my return to Anfield on Boxing Day. For weeks before the Liverpool-Newcastle fixture I wondered what it was going to be like. I didn't want to make a song and dance about it, because scores of footballers go back to their old clubs. I suppose you could say it's a bit like having a fight with your brother.

But I didn't enjoy the experience one bit. Above all I didn't enjoy us being beaten 2–0 by my old team-mates.

Much was made of the chants and songs directed at me. I ought to point out that most of them simply expressed typical Scouse humour: 'You should have signed for a big club!' and 'Where were you in Istanbul?!' They weren't abusive. But when you're being beaten 2–0 by your old club and your team's not playing well, it's just horrible. I felt ten inches smaller than I am. Liverpool were in my blood, but I would have loved to have scored against them.

Though I wasn't offended by the teasing, some Liverpool fans wrote to say they had been sickened by the chants. One even said they had given up their season ticket in disgust. People phoned and apologised. People very high up. I would have loved the Anfield crowd to give me a round of applause.

Ninety per cent of my family are from Liverpool and I was born half an hour down the road. I think my mum was a little hurt. But at least I understood the sense of humour. I've spent most of my life around Liverpudlians and the club. I recognised that sense of mischief.

Calamity then struck me five days later when I raced in to contest a ball with Paul Robinson in the match against Spurs at White Hart Lane on New Year's Eve. As soon as my England team-mate landed on my feet I heard a couple of clunks. As I stood up I felt it click and knew I'd broken a bone. The pain really arrived after an hour, accompanied by the swelling. That 's when the throbbing started. Back in Newcastle that night I saw a specialist, took some extra advice from the Newcastle medical stuff plus Gary Lewin, the England physio, and players who had broken a metatarsal – Gary Neville, David Beckham – and came to the conclusion that an operation would be the appropriate course.

It was a shocking blow. I had scored seven times in ten games. The timing was abysmal. I sat there feeling sorry not for myself but for Newcastle, who had paid such a big fee and invested so much hope in me. I wasn't bothered about me. The fans had only seen me ten times. Frankly, I felt guilty. The only consolation was that the team had a good winning record when I was on the pitch. Had I played ten games and done bugger-all I would have accepted people being frustrated at seeing me on an exercise bike for three months.

Naturally the thought flashed through my mind that a random accident might cost me my World Cup place. I'm not going to hide that. Obviously my first duty was to get back for Newcastle, who pay my wages. Newcastle fans didn't want to hear me talking about the World Cup ahead of my club. However, the first question you're asked in those situations is: 'Are you going to be fit for the World Cup?' You can answer ten questions about Newcastle and one about England and the press will all focus on England.

Understandable, I suppose. But I did feel uncomfortable doing interviews, talking about Newcastle and then seeing England headlines. That increased my guilt. I was acutely aware who was paying my salary, and I wanted the club to know that I was fighting to get fit for Newcastle United. There I was wanting to play club football again and New-castle fans were picking up newspapers saying: 'Michael Owen will be back in time for four club matches to prepare him for the World Cup.' Great!

I was in the gym doing my rehab one day when a colleague poked his head round the door and said, 'The gaffer's been sacked!' We assembled in the canteen and saw the news confirmed on TV. Graeme then joined us to say thanks. I was massively impressed with the way he handled his departure. Like a proper man. He shook everyone's hand and herded the kids into a corner to give them some final advice. He offered no excuses. He thanked us for trying so hard for him. He came over really well. Glenn Roeder took charge, with Alan lending support as a temporary assistant.

There was one other managerial drama to come, this time involving fake sheikhs and stings. I picked up the *News of the World* one Sunday morning to find Sven-Goran Eriksson plastered all over the front and back pages, having been lured by undercover reporters into discussing some of the England players and his employment options after the World Cup. My phone had been switched off overnight so I'd had no warning. Reading it, I suddenly saw my name, and the quotes attached to it, and thought: 'Oh, no, I'm in trouble here with the Newcastle supporters!'

I turned my phone on and almost straight away Sven called me to explain that he'd been deceived. He was at pains to say that he hadn't said anything negative about me, and even joked that he'd advised the undercover journalists to buy me one day! 'It came out wrong and I can only apologise,' he said.

I then spoke to the chairman, Freddy Shepherd, who said he totally understood. Things get twisted. I hadn't spoken to the England manager about my time at Newcastle. The only conversation with him was when I was still at Real Madrid, and I was asking him what my position would be if I stayed in Spain. I discussed that issue with him in broad outline. At no point did I ever say I was unhappy at Newcastle.

Can you imagine me going to the England manager and saying: 'I hate it here but the money's great'? What would he think of me? I would never say that. To him or anyone else. Or even think it. Sven was probably just trying to tell his hosts that Newcastle had offered a lot of money for me at a time when I was expressing a desire to go back to Liverpool – and it simply came out wrong.

I wasn't quite sure how to respond publicly. I didn't want to start a big debate about it and give the story legs. But finally now I can tell the Newcastle fans how Sven's words came to be interpreted in that way. At the time, I just had to take it on the chin.

On the playing front, we qualified for the World Cup and enjoyed a thrilling 3–2 victory over our old enemy Argentina, in which I scored twice to take my international goals tally to 35. My thoughts inevitably strayed towards Sir Bobby Charlton's all-time record of 49. To be the leading all-time goalscorer for England might just be the ultimate achievement. People talk about you being the youngest this and the youngest that, and all those milestones are lovely. There are one or two you're not bothered about. Being European Footballer of the Year meant a huge amount to me. When I retire it will be even bigger. It's only just sinking in now what an honour that is. And to be the leading scorer for such a prestigious country as England would be a proper record to hold.

On a personal level, Louise and I got married in June 2005 with all the people we love and care about with us, close to where we grew up. The wedding was fantastic. We had a big marquee with a dancefloor put up in the back garden. It was just perfect for what we wanted. Steven Gerrard, Wayne Rooney, Carra, Danny Murphy and Didi Hamann were among our guests. It was so special, you could only stage that kind of day and have those feelings once in your life. We did the paperwork at a hotel the day before, because our home wasn't licensed, but we exchanged vows and rings in a ceremony at the house. We're not ones for going over the top but it was lavish enough to be memorable. We had 60 people at the wedding and around 200 at the reception.

Within a year we had become a family of four with a son to raise alongside our daughter Gemma. As ever with births, there was a story attached to the arrival of James Michael Owen just after lunchtime on 6 February 2006.

Newcastle were extremely generous with time-off when Louise was due to deliver. On the day, her feeling was that I should stay at home with Gemma and she would give me a call from the hospital when she started to go into labour.

I got the call alright, from Louise's mum Sue, who said the first small contractions had started. I took Gemma round to my mum and dad's house thinking it would be at least an hour before Louise began experiencing any serious tremors. I reckoned I could be there within 45 minutes, so there was no cause for panic.

After three-quarters of an hour, when I was still 15 minutes from the hospital, I got a call from Sue. 'Where are you?' she said, slightly agitated.

'About 15 minutes away,' I replied.

'Well, quick,' Sue said. 'She's started.' I dropped the car down a gear and started bombing towards the Countess of Chester hospital. By now I was in a state.

I legged it to the delivery room and poked my head round the door to find the baby had been out for 15 seconds.

I'd missed it. He was still in all his glory, with the cord being cut. He weighed 7st 10lb. Unbelievable, given that I had been so relaxed earlier in the day. The labour had taken less than an hour from the first strong contractions to the baby being out.

Louise wasn't cross. She was apologetic. She did say, 'Well, you were a bit more than 45 minutes!' but overall she was just sympathetic.

I started this book by describing how I took over the family goalscoring business from my dad. Throughout Louise's second pregnancy, I was expecting a boy, even though we didn't know. As I looked at him in the delivery room, I felt exactly as I had when I studied Gemma. It goes without saying that I love them just the same. I'm delighted to have one of each.

I'm so excited for the future. I was asked the other day whether James might take the torch from dad and me and become a striker.

You just never know.

Career Record

*Compiled by Mark Baber of the Association of
Football Statisticians up to 31 March 2006.*

PERSONAL SUMMARY

Full name: Michael James Owen
Place and Date of Birth: Chester, 14 December 1979
Position: Forward
Height 5ft 8in
Weight 10st 9lb
Parents: Terry and Janette
Brothers: Terry, Andrew
Sisters: Karen, Lesley
Children: Gemma Rose Owen and James Michael Owen
Married to: Louise Bonsall on 24 June 2005

EARLY CAREER

Played for Deeside Primary Schools in North Wales.
At 14, joined the FA School of Excellence at Lilleshall.
Played for England Under-15s, beating the goal-scoring
    record of Kevin Gallen and Nick Barmby.
In 1996 won the FA Youth Cup with Liverpool, scoring a
    hat-trick in the final against Manchester United.
Signed professional forms with Liverpool on 18 December
    1996.

CAREER BREAKDOWN

Totals by Competition

Competition	Total Apps	On as sub	Subbed off	Goals	Yellow	Red
Premiership	226	23	55	125	7	1
UEFA Cup	33	3	11	12	0	0
European Cup	16	1	3	9	0	0
FA Cup	15	1	4	8	1	0
League Cup	14	2	6	9	1	0
FA Community Shield	2	0	1	1	0	0
European Super Cup	1	0	1	1	0	0
Primera Liga	35	15	13	13	1	0
Copa del Rey	4	0	0	2	0	0

HONOURS

Team

2001	UEFA Cup
2001	FA Cup
2001	League Cup
2001	European Super Cup
2001	FA Community Shield
2003	League Cup

Personal

1997–98	PFA Young Player of the Year
1997–98	Premier League Top Scorer
1997–98	Carling Premiership Player of the Year
1998	August Carling Premiership Player of the Month
1998	BBC Sports Personality of the Year
2001	European Footballer of the Year ('Balon d'Or')
2001	*World Soccer* World Player of the Year

Club Goals – Liverpool

Season	Date	Competition
1996–97	06/05/1997	Premiership
1997–98	09/08/1997	Premiership
1997–98	23/08/1997	Premiership
1997–98	16/09/1997	UEFA Cup
1997–98	08/11/1997	Premiership
1997–98	18/11/1997	League Cup
1997–98	13/12/1997	Premiership
1997–98	20/12/1997	Premiership
1997–98	26/12/1997	Premiership
1997–98	07/01/1998	League Cup
1997–98	20/01/1998	Premiership
1997–98	07/02/1998	Premiership
1997–98	14/02/1998	Premiership
1997–98	28/02/1998	Premiership
1997–98	07/03/1998	Premiership
1997–98	10/04/1998	Premiership
1997–98	19/04/1998	Premiership
1997–98	02/05/1998	Premiership
1997–98	06/05/1998	Premiership
1998–99	16/08/1998	Premiership
1998–99	30/08/1998	Premiership
1998–99	15/09/1998	UEFA Cup
1998–99	24/10/1998	Premiership
1998–99	10/11/1998	League Cup
1998–99	24/11/1998	UEFA Cup
1998–99	29/11/1998	Premiership
1998–99	19/12/1998	Premiership
1998–99	26/12/1998	Premiership
1998–99	28/12/1998	Premiership

Home Team	Away Team	Goals	Time
Wimbledon	Liverpool	1	74
Wimbledon	Liverpool	1	71
Blackburn Rovers	Liverpool	1	52
Celtic	Liverpool	1	6
Liverpool	Tottenham	1	86
Liverpool	Grimsby	3	28, 45, 57
Crystal Palace	Liverpool	1	56
Liverpool	Coventry City	1	14
Liverpool	Leeds United	1	46
Newcastle United	Liverpool	1	95
Liverpool	Newcastle United	1	17
Liverpool	Southampton	2	24, 90
Sheffield Wed	Liverpool	3	27, 73, 78
Aston Villa	Liverpool	1	6
Liverpool	Bolton Wanderers	1	65
Manchester Utd	Liverpool	1	36
Coventry City	Liverpool	1	33
Liverpool	West Ham United	1	4
Liverpool	Arsenal	1	40
Southampton	Liverpool	1	73
Newcastle United	Liverpool	3	17, 18, 32
FC Kosice	Liverpool	1	59
Liverpool	Nottm Forest	4	10, 38, 71, 77
Liverpool	Tottenham	1	81
Celta Vigo	Liverpool	1	35
Liverpool	Blackburn Rovers	1	33
Liverpool	Sheffield Wed	1	34
Middlesbrough	Liverpool	1	17
Liverpool	Newcastle United	2	67, 80

Season	Date	Competition
1998–99	03/01/1999	FA Cup
1998–99	16/01/1999	Premiership
1998–99	24/01/1999	FA Cup
1998–99	06/02/1999	Premiership
1998–99	20/02/1999	Premiership
1998–99	27/02/1999	Premiership
1998–99	05/04/1999	Premiership
1999–00	18/09/1999	Premiership
1999–00	13/10/1999	League Cup
1999–00	20/11/1999	Premiership
1999–00	18/12/1999	Premiership
1999–00	26/12/1999	Premiership
1999–00	28/12/1999	Premiership
1999–00	18/03/2000	Premiership
1999–00	01/04/2000	Premiership
1999–00	09/04/2000	Premiership
2000–01	26/08/2000	Premiership
2000–01	06/09/2000	Premiership
2000–01	09/09/2000	Premiership
2000–01	23/09/2000	Premiership
2000–01	09/11/2000	UEFA Cup
2000–01	13/12/2000	League Cup
2000–01	23/12/2000	Premiership
2000–01	15/02/2001	UEFA Cup
2000–01	11/03/2001	FA Cup
2000–01	15/03/2001	UEFA Cup
2000–01	18/03/2001	Premiership
2000–01	01/05/2001	Premiership
2000–01	05/05/2001	Premiership
2000–01	08/05/2001	Premiership
2000–01	12/05/2001	FA Cup

Home Team	Away Team	Goals	Time
Port Vale	Liverpool	1	34
Liverpool	Southampton	1	63
Manchester Utd	Liverpool	1	3
Liverpool	Middlesbrough	1	9
Liverpool	West Ham United	1	45
Chelsea	Liverpool	1	77
Nottm Forest	Liverpool	1	72
Leicester City	Liverpool	2	23, 39
Southampton	Liverpool	1	53
Sunderland	Liverpool	1	63
Liverpool	Coventry City	1	45
Newcastle United	Liverpool	2	31, 52
Liverpool	Wimbledon	1	58
Derby County	Liverpool	1	17
Coventry City	Liverpool	2	23, 37
Liverpool	Tottenham	1	61
Southampton	Liverpool	2	24, 64
Liverpool	Aston Villa	3	5, 14, 33
Liverpool	Manchester City	1	11
Liverpool	Sunderland	1	34
Slovan Liberec	Liverpool	1	82
Liverpool	Fulham	1	105
Liverpool	Arsenal	1	62
AS Roma	Liverpool	2	46, 72
Tranmere	Liverpool	1	27
Liverpool	FC Porto	1	38
Liverpool	Derby County	1	52
Bradford City	Liverpool	1	47
Liverpool	Newcastle United	3	25, 72, 81
Liverpool	Chelsea	2	7, 60
Arsenal	Liverpool	2	83, 88

Season	Date	Competition
2000–01	19/05/2001	Premiership
2001–02	08/08/2001	European Cup
2001–02	12/08/2001	FA Community Shield
2001–02	18/08/2001	Premiership
2001–02	24/08/2001	European Super Cup
2001–02	11/09/2001	European Cup
2001–02	15/09/2001	Premiership
2001–02	27/10/2001	Premiership
2001–02	04/11/2001	Premiership
2001–02	17/11/2001	Premiership
2001–02	20/11/2001	European Cup
2001–02	01/12/2001	Premiership
2001–02	08/12/2001	Premiership
2001–02	29/12/2001	Premiership
2001–02	05/01/2002	FA Cup
2001–02	19/01/2002	Premiership
2001–02	03/02/2002	Premiership
2001–02	09/02/2002	Premiership
2001–02	30/03/2002	Premiership
2001–02	13/04/2002	Premiership
2001–02	20/04/2002	Premiership
2001–02	11/05/2002	Premiership
2002–03	02/09/2002	Premiership
2002–03	28/09/2002	Premiership
2002–03	06/10/2002	Premiership
2002–03	22/10/2002	European Cup
2002–03	26/10/2002	Premiership
2002–03	02/11/2002	Premiership
2002–03	12/11/2002	European Cup
2002–03	28/11/2002	UEFA Cup
2002–03	12/12/2002	UEFA Cup

Home Team	Away Team	Goals	Time
Charlton Athletic	Liverpool	1	80
FC Haka	Liverpool	3	56, 66, 88
Liverpool	Manchester Utd	1	16
Liverpool	West Ham United	2	18, 77
Bayern München	Liverpool	1	46
Liverpool	Boavista	1	29
Everton	Liverpool	1	31
Charlton Athletic	Liverpool	1	43
Liverpool	Manchester Utd	2	32, 51
Blackburn Rovers	Liverpool	1	30
Liverpool	Barcelona	1	27
Derby County	Liverpool	1	6
Liverpool	Middlesbrough	1	27
West Ham United	Liverpool	1	88
Liverpool	Birmingham City	2	17, 25
Liverpool	Southampton	1	8
Leeds United	Liverpool	1	90
Ipswich Town	Liverpool	2	62, 71
Liverpool	Charlton Athletic	1	36
Sunderland	Liverpool	1	55
Liverpool	Derby County	2	15, 89
Liverpool	Ipswich Town	1	46
Liverpool	Newcastle United	1	73
Manchester City	Liverpool	3	4, 64, 89
Liverpool	Chelsea	1	90
Spartak Moskva	Liverpool	3	29, 70, 90
Liverpool	Tottenham	1	86
Liverpool	West Ham United	2	28, 55
FC Basel	Liverpool	1	85
Vitesse Arnhem	Liverpool	1	26
Liverpool	Vitesse Arnhem	1	21

Season	Date	Competition
2002–03	11/01/2003	Premiership
2002–03	21/01/2003	League Cup
2002–03	23/02/2003	Premiership
2002–03	27/02/2003	UEFA Cup
2002–03	02/03/2003	League Cup
2002–03	08/03/2003	Premiership
2002–03	16/03/2003	Premiership
2002–03	23/03/2003	Premiership
2002–03	12/04/2003	Premiership
2002–03	19/04/2003	Premiership
2002–03	26/04/2003	Premiership
2003–04	17/08/2003	Premiership
2003–04	30/08/2003	Premiership
2003–04	13/09/2003	Premiership
2003–04	20/09/2003	Premiership
2003–04	24/09/2003	UEFA Cup
2003–04	28/09/2003	Premiership
2003–04	25/10/2003	Premiership
2003–04	11/02/2004	Premiership
2003–04	15/02/2004	FA Cup
2003–04	03/03/2004	UEFA Cup
2003–04	17/03/2004	Premiership
2003–04	04/04/2004	Premiership
2003–04	09/04/2004	Premiership
2003–04	08/05/2004	Premiership
2003–04	15/05/2004	Premiership

Total Number of Club Goals: 158

Home Team	Away Team	Goals	Time
Liverpool	Aston Villa	1	38
Liverpool	Sheffield Utd	1	107
Birmingham City	Liverpool	1	77
Liverpool	Auxerre	1	67
Liverpool	Manchester Utd	1	86
Liverpool	Bolton Wanderers	1	67
Tottenham	Liverpool	1	51
Liverpool	Leeds United	1	13
Liverpool	Fulham	1	59
Everton	Liverpool	1	30
West Bromwich	Liverpool	4	15, 49, 61, 67
Liverpool	Chelsea	1	79
Everton	Liverpool	2	39, 52
Blackburn Rovers	Liverpool	2	12, 68
Liverpool	Leicester City	1	20
Olimpija Ljubljana	Liverpool	1	78
Charlton Athletic	Liverpool	1	52
Liverpool	Leeds United	1	35
Liverpool	Manchester City	1	3
Liverpool	Portsmouth	1	2
Levski Sofia	Liverpool	1	11
Liverpool	Portsmouth	2	28, 58
Liverpool	Blackburn Rovers	2	7, 24
Arsenal	Liverpool	1	42
Birmingham City	Liverpool	1	29
Liverpool	Newcastle United	1	67

Club Goals – Real Madrid

Season	Date	Competition
2004–05	19/10/2004	European Cup
2004–05	23/10/2004	Spanish Primera Liga
2004–05	26/10/2004	Copa del Rey
2004–05	31/10/2004	Spanish Primera Liga
2004–05	07/11/2004	Spanish Primera Liga
2004–05	14/11/2004	Spanish Primera Liga
2004–05	28/11/2004	Spanish Primera Liga
2004–05	18/12/2004	Spanish Primera Liga
2004–05	16/01/2005	Spanish Primera Liga
2004–05	19/01/2005	Copa del Rey
2004–05	13/02/2005	Spanish Primera Liga
2004–05	02/03/2005	Spanish Primera Liga
2004–05	03/04/2005	Spanish Primera Liga
2004–05	10/04/2005	Spanish Primera Liga
2004–05	07/05/2005	Spanish Primera Liga
2004–05	28/05/2005	Spanish Primera Liga

Total Number of Real Madrid Goals: 16

Club Goals – Newcastle

Season	Date	Competition
2005–06	18/09/2005	Premiership
2005–06	24/09/2005	Premiership
2005–06	30/10/2005	Premiership
2005–06	17/12/2005	Premiership

Total Number of Newcastle Goals: 7

Home Team	Away Team	Goals	Time
Real Madrid	Dynamo Kiev	1	35
Real Madrid	Valencia	1	6
Leganes	Real Madrid	1	49
Real Madrid	Getafe	1	28
Malaga	RealMadrid	1	78
Real Madrid	Albacete	1	88
Real Madrid	Levante	1	86
Racing	Real Madrid	1	34
Real Madrid	Real Zaragoza	1	85
RealMadrid	Valladolid	1	55
Osasuna	Real Madrid	1	76
Real Madrid	Real Betis	1	10
Albacete	Real Madrid	1	45
Real Madrid	Barcelona	1	65
Real Madrid	Racing	1	29
Real Zaragoza	Real Madrid	1	22

Home Team	Away Team	Goals	Time
Blackburn	Newcastle	1	66
Newcastle	Man City	1	18
West Brom	Newcastle	2	46, 78
West Ham	Newcastle	3	5, 43, 90

ENGLAND PLAYING RECORD

Cat.	Date	Competition	Home
Y	23/07/1996	UEFA U18 XII FINALS gp B	England
Y	25/07/1996	UEFA U18 XII FINALS gp B	Italy
Y	27/07/1996	UEFA U18 XII FINALS gp B	England
Y	31/07/1996	UEFA U18 XII FINALS 3–4	England
Y	11/10/1996	UEFA U18 XIII gp 5	England
Y	13/10/1996	UEFA U18 XIII gp 5	England
Y	18/02/1997	U18	England
Y	29/04/1997	UEFA U18 XIII 2nd Rd gp 3	England
Y	13/05/1997	UEFA U18 XIII 2nd Rd gp 3	Portugal
Y	18/06/1997	WYC XI gp F	Ivory Coast
Y	20/06/1997	WYC XI gp F	UAE
Y	23/06/1997	WYC XI gp F	Mexico
Y	26/06/1997	WYC XI 2nd Round	Argentina
Y	09/09/1997	UEFA U18 PRELIM	England
U	17/12/1997	UEFA U21 XIV gp	England
A	11/02/1998	Friendly	England
A	25/03/1998	Friendly	Switzerland
A	22/04/1998	Friendly	England
A	27/05/1998	KING HASSAN II CUP	Morocco
A	29/05/1998	KING HASSAN II CUP	Belgium
A	15/06/1998	WC XVI FINALS Group G	England
A	22/06/1998	WC XVI FINALS Group G	Romania
A	26/06/1998	WC XVI FINALS Group G	Colombia
A	30/06/1998	WC XVI FINALS 2nd Rd	Argentina
A	05/09/1998	ENC XII gp 5	Sweden
A	10/10/1998	ENC XII gp 5	England
A	14/10/1998	ENC XII gp 5	Luxembourg
A	10/02/1999	Friendly	England
A	04/09/1999	ENC XII gp 5	England

Away	Home score	Away score	Pens	Goal time
Spain	0	0		
England	1	1		
Ireland	1	0		
Belgium	3	2		103
Finland	1	0		
N. Ireland	4	0		37, 39, 53, 71
Scotland	4	1		
Portugal	2	1		66
England	3	0		
England	1	2		5
England	0	5		51
England	0	1		66
England	2	1		
Yugoslavia	0	0		
Greece	4	2		60
Chile	0	2		
England	1	1		
Portugal	3	0		
England	0	1		59
England	0	0	4–3	
Tunisia	2	0		
England	2	1		79
England	0	2		
England	2	2	4–3	16
England	2	1		
Bulgaria	0	0		
England	0	3		19
France	0	2		
Luxembourg	6	0		90

Cat.	Date	Competition	Home
A	08/09/1999	ENC XII gp 5	Poland
A	10/10/1999	Friendly	England
A	13/11/1999	ENC XII Play off 1st Leg	Scotland
A	17/11/1999	ENC XII Play off 2nd Leg	England
A	27/05/2000	Friendly	England
A	12/06/2000	ENC XII Finals gp A	Portugal
A	17/06/2000	ENC XII Finals gp A	England
A	20/06/2000	ENC XII Finals gp A	England
A	02/09/2000	Friendly	France
A	07/10/2000	WC XVII EUROPE gp 9	England
A	28/02/2001	Friendly	England
A	24/03/2001	WC XVII EUROPE gp 9	England
A	28/03/2001	WC XVII EUROPE gp 9	Albania
A	25/05/2001	Friendly	England
A	06/06/2001	WC XVII EUROPE gp 9	Greece
A	15/08/2001	Friendly	England
A	01/09/2001	WC XVII EUROPE gp 9	Germany
A	05/09/2001	WC XVII EUROPE gp 9	England
A	27/03/2002	Friendly	England
A	17/04/2002	Friendly	England
A	21/05/2002	Friendly	South Korea
A	26/05/2002	Friendly	England
A	02/06/2002	WC XVII FINALS gp f	England
A	07/06/2002	WC XVII FINALS gp f	Argentina
A	12/06/2002	WC XVII FINALS gp f	Nigeria
A	15/06/2002	WC XVII FINALS 2nd Rd	Denmark
A	21/06/2002	WC XVII FINALS QF	Brazil
A	07/09/2002	Friendly	England
A	12/10/2002	ENC XIII gp 7	Slovakia
A	16/10/2002	ENC XIII Gp 7	England

Away	Home score	Away score	Pens	Goal time
England	0	0		
Belgium	2	1		
England	0	2		
Scotland	0	1		
Brazil	1	1		38
England	3	2		
Germany	1	0		
Romania	2	3		45
England	1	1		86
Germany	0	1		
Spain	3	0		
Finland	2	1		43
England	1	3		73
Mexico	4	0		
England	0	2		
Netherlands	0	2		
England	1	5		13, 48, 66
Albania	2	0		43
Italy	1	2		
Paraguay	4	0		4
England	1	1		26
Cameroon	2	2		
Sweden	1	1		
England	0	1		
England	0	0		
England	0	3		22
England	2	1		23
Portugal	1	1		
England	1	2		82
Macedonia	2	2		

Cat.	Date	Competition	Home
A	12/02/2003	Friendly	England
A	29/03/2003	ENC XIII Gp 7	Liechtenstein
A	02/04/2003	ENC XIII Gp 7	England
A	22/05/2003	Friendly	South Africa
A	03/06/2003	Friendly	England
A	11/06/2003	ENC XIII Gp 7	England
A	20/08/2003	Friendly	England
A	06/09/2003	European Championships	Macedonia
A	10/09/2003	ENC XIII Gp 7	England
A	18/02/2004	Friendly	Portugal
A	01/06/2004	Friendly	England
A	05/06/2004	Friendly	England
A	13/06/2004	European Championships	France
A	17/06/2004	European Championships	England
A	21/06/2004	European Championships	Croatia
A	24/06/2004	ENC XIII FINALS QF	Portugal
A	18/08/2004	Friendly	England
A	04/09/2004	WC XVIII Prelim UEFA Gp 6	Austria
A	08/09/2004	WC XVIIIPrelim UEFA Gp 6	Poland
A	09/10/2004	WC XVIII Prelim UEFA Gp 6	England
A	13/10/2004	WC XVIII Prelim UEFA Gp 6	Azerbaijan
A	17/11/2004	Friendly	Spain
A	09/02/2005	Friendly	England
A	26/03/2005	WC XVIII Prelim UEFA Gp 6	England
A	30/03/2005	WC XVIII Prelim UEFA Gp 6	England
A	31/05/2005	Friendly	Colombia
A	17/08/2005	Friendly	Denmark
A	12/10/2005	WC XVIII Prelim UEFA Gp 6	England
A	12/11/2005	Friendly	Argentina

Total Number of England Goals as a full international: 35
Total Number of England Caps: 75

Away	Home score	Away score	Pens	Goal time
Australia	0	0		
England	0	0		28
Turkey	0	0		
England	0	0		
Serbia & Montenegro	2	1		
Slovakia	2	1		62, 73
Croatia	3	1		51
England	1	2		
Liechtenstein	2	0		46
England	1	1		
Japan	1	1		22
Iceland	6	1		
England	2	1		
Switzerland	3	0		
England	2	4		
England	2	2	6–5	3
Ukraine	3	0		50
England	2	2		
England	1	2		
Wales	2	0		
England	0	1		22
England	1	0		
Netherland	0	0		
Northern Ireland	4	0	52	
Azerbaijan	2	0		
England	2	3		36,42,58
England	4	1		
Poland	2	1		43
England	2	3		86, 90

England goal average: 1 goal every 2.1 games

GOAL TYPE

	Penalty	Left Foot	Right Foot	Header	Other (Knee)	Total
Liverpool	13	20	113	12	0	158
Real Madrid	0	0	15	1	1	16
Newcastle	0	1	4	2	0	7
England	1*	2	22	9	1	35
%	6.5%	11.1%	70.8%	11.1%	0.5%	

* Does not include penalty shoot-outs.

Index

Abramovich, Roman 307
Adams, Tony 160
  Euro 2000 156
  Euro 2000 qualifiers
    149
  FA Cup 2001 182
  star of England team 77
  World Cup 1998 91
Anderton, Darren 88, 91,
  97–98
Anelka, Nicolas 212–213
Armfield, Jimmy 51
Atkins, Isabel 9–10
Atkins, Roland 9, 136
Ayala, Roberto 94, 95, 100,
  324

Babb, Phil 61
Babbel, Markus
  2000–2001 season 170
  FA Cup 2001 182
  signed by Liverpool 166
  UEFA Cup 2001 186
Ball, Michael 36
Ballack, Michael 192, 216,
  241
Banks, Tony 145

Barmby, Nick
  2000–2001 season 170, 172,
    176
  England youth scoring record
    44
  Lilleshall football academy 36
  signed by Liverpool 166
  World Cup 2002 qualifiers
    193, 195
Barnes, John 55
  Liverpool star player 82, 188
  Owen's League debut 59
  Owen's views on 68
Baros, Milan 260
Bascombe, Chris 288
Batistuta, Gabriel 91–92
Batty, David 98, 101
Bayliff, Simon 269
Beardsley, Peter 153
Becker, Boris 123
Beckham, David
  birth of children 269
  broken foot 214, 218
  career shaped by Ferguson 46
  courting publicity 255–256
  Euro 2000 154, 156–158
  Euro 2000 qualifiers 149

Beckham, David – *cont.*
  Euro 2004 314–315, 321,
    328–329
  Euro 2004 build-up 312
  Euro 2004 qualifiers 258
  free-kick against Greece 238
  friction with Hoddle 88–89,
    114–116
  idolized by Japanese fans
    217–218
  Keegan criticizing Owen
    157–158
  move to Real Madrid
    253–254, 267
  Owen's views on 255–256
  public acclaim for Rooney
    323
  relationship with Owen 254
  security scares 288
  sending-off incident 96–97,
    224
  Stephens as agent 56, 57
  World Cup 1998 88–89, 94,
    96–97, 101, 103
  World Cup 2002 218–219,
    226–227
  World Cup 2002 qualifiers
    178, 193, 194, 210
Beckham, Victoria 89, 219, 256
Bellamy, Craig 160
Benitez, Rafael
  appointed Liverpool manager
    318
  meeting Liverpool star players
    318–319
  Owen transfer 2–5
  vision for Liverpool 2
Berger, Patrik 182, 186
Bergkamp, Dennis 75
Bergues, Patrice 58, 108–109
Berry, Alan 135

Bevington, Adrian 329–330
Bielsa, Manuel 225
Bjornbye, Stig Inge 59
Blunt, Keith 35, 36, 38, 39
  Owen's aggression 72
Bohme, Jorg 195, 200
Bonsall, John 51
  birth of Gemma 272
  Louise's riding accident 274,
    276, 278
Bonsall, Louise
  birth of Gemma 268–271
  breeding racehorses 138, 143
  dislike of celebrity 141, 219,
    256
  engagement to Michael 52
  Euro 2004 319–320
  FA Cup 2001 185
  Gemma speaking on phone
    313
  giving up competitive riding
    282
  going racing 140
  hospital stay 277–281
  house renovation 286–287
  Michael owning racehorses
    129–130
  Michael's childhood
    sweetheart 51–52
  Michael's gambling 245, 249
  Michael's head injury 168
  Michael's riding style 131
  parenting skills 271–272,
    282–283
  planned marriage to Michael
    2–3
  relationship with Michael 35,
    51–54
  riding accident 3, 274–278,
    308
  schooling horses 135

Bonsall, Sue
  birth of Gemma 272
  Louise's riding accident 274,
    276, 278, 283
Branch, Michael 264
Bridge, Wayne
  card schools 248
  World Cup 2002 228
Browes, Dave 124
Brown, Wes 36, 38
Butt, Nicky
  dropped from England team
    312
  World Cup 2002 225

Cadamarteri, Danny 264
Camara, Titi 67, 119
Campbell, Sol
  Euro 2000 qualifiers 149
  Euro 2004 327
  Lilleshall football academy 36
  World Cup 1998 91, 98
  World Cup 2002 222
  World Cup 2002 qualifiers
    193
Carragher, Jamie
  2000–2001 season 170
  Antonelli's restaurant 10
  England youth football 69
  Euro 2004 316, 324
  Euro 2004 build-up 312
  Everton fan 33
  fanatical about football 41–42
  friendship with Owen 40–41,
    255
  Gerrard staying at Liverpool
    330
  Houllier sacked as Liverpool
    manager 291
  Liverpool youth side 39–40
  meeting Benitez 318–319

Owen's goal celebrations 199
Owen's views on 40–42
Carroll, John 136–137, 142
Chamot, José 95
Channon, Mick 139
Cheyrou, Bruno 257
Christie, Linford 123
Cole, Andy 75, 167
  Euro 2000 152
  Lilleshall football academy 36
  World Cup 2002 qualifiers
    164
Cole, Ashley 193, 296
Collina, Pierluigi 196
Collymore, Stan 213
  clash with Harkness 145
  leaving Liverpool 69
  Liverpool star player 82
  Owen's League debut 59
  Owen's views on 61
  rift with Evans 60–61
Community Shield 2001 207
Costa, Rui 327
Costinha, Francisco 325
Cotton, Ian 283
Cox, Arthur 153, 163
Crevoissier, Jacques 58
Cruyff, Jordi 186
Curtis, John 39

Dailly, Christian 168
Damiano, Cristian 58
Deisler, Sebastian 192, 195
Desailly, Marcel 266
  sprinting speed 32
Dettori, Frankie 131, 136–138,
    140, 289
Diao, Salif 257
Diouf, El-Hadji
  2002–2003 season 260
  missing penalties 302

Diouf, El-Hadji – *cont.*
  signed by Liverpool 213,
    257
Dixon, Lee 117, 182
Donnelly, Terry 73
Douglas, Malcolm 57
Dublin, Dion 75
  Owen's England debut 79
  World Cup 1998 build-up 80
Dudek, Jerzy 209
  2002–2003 season 260, 261
Dunne, Richard 15
Dyer, Kieron 244, 248

Elvstone, Barry 140
England
  Beckham's contribution to
    team 256
  card schools 246–249
  Eriksson appointed manager
    175–176
  Euro 2000 152–162
  Euro 2000 qualifiers 114,
    117–118, 146–149
  Euro 2004 1, 310–330
  Euro 2004 qualifiers 174,
    257–259, 267, 297–298
  Ferdinand's suspension
    298–300
  football hooligans 257–258
  Hoddle sacked as manager
    114–115, 117
  Keegan appointed manager
    117–118
  Keegan resigning as manager
    162–163
  Owen as captain 214–215
  Owen's debut 73–74, 76–79
  Owen's views on 4–5
  penalty shoot-outs 1,
    310–311, 328–329

  Rooney's debut 263
  support from fans 196
  World Cup 1998 1, 80–104
  World Cup 2002 125–126,
    217–243
  World Cup 2002 qualifiers
    162–164, 177–178,
    190–202, 209–210
  youngest players 78
  youth football 68–69, 71
Eriksson, Sven-Goran 146, 162
  appointed England manager
    175–176
  calm manner 242–243
  card schools 249
  consistently picking Owen
    207
  consulting with senior players
    254–255
  defeats for England team 4
  discussions with Chelsea
    307–308
  encouragement for players
    177
  Euro 2004 310, 314–315,
    318–321, 326–330
  Euro 2004 qualifiers 258–259
  faith in players 148
  Ferdinand's suspension
    298–300
  injury worries 214–215
  Owen's admiration for 176
  Owen's views on 221–222
  praise for Owen 202
  public acclaim for Rooney
    324
  relationship with Jonsson 221
  relaxed management style 83
  reserved attitude 153
  supporting young players 77
  World Cup 2002 222–243

World Cup 2002 qualifiers
177–178
Euro 2000 152–162
qualifiers 114, 117–118,
146–149
Euro 2004 1, 310–330
qualifiers 174, 257–259, 267,
297–298
Evans, Roy
clash with Houllier 110–111
Houllier appointed Liverpool
manager 105, 107–108
managerial skills 74
Owen's League debut 58–59
picking Owen for penalties
69–70
rift with Collymore 60–61
sacked by Liverpool 112

FA Cup 2001 2, 172–172, 178,
180–185
FA Youth Cup 1996 39–40
Faldo, Nick 113
Fallon, Kieren 289–290
Fazackerly, Derek 153, 163
Ferdinand, Les 159
Ferdinand, Rio
consulted by Eriksson 254
playing style 32–33
suspension for missing drugs
test 298–300
World Cup 1998 83
World Cup 2002 232,
234–235, 242
World Cup 2002 qualifiers
193
youth football 40
Ferguson, Sir Alex 292
Owen's trial for Manchester
United 46–48
racehorse owner 128–129

Figo, Luis 155, 253
Flynn, Mike 283–285, 290,
308
Flynn, Sue 283–284
football
counter-attacking style of play
294
crowding of referees 30–31
fads in 30–31
hooligans 84–85, 257–258
improving standards 74–75
Lilleshall football academy
35–39, 51
penalties 91–94
scouting for teenage talent
44–45
Fortune, Jimmy 137
Fowler, Robbie
2000–2001 season 170, 188
2001–2002 season 203
cocaine prank 66
comparisons with Owen 264
England squad 77
FA Cup 2001 182, 183
Heskey signed by Liverpool
149
injury 69, 74, 78
Liverpool star player 61, 65
number 9 shirt 55
Owen's views on 65–67
pranks 63, 66
rift with Houllier 170–171
rift with Thompson 208–209
support from Liverpool fans
107
UEFA Cup 2001 186
World Cup 1998 82
World Cup 2002 qualifiers
164, 201
Worthington Cup 2001 174
Francis, Trevor 175

Gallen, Keith 44
Galley, Dave 124, 204
Gascoigne, Paul
  dropped from England squad
    80–81
  Owen's views on 81–82
Gerrard, Steven
  2000–2001 season 170
  appointed Liverpool captain
    303
  Euro 2000 156
  Euro 2004 316, 324
  Euro 2004 build-up 311–312
  friendship with Owen 40
  Houllier sacked as Liverpool
    manager 291–292
  injury 220–221
  meeting Benitez 318–319
  missing penalties 302–303
  staying at Liverpool 330–331
  support for Rooney 264
  UEFA Cup 2001 186
  World Cup 2002 qualifiers
    192, 193, 196–198
Giggs, Ryan 294
  booed by fans 67
  career shaped by Ferguson
    46
Gomes, Nuno 155
Gorman, John 78, 116
Gosden, John 129–133, 136,
  138
Graf, Steffi 123
Graham, George 48
Gray, Andy 106
Gregory, John 144
Griffiths, Gilly 140
Gronkjaer, Jesper 266

Hamann, Didi
  Euro 2004 317–318

friendship with Owen 40, 41,
  119–120, 255
golf playing 28
Owen owning racehorses 136,
  140
pranks 63
signed by Liverpool 119
star German player 241
training regime 262
World Cup 2002 qualifiers
  162, 192–193, 198, 199,
  201
Hargreaves, Owen
  fitness tests 215
  World Cup 2002 225
Harkness, Steve
  clash with Collymore 145
  pranks 63
Harley, Jon 36
Harrison, Dave 57
Hasselbaink, Jimmy Floyd
  75
  Golden Boot award 118
Heggem, Veggard 168–169
Heighway, Steve 43, 50
Henchoz, Stéphane
  2000–2001 season 170
  FA Cup 2001 184
  signed by Liverpool 119
Henry, Thierry 75, 180, 211,
  232
  Euro 2004 315–316
  Owen's admiration for 301
Herrera, Martin 186
Heskey, Emile
  2000–2001 season 170, 173
  2001–2002 season 203
  2002–2003 season 260
  Euro 2000 152, 155–156
  Euro 2000 qualifiers 148
  Euro 2004 316

goal celebration 170
leaving Liverpool 295–296
missing penalties 302
Owen's head injury 168
signed by Liverpool 149, 213
World Cup 2002 225, 227,
  232, 236
World Cup 2002 qualifiers
  164, 192, 193, 197, 199
Worthington Cup 2001
  174–175
Hoddle, Glenn
BBC Sports Personality of the
  Year event 113
coaching technique 78
encouragement for players
  177
England get-togethers 178
friction with Beckham 88–89,
  114–116
Owen's England debut 77–78
Owen's trial for Chelsea 49
Owen's views on 114–117
sacked as England manager
  114–115, 117
selecting World Cup 1998
  squad 74, 80–81
supporting young players
  76–77
views on penalties 93
World Cup 1998 82, 87–89,
  91, 93
Holyfield, Evander 147
Hood, Rachel 130
Houllier, Gérard 2, 62
appointed Liverpool manager
  105, 107–108
clash with Evans 110–111
death threats 288
defended by Gerrard 303
disciplinarian 109–110

dropping Owen for Valencia
  game 259–260
encouragement for Owen 177
Evans sacked by Liverpool
  112–113
FA Cup 2001 180–181
heart problems 203–207,
  210–211, 216
Louise's riding accident 278
Owen missing penalties
  301–302
Owen's contract renewal 305
Owen's head injury 169
Owen's views on 206–207,
  293–295
return to work 213–214
rift with Fowler 170–171
sacked as Liverpool manager
  291–293, 309
sacking players 119
signing Anelka 212–213
signing Heskey 149
signing new players 166, 257
targets 166
views on Owen's hamstring
  injury 122
Worthington Cup 2001
  174–175
Houllier, Isabel 203
Hurst, Sir Geoff 145, 190
Hutchison, Don 148
Hyypia, Sami
2000–2001 season 170
2002–2003 season 266
FA Cup 2001 183, 184
signed by Liverpool 119

Ince, Paul
England squad 77
Euro 2000 qualifiers 149
house in Algarve 22

Ince, Paul – *cont.*
  leaving Liverpool 119
  Liverpool debut 69
  Owen's views on 67–68
  World Cup 1998 82, 91, 98,
    99, 101

James, David
  card schools 248
  Euro 2004 1, 315–316, 325
  leaving Liverpool 119
  lively personality 62–63
Jancker, Carsten 193–195
Jeffers, Francis 264
Jevons, Phil 264
Johnsen, Ronny 72–73, 142
Johnson, Andrew 175
Jones, Bryn 24–25
Jones, Michael 27–28, 140
Jones, Vinnie 69

Kahn, Oliver 192–193, 195, 198
Kanchelskis, Andrei 294
Keegan, Kevin
  appointed England manager
    117–118
  card-playing sessions 153–154
  coaching technique 78
  criticizing Owen 157,
    161–162
  England get-togethers 178
  Euro 2000 152–162
  Euro 2000 qualifiers 146–147
  European Footballer of the
    Year 211
  Gerrard's injury 220
  lack of encouragement for
    players 177
  Manchester City manager 257
  resigning as England manager
    162–163

rift with Owen 3, 151–162,
  164, 167
Kenyon, Peter 307–308
Keown, Martin
  Euro 2000 156
  FA Cup 2001 182
  sprinting speed 32
Kewell, Harry 203
Kidd, Brian 47
King, Ledley 313
Kirkland, Chris 261
Klinsmann, Jurgen 123

Lampard, Frank
  Euro 2004 314, 327
  Euro 2004 build-up 312
  youth football 40
Le Saux, Graeme 91
Leather, Mark 122
Lee, Sammy 58, 318–319
Leonhardsen, Oyvind 119
Lewin, Gary 233
Lewis, Lennox 147, 229
Lilleshall football academy
  35–39, 51
Lineker, Gary
  Owen's idol 33–34
  TV presenter 140
Litmanen, Jari
  ankle problems 171–172
  signed by Liverpool 166
Livermore, Doug 77
Liverpool FC
  1997–1998 season 69–74
  1998–1999 season 105–113,
    118–119
  1999–2000 season 144–145,
    149–150
  2000–2001 season 166–176,
    178–189
  2001–2002 season 203–216

2002–2003 season 256–257, 259–266
2003–2004 season 296–305
Benitez appointed manager 318
Champions League 2001–2002 204–205, 211, 213–214, 216
Champions League 2002–2003 259–261
Christmas party incident 109–110
coaches 58
Community Shield 2001 207
European goal-scoring records 265–266, 296
FA Cup 2001 172–173, 178, 180–185
Gerrard appointed captain 303
Houllier sacked as manager 291–293
Houllier's heart problems 203–207, 210–211, 216
Owen's contract renewal 304–305
Owen's League debut 59–60
Owen's record with 2
Rush appointed as coach 261–262
sacking Evans 112–113
sacking Houllier as manager 309
sacking players 119
signing Heskey 149
signing new players 119, 166
signing Owen 46, 50, 55
'Spice Boys' team spirit 61–63
takeover battle 306–307
training regime 63–64
Treble victory parade 189

UEFA Cup 2001 173–174, 178–170, 185–187
UEFA Cup 2003 265
UEFA Cup 2004 296, 300
UEFA Super Cup 2001 207–208
Worthington Cup 2001 174–175
Worthington Cup 2003 262–263
youth side 39–40
Ljungberg, Freddie 181, 214
Lopez, Claudio 91
Lucio 214, 236
Lunt, Kenny 36

Magnier, John 128
Makelele, Claude 316
Mandela, Nelson 266–267
Mansell, Nigel 113
Maradona, Diego 55
Marsh, Simon 56, 57, 181, 185
Martyn, Nigel 164
Matthews, Sir Stanley 184
McAllister, Gary
  2000–2001 season 170
  FA Cup 2001 182
  signed by Liverpool 166
  UEFA Cup 2001 179, 186, 187
McCauley, Hugh 50
McClaren, Steve 320
McManaman, Steve
  England squad 77
  Euro 2000 155, 156
  friendship with Fowler 65
  leaving Liverpool 119
  Liverpool star player 188
  Owen's views on 67
  World Cup 1998 82

McManaman, Steve – *cont.*
World Cup 1998 build-up 80, 82
McManus, J. P. 128
Meier, Urs 327
Meijer, Erik 119
Merson, Paul 99
Milner, James 263
Moldovan, Viorel 86
Moores, David 189
Moran, Ronnie 55, 58, 293
Moreno, Javi 186
Morgan, Steve 287, 306
Morrison, Clinton 172
Motson, John 195, 198
Murphy, Danny
2000–2001 season 170, 188
2002–2003 season 260
friendship with Owen 40, 255
taking penalties 303

Neuville, Oliver 194
Neville, Gary
career shaped by Ferguson 46
consulted by Eriksson 254
Euro 2000 157–158
foot injury 218
Keegan criticizing Owen 157–158
World Cup 1998 89, 91
World Cup 2002 qualifiers 177, 193
Neville, Phil 46
Newman, Paul 215
Nicholas, Dave 24
Nielsen, Kim 97

Olazabal, José-Maria 123
Ortega, Ariel 91, 225
Owen, Andy (brother) 8
bought house by Michael 21

childhood football 13–14
footballing skills 31–32
World Cup 1998 87
Owen, Gemma (daughter) 2, 21, 35, 52–54, 83, 143, 245, 274
babyhood 271–273
birth of 268–271
Euro 2004 319–320
Louise's hospital stay 279, 281
Louise's riding accident 277, 282–283
Sardinia trip 311
speaking on phone 313
Owen, Janette (mother)
birth of Michael 7
birth of Gemma 268, 272
bought house by Michael 21
Euro 2004 319–320
FA Cup 2001 185
family values 15–16
Louise's hospital stay 280
Louise's riding accident 283
Michael owning racehorses 132–133, 136
Michael voted BBC Sports Personality of the Year 113–114
Michael's gambling 245–246
Michael's hat-trick against Germany 199
Michael's head injury 168–169
renovation of Michael's house 284, 287
support for Michael 11, 45
views on gambling 250–251
working life 10
World Cup 1998 87–89, 102

Owen, John (uncle) 10
Owen, Karen (sister) 8, 11
  bought house by Michael 22
  career as solicitor 14
  Louise's riding accident 283
  security scares 288–289
Owen, Les (grandfather) 9
Owen, Lesley (sister) 8
  bought house by Michael 22
  interior designer 14
  Louise's riding accident 274,
    283
  Michael owning racehorses
    129–130
  support for Michael 11
  World Cup 1998 87
Owen, Margaret (aunt) 10
Owen, Michael
  1997–1998 season 69–74
  1998–1999 season 105–119
  1999–2000 season 144–150
  2000–2001 season 166–189
  2001–2002 season 203–216
  2002–2003 season 256–266
  2003–2004 season 296–298,
    300–305
  2006 World Cup bid 145–146
  admiration for Eriksson 176
  aggressive streak 71–73,
    144–145
  Antonelli's restaurant 10
  appointing Stephens as agent
    56–57
  avoiding paparazzi 279–280
  BBC Sports Personality of the
    Year 113–114
  birth of 7
  birth of Gemma 268–271
  boxing 28–30
  breeding racehorses 135–136,
    138

interior designer's suicide
  283–285, 290, 308
bullied at school 27, 30,
  38–39
buying houses for family
  21–22
card schools 153–154,
  246–249
childhood football 13–15
childhood pranks 16
Christmas party incident
  109–110
Community Shield 2001
  207
comparisons with other
  players 264
competitive nature 249–250
consulted by Eriksson 254
cricket player 20
criticized by Keegan 157,
  161–162
Deeside goal-scoring record
  25–26
Deeside Schools team 24–25
dietary regime 223–224
dislike of celebrity 53, 105,
  140–141, 143, 218, 219,
  255–256, 279–280
dropped for Valencia game
  259–260
engagement to Louise 52
England captain 214–215
England debut 73–74,
  76–79
England youth football 44,
  68–69, 71
Eriksson's relationship with
  Jonsson 221
Euro 2000 152–162
Euro 2000 qualifiers 114,
  118, 146–149

Owen, Michael – *cont.*
 Euro 2004 1, 310–330
 Euro 2004 qualifiers
  257–259, 267, 297–298
 European Footballer of the
  Year 211–212
 Everton fan 33
 FA Cup 2001 2, 172–173,
  180–185
 FA Youth Cup 1996 39–40
 family background 8–10
 family values 3, 6, 18, 20–21
 Ferdinand's suspension
  298–300
 friendship with Carragher
  40–41, 255
 friendship with Hamann
  40–41, 119–120, 255
 gambling stories 244–245,
  289–290
 Gascoigne dropped from
  England squad 80–81
 Gemma speaking on phone
  313
 Gerrard staying at Liverpool
  330–331
 goal against Brazil 236–238
 Golden Boot award 75, 118,
  121
 golf caddy 17–18
 golf player 18–19
 hamstring injury 118,
  121–127, 232–236
 hand-warming goal
  celebration 198–199
 hat-trick against Germany
  195–199
 hat-trick against Newcastle
  106
 Hawarden Rangers 26–27
 head injury 168–169, 278

Houllier sacked as Liverpool
  manager 291–293
 Houllier's heart problems
  203–207, 210–211, 216
 house renovation 284–287
 idolized by Japanese fans
  217–218
 interest in racing 132–143
 international record 2
 investing in property 21–22
 Lancashire Oaks incident
  142–143
 League debut 59–60
 Lilleshall football academy
  35–39, 51
 Liverpool European goal-
  scoring record 265–266, 296
 Liverpool signing Anelka
  212–213
 Liverpool youth side 39–40
 Louise as childhood
  sweetheart 51–52
 Louise's hospital stay
  277–281
 Louise's riding accident
  274–278
 loyalty to Liverpool 305–306
 match memorabilia 202
 meeting Benitez 318–319
 meeting Mandela 266–267
 memorable goals 45–46
 Mold Alexander 24
 nationality 7, 42–44
 newspaper column 58
 number 10 shirt 55
 penalty shoot-outs 98–101
 planned marriage to Louise
  2–3
 plans for future 138–140
 playing style 32–33
 pranks 63

problems with penalties
301–303
public acclaim for Rooney
323–324
racehorse owner 128–143,
251–252
rebellious nature 15
record with Liverpool 2
red cards 71–73
relationship with Beckham
254
relationship with Louise 35,
51–54
riding style 131
rift with Keegan 3, 151–162,
164, 167
schoolboy football 24–25
schooldays 27–28, 37
security scares 288–289
shin bone injury 296–297
shirt-swapping incident
200
signed by Liverpool 46, 50,
55
snooker playing 19
somersault goal celebration
183, 198
speculation about contract
renewal 304–306
'Spice Boys' team spirit 61–63
sponsors 57–58
sprinting speed 31, 32
support from family 11–13,
16–17, 20, 45, 283
training regime 262
transfer to Real Madrid 1–6
trial at Arsenal 48–49
trial at Chelsea 49
trial at Manchester United
46–48
TV analyst 210

UEFA Cup 2001 173,
185–187
UEFA Super Cup 2001
207–208
Umbro sponsorship 30, 56,
57, 111, 180–181, 306
views on alcohol 63–64
views on Barnes 68
views on Beckham 255–256
views on Carragher 40–42
views on Collymore 61
views on England team 4–5
views on Eriksson 221–222
views on fatherhood 271–273
views on football hooligans
84–85
views on football standards
74–75
views on footballing fads
30–31
views on Fowler 65–67
views on friends 290
views on gambling 245–249
views on Gascoigne 81–82
views on German team 241
views on Hoddle 114–117
views on Houllier 206–207,
293–295
views on Ince 67–68
views on Liverpool fans 107
views on McManaman 67
views on money 111–112
views on penalties 91–94
views on Redknapp 183–184
views on Rooney 263–265,
324–325
views on rough play 71
views on shirt swapping 229
views on Zidane 316–317
'wonder goal' 94–96
World Cup 1998 1, 80–104

Owen, Michael – *cont.*
World Cup 2002 125–126,
217–243
World Cup 2002 qualifiers
162–164, 177–178,
190–202, 209–210
Worthington Cup 2001
174–175
Worthington Cup 2003
262–263
youngest England goal scorer
79–80
youngest England player 78
Owen, Rose (grandmother)
10
Owen, Terry (brother) 8
bought house by Michael 22
childhood football 13–14
footballing skills 31–32
Owen, Terry (father)
birth of Gemma 269, 272
bought house by Michael 21
disciplining Michael 16–17
Euro 2004 319–320
Everton player 49–50
FA Cup 2001 185
football career 3, 8–9, 49–50
football scouts 43
gambling 250–251
goal-shooting style 312
golf player 17–18
Hawarden Rangers incident
26–27
Keegan's criticism of Michael
159–160
Lancashire Oaks incident
142–143
Michael appointing agent 56
Michael as boxer 28, 30
Michael owning racehorses
129–130, 133, 135–136

Michael's England debut 77,
78
Michael's gambling 245
Michael's hat-trick against
Germany 199
Michael's head injury 169
Michael's nationality 43
Michael's red card incident
71
settling in Flintshire 2
snooker playing 19
support for Michael 7, 11–13,
16–17, 45
working life 10–11
World Cup 1998 87–89, 102
Owen, Tommy (uncle) 10

Paisley, Bob 59
Parry, Rick 3, 291
Peacock, Gavin 49
Pearce, Stuart 98, 106
Pelé 55, 324
Perry, Chris 113
Petrescu, Dan 87
Pickering, Gilly 38
Pickering, Tony 38
Pinto, Joao 155
Platt, David
horses 132
Stephens as agent 56, 57
Poll, Graham 72–73
Postiga, Helder 326
Prothero, Martin 57
Purse, Darren 175

Quinn, Mickey 48
Quinn, Stuart 40

Ratcliffe, Kevin 33
Raul 253
Real Madrid 1–6

Redknapp, Jamie
  2000–2001 season 170
  FA Cup 2001 183–184
  friendship with Collymore 61
  Owen's views on 183–184
Ricardo 1, 327
Riedle, Karlheinz
  1997–1998 season 69
  1998–1999 season 105
  leaving Liverpool 119
  Owen's hamstring injury 123
Rivaldo 229, 238–239
Roa, Carlos 95, 99–100
Robinson, Peter 55–56, 58
Ronaldinho 238–240
Ronaldo 239, 253
Rooney, Wayne
  aggressive play 324–325
  England debut 263
  Euro 2004 314–315, 321–324
  Euro 2004 build-up 312
  Owen's views on 263–265,
    324–325
  public acclaim 2, 323
  youngest England goal scorer
    79
  youngest England player 78
Royle, Joe 49
Ruddock, Neil 109
Rush, Ian
  Deeside goal-scoring record
    25–26
  goal-scoring ability 115
  Liverpool coach 261
  Liverpool European goal-
    scoring record 265–266, 296
  Liverpool legend 65

Salas, Marcelo 79
Samuel, Walter 33, 225
Schmeichel, Peter 72

Scholes, Paul
  career shaped by Ferguson 46
  consulted by Eriksson 254
  Euro 2000 154, 155
  Euro 2000 qualifiers 118,
    147–149
  Euro 2004 build-up 312
  World Cup 1998 91, 95, 97
  World Cup 2002 225, 227
  World Cup 2002 qualifiers
    193, 194, 197
Seaman, David
  Euro 2000 qualifiers 149
  Euro 2004 qualifiers 258
  FA Cup 2001 182
  Gascoigne dropped from
    England squad 81
  retirement from international
    football 258–259
  World Cup 1998 91–92
  World Cup 2002 239–240
  World Cup 2002 qualifiers
    164, 177, 193, 195
Shankly, Bill 59
Shannon, Dave 50
Shearer, Alan
  commitment to game 241
  Euro 2000 152–153,
    156–157, 162
  Euro 2000 qualifiers 147–149
  goal celebration 198
  not coming off voluntarily
    232
  number 9 shirt 55
  playing style 159
  public acclaim for Rooney
    323
  retirement from international
    football 259
  star of England team 34, 76,
    77

Shearer, Alan *cont.*
  Stephens as agent 56, 57
  World Cup 1998 85, 86, 91, 94, 97, 98–99
  World Cup 1998 build-up 79
Sheedy, Kevin 33
Sheringham, Teddy
  card schools 248
  England squad 76
  Owen's England debut 79
  World Cup 1998 85
  World Cup 1998 build-up 79
  World Cup 2002 227–228
  World Cup 2002 qualifiers 164
Shinawatra, Thaksin 307
Silvestre, Mikael 315
Simeone, Diego 91, 97, 225
Simmons, Craig 38
Smith, Richard 233–236
Smith, Steve 320
Southall, Neville 33
Southgate, Gareth 98, 267
Spackman, Nigel 153
Speed, Gary 25
Spencer, John 49
Stam, Jaap 33
Stanley, Peter 140
Stephens, Tony
  appointed as Owen's agent 56–57
  Bayliff as assistant 269
  Beckham's move to Real Madrid 254
  Michael owning racehorses 251
  Owen owning racehorse 128–129, 132
  Owen transfer to Real Madrid 1, 2

Owen's contract renewal 305
Owen's head injury 169
Owen's low patch 302
Steven, Trevor 33
Stubbs, Ray 113
Sutton, Chris 75

Taylor, Peter 176
Terry, John 314
  Euro 2004 327
  playing style 32
Thompson, David 39
Thompson, Phil 180–181
  able substitute manager 210
  Houllier's heart problems 204, 205, 210
  Houllier's return to work 213–214
  leaving Liverpool 318
  rift with Fowler 208–209
Tigana, Jean 58
Tyldesley, Clive 184
Tyson, Mike 229–230

UEFA Cup
  2001 173–174, 178–179, 185–187
  2003 265
  2004 296, 300
UEFA Super Cup 2001 207–208

Van Nistelrooy, Ruud 75, 232, 302, 315
Vassell, Darius
  Euro 2004 314–315, 321, 328
  Euro 2004 build-up 312
  World Cup 2002 225, 228
Vaughan, David 19
Venables, Terry 42, 176

Veron, Juan Sebastian 91, 225
Vieira, Patrick 180, 182, 212

Waddle, Chris 98
Walker, Ian 36
Waller, Dr Mark 123–124,
    168–169, 204, 214,
    276–277
Warner, Tony 119
Weir, David 144
Wenger, Arséne 108, 160, 242,
    292
Westerveld, Sander 209
Wetherall, David 150
Wilkinson, Howard 71, 117,
    176
  unusual managerial
    techniques 163–164
Wise, Dennis
  Euro 2000 156, 162
  Owen's trial for Chelsea 49
Wohlfahrt, Dr Hans-Muller
    123–124
Woods, Tiger 239
World Cup
  1998 1, 80–104

2002 217–243
2002 qualifiers 162–164,
    177–178, 190–202,
    209–210
Worthington Cup
  2001 174–175
  2003 262–263
Wright, Ian
  Owen's trial for Arsenal 48
  World Cup 1998 build-up
    79–80

Yakin, Hakan 320
Yorke, Dwight
  Golden Boot award 118
  Stephens as agent 56, 57

Zanetti, Javier 96
Zico 55
Zidane, Zinedine 5, 211, 253
  Euro 2004 314, 316–317
  Owen's views on 316–317
Ziege, Christian
  2000–2001 season 167
  shirt-swapping incident 200
  signed by Liverpool 166

PHOTOGRAPHIC ACKNOWLEDGMENTS

All photographs supplied by Michael Owen with the
exception of the following:

Page 4 (centre and bottom) © John Sibley/Action Images;
age 6 (bottom) © Popperfoto; **Page 7** (top) © PA Photos, (bottom)
© Action Images; **Page 8** © Andrew Crowley/Camera Press;
Page 9 (top) © Martyn Hayhow/PA Photos, (bottom) © Stuart
Atkins/All Action; **Page 10** (top) © Rui Vieira/PA Photos, (centre left
and right) © Action Images, (bottom) © Witters/Empics;
Page 11 (top) Richard Sellers/Sportsphoto/Popperfoto, (centre) © Rui
Vieira/PA Photos, (bottom) © Darren Walsh/Action Images;
Page 12 (top) © Phil Knot/Camera Press, (centre right) © Eamonn
Clarke/All Action, (centre left) © Cruise Pix/All Action, (bottom) ©
Colin Mason/London Features; **Page 13** (centre) © John Stillwell/PA
Photos, (bottom) © Phil Noble/PA Photos; **Page 14** (top) © Phil
Noble/PA Photos, (centre) © Gareth Copley/PA Photos, (bottom)
© John Stillwell/PA Photos; **Page 15** (bottom centre) © Michael
Steele/Empics, (bottom) © Dave Joyner/Popperfoto; **Page 16** (top) ©
John Sibley/Action Images, (top centre) © Corbis; **Page 17** (centre
left) © John Giles/PA Photos, (centre right) © Martin Rickett/PA
Photos, (bottom) © David Davies/PA Photos; **Page 18** (top) © Dave
Joyner/Popperfoto, (centre) © Matthew Ashton/Empics, (bottom)
© Michael Regan/Action Images; **Page 19** (top) © EPA/PA Photos,
(centre right) © Tim De Waele/Corbis, (centre left and bottom) ©
Laurence Griffiths/Getty Images; **Page 20** (top) © Reuters/Corbis,
(centre right) © Neal Simpson/Empics, (centre left) © Alex
Morton/Action Images, (bottom) © Ben Radford/Getty Images;
Page 21 (top) © Lluis Gene/Getty Images, (centre) © EPA/PA Photos,
(bottom) © Ross Kinnaird/Getty Images; **Page 23** (top) ©
Euroimages/London Features International, (bottom) © Christian
Liewig/Corbis; **Page 24** (top) © Lawrence Griffiths/Getty Images,
(centre) © Ian Horrocks/Newcastle Utd/Getty Images, (bottom) ©
Mike Hewitt/Getty Images.